DRINK, DRUGS
AND DRIVING

Second Edition

By

H. J. Walls, B.Sc., Ph.D.
*Formerly Director of the Metropolitan Police
Forensic Science Laboratory*

And

Alistair R. Brownlie, M.A., LL.B.
*Solicitor Supreme Courts
Edinburgh*

LONDON
SWEET & MAXWELL

EDINBURGH
W. GREEN & SON

1985

Published by
Sweet & Maxwell Limited of
11 New Fetter Lane, London
and W. Green and Son Limited of
St. Giles Street, Edinburgh
Computerset by Promenade Graphics Limited, Cheltenham
Printed and bound in Great Britain by
Hazell Watson and Viney Limited

British Library Cataloguing in Publication Data

Walls, H.J.
   Drink, drugs and driving.—2nd ed.
   1. Drunk driving—Great Britain
   I. Title   II. Brownlie, Alistair R.
   344.105'247   KD2618

   ISBN 0–421–29600–3

PREFACE

When the first edition of this book appeared in 1970 the whole field of drink-and-driving law enforcement had a short time previously been revolutionised: the Road Safety Act 1967 had created the completely new offence of driving or attempting to drive with more than a prescribed concentration of alcohol in the blood stream, regardless of whether or not driving ability was impaired. As is now well known, the concentration chosen for legislative enforcement was 80 milligrams of alcohol per 100 millilitres of blood, a figure representing in the opinion of the legislators a reasonable compromise between an unduly oppressive restriction of freedom and an unacceptable increase in liability to accident.

While the new law (later consolidated in the Road Traffic Act 1972) at first went a long way towards achieving its objective of reducing the toll of death and injury on the roads, it was perhaps inevitable that its very novelty brought problems. The chief of these were that faults in drafting were complicated by the description of the offence and left unforseen loopholes to legally permissible but sometimes unmeritorious defence pleas, while the question of how to deal with recidivist alcoholic or problem drinkers remained unsolved, and where the repetitive blood or urine analyses which the law made essential took up a great deal of skilled analysts' time.

These and other problems were examined by the Departmental Committee on Drinking and Driving (the Blennerhassett Committee) which reported to the Minister for Transport in 1976 and recommended a number of solutions, most of which were included in the Transport Act 1981 and incorporated in the restated code of law. It is noteworthy that in neither the Report nor the Act was any change recommended or enacted in the permissible maximum blood-alcohol level; the figure of 80mg/100ml had and has apparently been accepted as the best compromise, and it seems unlikely that it will be changed now. There has however been a well publicised major change in analytical methodology. Of all the changes introduced by the 1981 Act the most far-reaching in its effects on the practice of law enforcement is the substitution of breath for blood or urine as the body substance of first choice for analysis. This, while not revolutionary in the sense that the 1967 enactment of a maximum permissible figure was, has nevertheless resulted in a situation comparable with that following the 1967 Act as far as general comprehension of the scientific background is concerned.

Just, therefore, as the present authors tried in their first edition to give some helpful guidance to non-scientists enmeshed in the toils of that new legislation, they have attempted in this second to give similar help to those concerned with the understanding of the changes made by the 1981 Act. The general plan of the book, with its natural division into legal and scientific sections, has necessarily remained unaltered. In the legal section, to avoid constant repetition, we cite the Road Traffic Act 1972 in its amended form following the substitutions of the Transport Act 1981. We describe the two principal offences in their original and amended forms, and we deploy so much of the case law as seems likely to remain relevant despite the altered definition of the prescribed-level offence and the seeming abolition of the principle of *Scott* v. *Baker* [1969] 1 Q.B. 659.

In the scientific section, considerable changes have been made. Notice has been taken of the changes in the law about alcoholic drinks consequent upon British entry into the E.E.C. Less space has been given to the now less often necessary collection, transport and analysis of blood or urine specimens, and more to the now more important subject of the correct relationship of blood and breath alcohol. Some account is given of the theory and practice of the new analytical techniques. Finally, the extensive new researches since 1970 into the effects of drugs on driving have entailed the complete re-writing and considerable enlargement of the chapter on that topic.

Proper names appearing in the text in italics indicate authorities cited by us; a complete list of all such scientific authorities appears as Appendix IV, and legal citations as Appendix III. Lists of suggested further reading appear at the end of each scientific chapter for those wishing to obtain more information on any topic than it has been possible to include in a book of this size.

The authors hope that this book will enable drivers and members of the public generally better to understand the effect of alcohol and other drugs on driving ability, and the procedures which must follow when these are abused, so making some small contribution to the improvement of road safety and the saving of life on the roads.

H. J. Walls

November 1984   Alistair R. Brownlie

ACKNOWLEDGMENTS

In the preparation of this book the authors have received generous help from many sources, and express here thanks to:

The late Dr. J. A. G. Clarke (Dudley) and Mr. G. C. Hands (Laboratory of the Government Chemist) for "vetting" certain scientific chapters, and Mr. V. J. Emerson (Home Office) for similar vetting and for arranging for the reproduction of certain Crown Copyright material.

Professors R. Bonnichsen (Stockholm), R. F. Borkenstein (Indiana) and Kurt M. Dubowski (Oklahoma) for copies of, and permission to, reproduce certain figures.

It would have been impossibly invidious to attempt to arrange in any "order of merit," the numerous other people and firms who have helped in various ways, mainly by supplying information and affording library facilities; and briefly in alphabetical order they are:

Professor Malcolm Cameron and his librarian, Mr. P. S. Hockney (London Hospital Medical College); Dr. H. de la H. Davies (Association of Police Surgeons); Dr. R. C. Denney (Thames Polytechnic); those Directors and their staffs who are not otherwise individually mentioned of all the Home Office, Metropolitan Police, Strathclyde and Northern Ireland Forensic Science Laboratories, and the Home Office Central Research Establishment; Dr. Bryan Finkle (Center for Human Toxicology, Utah); Dr. J. D. J. Havard (British Medical Association); Mr. S. V. Ivanov and Mr. V. A. Uljanov (Soviet Union Embassy London and Ministry of Internal Affairs of the Soviet Union respectively); S. Karger AG (Basel); Dr. D. M. Lucas (Toronto); Professor Keith Mant (Guy's Hospital); Mr. A. M. Mather (CAMIC Limited); Mr. D. Neylan (Home Office Forensic Science Service) for the hitherto unpublished figures quoted on p. 110; Messrs. Oliver and Boyd (Edinburgh); Professor J. P. Payne (Royal College of Surgeons); Penguin Books Limited; Miss B. E. Sabey (Transport and Road Research Laboratory); Mr. H. Whitfield (Draeger Safety

Limited); Dr. P. M. Williams (Lion Laboratories Limited); Professor Helmut T. Zwahlen (Ohio).

We also thank the authors—too numerous to mention individually—who supplied us with reprints of their publications. We would not like the superb typing by Mrs Peggy Butler of the scientific section and by Mrs Martha Brownlie of the legal section to go unacknowledged. Their help was invaluable.

We must finally express our gratitude to the staff of Sweet and Maxwell Limited for their patience and co-operation, and our apologies to anyone deserving of thanks but omitted by oversight.

H. J. Walls
Alistair R. Brownlie

CORRIGENDUM

page 108, paragraph 2

The first three sentences of paragraph 2 should be deleted and replaced with:

"The practice in the forensic science laboratories was and is then as follows. A standard deviation of 2 mg/100 ml is assumed. Determinations of 6 standards must agree to within $\pm$ 1·5 per cent. of the recorded mean value. Each body fluid specimen is analysed by two independent analysts using entirely separate sets of equipment, and their results, if within the critical region (i.e. 87 to 100 mg/100 ml inclusive for blood, or a comparable 115 to 133 mg/100 ml inclusive for urine) must agree to within $\pm$ 2 mg/100 ml of the mean. Outside the critical region the criterion is $\pm$ 3 per cent. of the mean."

WALLS and BROWNLIE: Drink Drugs and Driving, 2nd ed.

CONTENTS

Appendices

TABLE OF CASES

TABLE OF STATUTES

TABLE OF STATUTORY INSTRUMENTS

CHAPTER 1

INTRODUCTION

ALCOHOL AS DRUNK

Note: This introductory chapter deals solely with the factual background information about alcoholic liquors which is desirable for a complete discussion of drinking and its effects. Any reader who finds it oppressively technical can skip it without prejudice to his understanding of the succeeding chapters, and return to it later for such information as he requires.

To chemists the word "alcohol" means a member of a class of carbon compounds possessing a certain structural feature in common and having therefore certain predictable chemical properties. The structural feature is the presence in the molecule of one or more *hydroxyl* groups each attached to a carbon atom. (Hydroxyl is one oxygen and one hydrogen atom linked together, and written in chemical formulae as $-OH$.) This carbon atom (or atoms, if there is more than one hydroxyl group) is in turn part of a molecular skeleton having a certain specified structure.

Alcohols were formerly named by prefixing to the word "alcohol" the name of the carbon-atom skeleton to which the hydroxyl was attached: methyl alcohol; ethyl alcohol; propyl alcohol, etc.[1] In the now accepted nomenclature, however, alcohols are named by giving the suffix "–ol" to the accepted name of the parent carbon compound: thus, methanol, derived from methane; ethanol; propanol, etc.[2]

Thus a very large number, probably thousands, of alcohols are known to chemists. Compounds as diverse as methanol (wood

---

[1] The "–yl" ending of these words is pronounced "–ile," not "–il." In particular, ethyl is pronounced "eethile," with a marked stress on the first syllable, and not as "Ethel."

[2] The ending "–ol" also appears in the names of many *phenols*—another class of compounds also containing hydroxyl groups but attached to a different type of carbon-atom skeleton. No confusion need however arise here, as we shall have no further occasion to mention phenols.

alcohol, wood spirit), ethylene glycol (used in anti-freeze), gly-
cerol (glycerine), menthol and cholesterol are all alcohols. However, one member of the class is so overwhelmingly the most
important, best known and most exhaustively studied that it is
commonly without ambiguity referred to simply as "alcohol" (and
will usually be so referred to here)—that is, ethyl alcohol, or ethanol, the compound in which a hydroxyl group is attached to a skeleton of two carbon atoms which otherwise contains only
hydrogen. Its structural formula written in full is therefore,

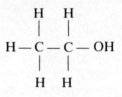

but chemists always use the briefer (and entirely unambiguous)
notation C_2H_5OH.

Ethanol is the alcohol present in, and responsible for the effect
of, fermented or distilled potable liquors. Pharmacologically, it is
therefore mankind's oldest and most widely used drug; we shall
return to that aspect of its properties. In its pure state, it is a colourless mobile liquid, with a sharp taste and a characteristic smell,
miscible with water in all proportions, boiling at 78°C, having a
density[3] of 0·788 gram per millilitre (g/ml) at 20°C, and burning
when ignited with a lambent colourless flame.

The alcohol in all potable liquors is derived from the ferment-
ing of a sugar by a yeast of the genus *Saccharomyces*. There is
however a limit to the alcoholic strength of any liquor made by
simple fermentation, in that yeasts cannot live in the presence of
more than a certain concentration of alcohol, and fermentation
therefore ceases when this concentration has been reached. The

[3] The *density* of a substance is defined as its mass per unit of volume. In the present context, mass is expressed in *grams* and volume in *millilitres*. Though a given
mass would *weigh* more on Jupiter, and less on the Moon, than on Earth, for all
practical present terrestrial purposes "weight" may be, and will be here, substituted for "mass." This seemingly academic point is mentioned because the Alcohol
Tables Regulations (S.I. 1979 No. 132) which define "alcohol strength by volume"
(%/vol) and "by mass" (% mass), and which are made under the European Communities Act 1972, specify "mass" when common usage would refer to "weight."

The density of water at 4°C is 1 gram per millilitre (0·997 gram per millilitre at
20°C), and the *relative density* of any substance, which is a dimensionless number, is
its density compared with that of water. "Relative density" is synonymous with the
formerly current and legally official term "specific gravity."

precise limit depends upon the species and strain of the yeast, but it lies very roughly somewhere around 15 per cent. of alcohol by volume.

Alcoholic liquors may therefore be divided into: (1) those made by fermentation only—namely, beers, cider and table wines; (2) those in which the alcohol concentration is increased by distillation—namely spirits and liqueurs; (3) "fortified" wines—that is, liquors such as port, sherry and vermouth, which are fermented wines strengthened alcoholically beyond the possible limit of fermentation by the addition of a distilled spirit, usually brandy.

The concentration of alcohol by distillation is made possible by the fact, already mentioned, that its boiling-point is lower than that of water. When a mixture of alcohol and water is heated to boiling, the greater volatility of the alcohol means that the vapour—and hence the condensed vapour, the distillate—contains relatively more alcohol than the original liquid. It is not however possible to separate alcohol and water completely by simple distillation; the purest alcohol that can be produced in this way still contains about 4·5 per cent. of water, and is usually known as *rectified spirit*. Other steps are necessary to prepare pure, or *absolute*, alcohol.

The most important fact about any potable liquor, from the points of view both of its effect upon the drinker and of the excise duty chargeable upon it, is the amount of alcohol it contains. This may be expressed in various ways. It is however ambiguous to refer simply to a percentage of alcohol present, without qualification, because of the different densities of alcohol and water. As the density of water is 0·997g/ml at 20°C, 100ml of water will therefore weigh very nearly 100g. The density of a dilute solution of alcohol will also have approximately the same value, and 100ml of it will also weigh approximatly 100g. Do then 100 grammes, or millilitres, of a "1 per cent." solution of alcohol contain 1g (1·27ml) or 1ml (0·788g) of alcohol? More concentrated solutions of alcohol will of course have themselves a density significantly less than that of water, and unqualified definition becomes even more ambiguous. A further complication arises from the fact that the admixture of alcohol and water produces a diminution in the gross volume; if one volume of alcohol and one volume of water are mixed, the mixture will occupy less than two volumes.

A "percentage" in this context will therefore have a definite meaning only if certain qualifying information is also given. Take for example a "10 per cent." solution. This may mean:

10% weight/weight (w/w):   10 g of alcohol in 100 g of solution
10% volume/volume (v/v):   10 ml of alcohol in 100 ml of solution
10% weight/volume (w/v):   10 g of alcohol in 100 ml of solution
10% volume/weight (v/w):   10 ml of alcohol in 100 g of solution

The last of these is never used in practice, but any of the first three may be.

If the concentration of a solution of alcohol is given as such-and-such a per cent. "by weight" or "by volume," these can be taken as meaning weight/weight and volume/volume, respectively. With comparatively dilute solutions, the relative density of which does not differ significantly from 1·0, the weight/weight and weight/ volume percentages will be practically the same; this will not be the case however with concentrated solutions such as distilled spirits.

In scientific contexts, the concentrations of alcohol solutions are always expressed in one of the above ways, or an equivalent, and since 1980 the first two have been prescribed by the Food Labelling Regulations 1980[4] for label indications of the strengths of liquors sold in the United Kingdom other than beer, cider and what the Alcoholic Liquor Duties Act 1979 describes as "made-wines" (*i.e.* liquors such as medicated wines, ginger wine, home-made fruit and vegetable wines). In practice, since section 2 of that Act requires that for excise purposes alcoholic strengths shall be computed as percentages by volume, this is nowadays the method normally encountered.

The determination and label declaration of alcoholic strengths is now to a great extent governed by EEC Regulations. Under the European Communities Act 1972 the determination is based on a table prescribing EEC Directive 766/1976 as validating Recommendation No. 22 of the Bureau Internationale de Métrologie Légale (OIML).

Until 1979 the alcoholic strengths of potable liquors were, in this country and in other members and ex-members of the Commonwealth, always calculated in terms of a hypothetical alcohol/water mixture known as *proof spirit*; the term is described in the 1979 Act and may still be encountered on labels. It has been defined since 1818 by its specific gravity at a particular temperature, and contains almost exactly 49 per cent. of alcohol by weight or 57 per cent. by volume. The strength of a liquor was then given as so

---

[4] S.I. 1980 No. 1849.

many "° proof," the figure being the number of volumes of proof spirit that could be made from the alcohol contained in 100 volumes of the liquor. To convert "° proof" into per cent. volume/ volume one simply divides by 1·75; for example, a liquor of 70° (the strength at which spirits are normally sold in this country) contains $\frac{70}{1·75}$ or 40 per cent. of alcohol v/v, and a vermouth, say, labelled as 30° proof will contain approximately 17 per cent. Pure alcohol is 175° (British) proof.

The strength of a beer is now occasionally given in terms of its *original gravity* ("O.G."), and may in future be normally so described if a code of practice proposed by the Brewers' Society is adopted. This figure is 1,000 times the specific gravity[5] of the wort before fermentation; it depends upon the sugar content of the wort, and the higher this is the more alcohol can be produced. There is no exact correlation between O.G. and the alcohol concentration of the beer, since the latter will depend also on the method of brewing—how far fermentation is allowed to proceed and so forth—but, very roughly, the third and fourth figures of the O.G. divided by 10 will give the approximate alcoholic strength: for example, an O.G. of 1,040 will usually yield about 4 per cent. v/v of alcohol, and barley wine with a declared O.G. of 1,085 will contain about 8·5 per cent.

Some cough mixtures and similar medicines also contain large amounts of alcohol.

Per cent. volume/volume is now used in almost every country to express alcoholic strengths. For example, a French *vin ordinaire* labelled as "9·5°" will contain 9·5 per cent. v/v of alcohol. The only important exception is the United States, which still measures alcoholic strengths in terms of a proof spirit. Unfortunately, U.S. proof is not the same as the traditional British one, which fact can cause considerable confusion, since the same liquor will have a higher proof strength in the United States than in Britain. In fact, U.S. proof spirit contains 50 per cent. of alcohol by volume; hence to convert U.S. proof to per cent. v/v one simply divides by two. 100°U.S. proof is equivalent to 87·4° British proof, and 100° British proof to 114·3°U.S.

Table 1 overleaf gives the approximate alcoholic strengths of the liquors most commonly consumed in Great Britain.

[5] See p. 2, n. 3.

TABLE 1

		%[6] Alcohol v/v	Approximate weight of alcohol per drink	
			Grams	Measure
Beer	Draught Bitter	2½–4½	11–20	Pint
	Draught Mild	2½–3	11–14	Pint
	Bottled (Light Ales, etc.)	2½–4	6–9	
	Bottled ("Export" and other strong Light Ales)	ca.4½	ca.10	Half pint
	Lagers	4–5½	9–12	
	Stout	3–4½	6½–10	
	Guinness	4½	10	
	Strong Ales ("Barley Wines")	8½–11	13–17	'Nip' (⅓ pint)
Cider	Commercial	3½–5	8–11	½ pint
	Farmhouse	Very variable 4–(10?)	11–(50?)	Pint
Table Wines[7]	Still	6½–15½	6–14	
	Claret, Burgundy	ca.11	ca.10	4-oz.
	Hock	ca.9	ca.8	(100ml)
	Sparkling (Champagne)	ca.10	ca.9	glass
Fortified Wines and Aperitifs	Sherry, Port, Madeira,	17–21	8–10	2-oz.
	Vermouths and Aperitifs (Dubonnet, etc.)	17–18	8–9	(100 ml) glass
Spirits	Whisky, Gin, Rum, Brandy, Vodka	40[8]	7½	British pub "single" (5/6 fl.oz.)[9]
Liqueurs	Alcoholic strengths vary widely	ca.15–55	Up to 10 grams, assuming a glass holding one English "single" spirit measure	

[6] For the alcoholic strengths of, and congeners present in, a very large number of fermented and distilled liquors, see *Bonte* (1978 and 1979). (Congeners are the trace constituents of a potable liquor which give it its characteristic flavour and bouquet.)

[7] By the Food Labelling Regulations 1980 (S.I. 1980 No. 1849), which have already been cited (p. 4), and which are based on EEC Regulations, the word "wine" without qualification may be applied only to plain fermented grape juice. There is also an EEC Regulation that "wine" may not contain less than 9 per cent. by volume of alcohol; this regulation is not, however, always observed. In Great Britain, for fiscal purposes wines are at present divided into four categories, namely: under 15 per cent. of alcohol by volume (*i.e.* all unfortified table wines); 15–18 per cent.; 18–22 per cent.; over 22 per cent. Within each category the duty payable does not depend on the alcoholic strength.

WARNING

About the only completely unqualified statement which can safely be made about the absorption and effects of alcohol is that when a sufficient quantity has been absorbed the drinker will show the familiar symptoms of intoxication, and that if no more alcohol is consumed the effects will gradually wear off again.

Vast numbers of researches have been made, and their results published in thousands of scientific papers, on the physiology, pharmacology, distribution in the body and effects of alcohol. Many of these have produced extremely interesting, valuable and significant results. It should however always be remembered that the personal factor—the individual characteristics of the drinker— represents the most important single variable in all of these experiments. Some experimenters have tended to forget this fact, and have sometimes drawn general conclusions which were simply not warranted by the comparatively small body of evidence upon which they were based. The results of any experiment based on a limited number of subjects can at the most, in the absence of conflicting results, be tentatively accepted as valid.

We must not nevertheless throw out the baby of common sense with the bath water of incompletely verified results. To take a crude but, we hope, adequate analogy, although the human skull varies very widely indeed in thickness and strength, that fact does not justify any doubt about the outcome in the case of an unfortunate individual who falls on his head from a tenth-floor window.

---

[8] Although 40 per cent. by volume is the strength at which spirits are normally sold in Britain, other strengths may be encountered. By the Food and Drugs Act 1955, s.3(4), the minimum legal alcoholic strength for spirits is 65° proof, which is about 37·25 per cent. alcohol by volume; cut-price spirits ("cocktail gin") may contain this legal minimum. Schnapps (Scandinavian "akavit") may contain up to 43 per cent., U.S. spirits and spirit-based "cordials" up to 50 per cent., and it is possible to obtain vodka containing up to 80 per cent. ("Polish spirit," used by amateur winemakers for fortification).

[9] By the Weights and Measures Act 1963, Sched. 4, Pt. 6, the measures by which spirits are sold for consumption on the premises shall be one-quarter, one-fifth, or one-sixth of a gill. The customary "single" is five-sixths of a fluid ounce—that is, one-sixth of a gill. The "single" formerly customary in Scotland was one twenty-second of a bottle—that is, 1·21 fluid ounce, or approximately one quarter of a gill—and contained 10 g of alcohol.

FURTHER READING

Further information about potable liquors will be found in:

Alexis Lichine, *Encyclopaedia of Wines and Spirits*, (Cassell, London, revd. ed. 1974).

Michael Jackson (Ed.), *The World Guide to Beer* (Mitchell Beazley, London, 1977).

Both of these should be available in any good reference library.

Much information about *congeners* will be found in *Kricka and Clark*, Chap. 4 (see Scientific References, *post*, p. 261).

Chapter 2

THE ABSORPTION AND ELIMINATION OF ALCOHOL

For alcohol to produce its well-known effects, desired or otherwise, it must reach the brain. To do so after having been drunk it must first pass into the bloodstream by absorption through the walls of the alimentary tract. This is a straightforward physicochemical process of diffusion, which will continue as long as the concentration of alcohol within the alimentary tract is higher than that in the blood.

The alcohol first passes in this way from the stomach and duodenum into the portal vein, the blood in which carries it to the liver. This blood then passes from the liver to the right side of the heart, thence to the lungs, back as arterial blood to the left side of the heart, and from there into the general systemic circulation, by which means it eventually reaches the brain. As the liver has also its own supply of arterial blood, the alcohol in the general systemic circulation reaches it again by that route. Since about 75 per cent. of the total blood reaching the liver comes via the portal vein and only about 25 per cent. via the hepatic artery (*Brettel*, 1975), a small amount of the alcohol absorbed from the alimentary tract is oxidised before it can reach the general circulation and never appears there. (German writers refer to this as the "absorption deficiency.")

As soon as any alcohol is present in the bloodstream, various mechanisms for its removal come into action, by far the most important of these being the destructive oxidation in the liver mentioned in the previous paragraph. The overall rate of its removal is practically constant, and is considerably less than the rate at which alcohol initially enters the blood by diffusion. Therefore, a graph in which blood-alcohol concentration is plotted against time (the well-known *blood-alcohol curve*) should show:

1. A sharply rising portion, during which absorption is faster than elimination. (The *absorption phase*.)
2. A point of inflexion, which represents the moment at which

the gradually diminishing rate of absorption becomes slower than the constant rate of elimination. (The maximum or *peak*.)

3. A gently falling portion, which is approximately a straight line and represents the elimination of alcohol from the blood-stream at a constant rate. (The *elimination phase*.)

The "typical," idealised blood-alcohol curve therefore appears as shown in figure 1, and two actual experimentally determined ones are shown in figure 2.

EXPRESSION OF BLOOD-ALCOHOL CONCENTRATIONS

In any meaningful discussion of the effects of alcohol and its distribution in the body, it is necessary to specify the actual concentrations in the blood and other body fluids. These concentrations will always be vastly smaller than those in the alcoholic drinks mentioned in Chapter 1. (The concentration of alcohol in the blood of a very drunk man is about one-tenth of that in a very weak beer.) It is therefore convenient to use different units from those suitable for alcoholic drinks.

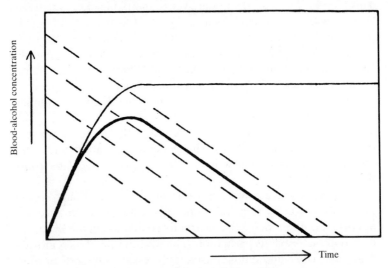

Figure 1. The Blood-Alcohol Curve: Theory

Alcohol is rapidly absorbed from the alimentary tract into the bloodstream. If there were no mechanism for its removal, its concentration in the blood would therefore rise to and remain at a level determined by the quantity absorbed (thin solid line). However, in fact oxidation in the liver removes it at a nearly constant rate, so that the blood concentration would fall regularly from any given initial concentration (sloping broken lines). The resultant of these two opposing processes is the *blood-alcohol curve* (thick solid line).

In general three systems are or have been used throughout the world.

1. A percentage figure, as used in the United States, and (formerly) in Great Britain. This has the advantage that everyone is familiar with percentages, but it has two disadvantages:

(a) The figure is ambiguous unless it is clearly specified whether it is weight/weight, weight/volume or volume/volume (see p. 4). Per cent. weight/volume is most commonly used, and may be assumed if not stated. However, errors have arisen from failure to be specific on this point.
(b) The figure is always a fraction (*i.e.* less than 1·0) and often indeed has a zero after the decimal point. Serious mistakes could therefore arise from printing errors leading to the misplacement of the decimal point or to the presence of too few or too many zeros.

2. A figure expressing grams (of alcohol) per litre (of blood or other body fluid). This is therefore parts per thousand, weight/volume, and is commonly used on the Continent with the designa-

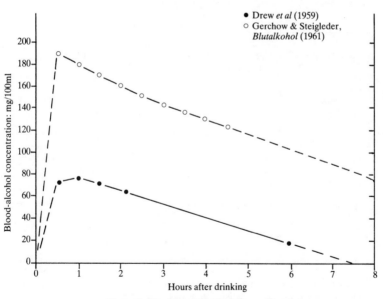

Figure 2. The Blood-Alcohol Curve: Practice

Two actual blood-alcohol curves, for a large and a small amount of alcohol, based on figures recorded from experiments performed in Germany and Britain respectively.

tion "pro mille" (contracted as ‰). This system is convenient, but suffers also from the disadvantage that a decimal point almost always has to be used.

3. The system now general in this country and adopted by statute, in which the weight/volume concentrations are expressed in milligrams per 100 millilitres (mg/100ml). The use of such units may be prima facie less familiar, but the system has the immense advantage that the relevant concentrations are always fairly large whole numbers with which it is never necessary to use decimal points. This system will be adopted throughout this book.

There seems to be little hope of a uniform system being adopted throughout the world. One of the present writers was, as it happens, secretary of a working party which met to discuss this very matter at two international conferences, and the party finally disbanded with the conviction that each country was too firmly wedded to its own system for any change to be practicable.[1]

Should it be necessary to convert from one system to another, Table 2 shows the simple arithmetic necessary.

TABLE 2

To convert To From	Milligrams per 100 millilitres (mg/100ml)	Parts per 1,000 (Pro mille) ‰	Per cent. w/v
Milligrams per 100 millilitres (mg/100ml)		Divide by 100	Divide by 1,000
Parts per 1,000 (Pro mille) ‰	Multiply by 100		Divide by 10
Per cent. w/v	Multiply by 1,000	Multiply by 10	

[1] That sentence was written some years ago, but until recently there was no evidence that it was not still true. Now, however, some American writers have started to use milligrams/deciliter (mg/dl), which is the same as the British system, but with a different name for the unit of volume. (1 deciliter (U.S.) or decilitre (British) = 100 millilitres).

The Blood-Alcohol Curve: Absorption and the "Peak"

In the present context, the three most important quantities of which the blood-alcohol curve is an expression are:

1. The time until the peak – that is, the time after drinking starts at which the highest concentration is reached. According to the type of drink and circumstances of drinking, this may be as short as 20 minutes or as long as several hours. (*Zink and Reinhardt* (1975) put the maximum time at about two hours; *Payne* (1970) at about three.) Most commonly, however, the time will be of the order of 30–60 minutes.

2. The concentration at the peak—that is, the highest concentration reached in the blood after drinking.

3. The rate of fall of the blood-alcohol concentration after the peak.

As 1. and 2. are closely connected, and indeed to some extent interdependent, they will be considered together. It should be obvious from what has been said above that there will be at least some connection between time-to-peak and peak height; if absorption is rapid, the maximum quantity of alcohol will pass into the blood before any significant degree of elimination has taken place; whereas, if absorption is slow, a significant quantity of alcohol will have been eliminated from the blood before absorption is complete.

To begin with, the theoretical maximum possible peak concentration is easily calculated, provided that one:

1. Assumes that all the alcohol has been absorbed before any significant degree of elimination has taken place.

2. Assumes that the alcohol is uniformly distributed throughout all the water in the body.

3. Knows the total quantity of water in the body.

4. Knows the total quantity of alcohol consumed.

This subject was extensively studied in the pioneering work of *E. Widmark* in Sweden (1914 onwards), and he produced the simple formula:

$$a = c \times p \times r$$

where a is the total amount of alcohol taken, c is the peak concentration in the blood, p is the weight of the drinker, and r is a factor derived from the proportion of the total body mass over which the alcohol can be distributed. r is in fact the ratio of the water content

of the entire body to that of the circulating blood. Widmark himself referred to it as the "reduced body weight," but it is now more
commonly referred to simply as the "Widmark factor."

Blood contains 80–85 per cent. of water; 83 per cent. may be
taken as a fair average figure. The proportion of water in the body
as a whole depends on age, sex and body habit, and varies from
slightly under 50 to slightly over 60 per cent. (It is not necessary
here to specify whether these percentages are weight/weight,
weight/volume or volume/volume, since the specific gravities of
blood and of the body as a whole may be assumed for the purpose
of this calculation to be the same as that of water.) Fat does not
absorb alcohol to any significant extent (see. for example, *Grüner*
1959), and fatty tissue and bone contain less water than other tissues; the combined effects of these facts is that the proportion of
water in the body is higher in the young than in the old, in the lean
than in the obese, and in men than in women (whose bodies contain a higher proportion of fat). The theoretical values of *r* will
therefore be 60/83 (*i.e.* 0·72) for a body containing 60 per cent. of
water, and 50/83 (*i.e.* 0·60) for a body containing 50 per cent. of
water. The mean values of *r* found experimentally by Widmark
himself were 0·68 for men and 0·55 for women. These figures
agree reasonably well with the theoretically derived ones. They
have also been more recently confirmed, within a reasonable margin, by *Zink and Wendler* (1978) using an examination of over 900
previously published blood-alcohol curves, and, as long as the
measurements were made only with drink taken on an empty stomach, by *Batt and Couchman* (Melbourne 1977, p. 200).

If therefore, to take one simple example, an 11-stone man
drinks two double whiskies, his theoretical peak blood concentration will be given by (turning the Widmark equation around):

$$c = \frac{a}{p \times r}$$

Since a single whisky contains approximately 7·5 g of alcohol
(p. 6), *a* will be 30g, and *p* (11 stones = 154lbs.) is approximately
70kg. Therefore, taking *r* as 0·68,

$$c = \frac{30}{70 \times 0·68}$$

$$= 0·063 \text{ per cent. w/v}$$

$$= 63 \text{ mg/100 ml}$$

Any experimentally determined blood-alcohol curve will always (for an initially sober subject) start at zero, rise to a maximum and fall to zero again. For a number of reasons, however, the peak concentration may in practice differ considerably from the theoretical value given by the above simple equation. The inevitable slight "absorption deficiency" has already been mentioned (p. 9), as has the fact that slow absorption is bound to lead to a lower peak. On the other hand, a short-lived higher-than-theoretical peak may occur as a temporary "overshoot" if the absorption is very rapid (fairly strong drink on an empty stomach: see p. 16 below). This will occur if absorption is so rapid that alcohol initially enters the blood stream faster than it can diffuse from there into the tissues. Lastly, the blood-alcohol level may in some circumstances rise to a "plateau" rather than a peak; this may happen after drinking beer, when a large quantity of dilute alcohol is absorbed rather slowly.

As mentioned below (p. 18), alcohol is absorbed more quickly from the duodenum (the first part of the small intestine) than the stomach. It is well established that, in consequence of that fact, persons who have undergone partial or complete gastrectomy absorb alcohol much more quickly than normal healthy persons do, and show a pronounced overshoot as defined in the previous paragraph. (See, for example, *Brinkmann et al.* 1970.)

In short, a prediction of the peak concentration based on the Widmark equation cannot be more than a rough guide. In an elaborate series of tests undertaken by the Royal Air Force Institute of Pathology (*Flanagan et al.* 1979), in which the amounts drunk by 131 test subjects at 12 social functions were accurately noted, it was found that in many cases the actual blood-alcohol levels differed very considerably from those predicted by Widmark calculations.

We shall consider in the following paragraphs the factors which may modify the course of the blood-alcohol curve and the peak concentration resulting from the consumption of a given amount of alcohol.

Duration of drinking

It is obvious that, if the drink is taken sufficiently slowly, the alcohol can be eliminated as fast, or nearly as fast, as it enters the blood, and the highest concentration actually reached may be only a small fraction of that calculated as above. If, to anticipate (*cf.*

pp. 19–20), we assume that an average man can eliminate the equivalent of one single whisky per hour, then, if the two doubles of the above example were taken as four singles at hourly intervals, the blood concentration would never rise above that corresponding to a single whisky—approximately 16mg/100ml. As a rough-and-ready rule of thumb, it can be taken that any drinking time longer than an hour will significantly reduce the peak blood-alcohol concentration below that reached if the drink were taken all at once.

Nature of liquor consumed

There has been a great deal of experimental work on this point, and the results have not always been free of contradictions. However it can be taken as established that:

1. In general, up to a certain point (but see 2., below) the more concentrated the alcohol the faster it is absorbed and the higher, therefore, is the peak concentration.

2. The maximum rate of absorption appears to occur when the drink contains somewhere about 20 per cent. volume/volume of alcohol. *Newman* (cited *Drew et al.* 1959) suggests that higher concentrations than this (*i.e.* neat spirits on an empty stomach) irritate the gastro-intestinal tissues and cause the absorptive surfaces to be coated and protected by the secretion of mucus. He also suggests that the motility of the stomach is decreased. *Wayne* (1962) states that concentrated alcohol tends to inhibit the opening of the pyloric sphincter between the stomach and the duodenum; both this and Newman's second suggestion would mean that the passage of the alcohol into the duodenum (where it is absorbed most rapidly—see p. 18) is delayed, so that the rate of absorption falls.

3. The alcohol is absorbed rather more rapidly from carbonated (sparkling) drinks—which is why one gets a bigger "kick" from champagne than from a still wine of equal alcoholic strength.

4. Absorption is much delayed or reduced by the presence of soluble nutrients in the drink. In particular, absorption is much slower from beer, which contains various carbohydrates, etc., than from spirits diluted with water or soda to the same actual alcoholic strength. (See, for example, *Mallach* 1966.) In a later test *Dussault and Chappel* (Toronto 1974, p. 365) gave their subjects various doses of alcohol ranging from 0·25 to 1·5 grams per kilogram body-weight and measuring the blood-alcohol levels subsequently

reached. They found that the beer peak was consistently about an hour later and 25 per cent. lower than the whisky one, and that the difference tended to be larger the higher the dose of alcohol. This effect has in fact been found to be so general that, if the alcohol is drunk as a heavy beer, the peak blood-alcohol concentration may be as little as one-third of the theoretical maximum for the alcohol taken.

The presence or absence, and nature, of food in the stomach

It is a well-known fact that alcohol taken with food usually has less effect than that taken on an empty stomach. This has been borne out by many experimental investigations, although quantitatively the results have differed somewhat. However, to take a few examples, *Abele and Kropp* (1958), *Lin et al.* (1976), *Welling et al.* (1977) and *Batt and Couchman* (Melbourne 1977, p. 200), using various combinations of alcohol dosages and time lapse between eating and drinking, all found that a full meal taken before drinking could reduce the blood-alcohol level to about half that produced by the same quantity of liquor on an empty stomach. *Welling*, who recorded the largest effects in proportion to the quantity of alcohol taken, suggests that some of the alcohol may be oxidised by the food in the gastro-intestinal tract before absorption can occur.

The evidence as to which types of food are most effective in this respect is somewhat conflicting, and some of the claims which have been made are probably exaggerated and possibly not disinterested. Olive oil, milk, yoghourt and mashed potatoes have all found their champions. In general, both fats (including vegetable oils) and carbohydrates seem to show this effect. Fats have generally been considered particularly effective but *Welling (loc. cit.)* found carbohydrates even more so.

It should perhaps be noted that results such as these cited above really apply only to alcohol consumed as wines or spirits; the absorption from beer is in any case so much retarded that the additional effect of food is relatively much less important.

Some evidence has even been found that eating after absorption is complete increases the rate of metabolism of alcohol. This is discussed in *Cooper, Schwar and Smith* pp. 128–29. *Etzler et al.* reporting in 1968 had detected this effect, but, according to their results, it was so small as to be barely significant and occurred only when the blood alcohol had already fallen to a low level.

Physiological factors

When all of the above factors have been taken into account, there will still remain, as a factor influencing the rate of absorption, the anatomical and physiological characteristics of the drinker. There are probably variations, both between different people and between different times for the same person, in such things as stomach-wall permeability and the blood supply to the alimentary tract. These causes affecting the absorption rate are, however, not open to experimental investigation, and their combined effects must simply appear as the scatter of the results normal in all biological experimentation.

However, the most important factor of this type, of which there has been some investigation, is the rate at which the stomach contents pass into the duodenum. It has been shown that absorption through the duodenal wall is much faster than through the stomach wall. Therefore the overall rate of absorption will depend on how fast and how soon the stomach contents pass into the duodenum, and this in turn will depend on the opening and closing of the pyloric sphincter, which controls the opening between these two organs. This also accounts for the well-known fact that persons who have undergone gastrectomy are more easily and more quickly affected by alcohol taken.

This factor may well account for the irregular course sometimes shown by experimentally determined blood-alcohol curves (*Ponsold*, Indiana 1965, p. 127); the sudden passage into the duodenum of alcohol-laden liquid in the stomach would be expected to result in a temporarily raised rate of absorption. It has also been shown that in certain circumstances the intake of food may, contrary to the normal rule described above, temporarily raise the absorption rate, since its entry into a stomach empty except for some alcohol-laden liquid may cause the closed sphincter to open. *Batt and Couchman* (*loc. cit.*) also emphasise the importance of the role of the pyloric sphincter in regulating the rate of absorption, and suggest that the personal variability of its actions may be a main cause of unexpected irregularities in blood-alcohol levels following given doses of alcohol.

THE BLOOD-ALCOHOL CURVE: ELIMINATION

Oxidation in the liver, which eliminates 90 per cent. or more of the alcohol absorbed, takes place in two stages:

alcohol → acetaldehyde → acetic acid,

each stage being catalysed by the appropriate enzyme, that responsible for the first stage of the conversion being known as *alcohol dehydrogenase* (ADH). The concentration of acetaldehyde in the blood remains practically constant at a level dependent on the overall rate of alcohol metabolism until all the alcohol has been metabolised (*Machata and Prokop* 1971 and 1978). Since, however, the second stage of the conversion is very much faster than the first, this concentration remains minute. (There is some evidence that in alcoholics some drugs may affect the rate of the alcohol-acetaldehyde reaction. See *Kolenda* 1975. The action of drugs given to alcoholics for aversion therapy is to block the second stage of the conversion, so that the accumulation of rather toxic acetaldehyde makes the drinker feel very ill.) The end product, acetic acid, is finaly oxidised to carbon dioxide and water. Alcohol may therefore be regarded as a food in the sense that its metabolism produces energy, and it can replace to some extent energy-giving foods such as fats and carbohydrates.

The other routes of elimination are by excretion of unchanged alcohol which has diffused into the urine via the kidneys, into expired breath via the lungs, and into sweat via the sweat glands. All of these taken together probably do not in normal circumstances account for more than 5–10 per cent. of the alcohol ingested; it is fallacious to suppose that alcohol can be got rid of to any significant extent by "sweating it out" or by copious urination, since the greatest quantities of urine or sweat that can be produced are barely significant in comparison with the total quantity of water in the body. To a first approximation, therefore, the elimination of alcohol from the blood will proceed at a constant rate determined by the oxidative capacity of the liver enzymes, and not affected by the peak blood-alcohol level reached.

Numerous series of experiments have been made to determine this rate of fall, and the results have agreed remarkably closely. *Elbel and Schleyer* (p. 61) give a mean value based on numerous tests made during the years 1930–55 which, converted to our notation for concentration, corresponds to a fall of 13·8 mg/100 ml per hour. *Jacobsen* (1952) gives 15±5 mg/100 ml per hour. Some more recent results (all expressed as mg/100 ml per hour) are:

Drew et al. (1959): approximately 16 (mean)
Coldwell and Smith (1959): 13±5

Ponsold and Heite (1960): Mean 17·2, with scatter of "up to 50 per cent." on either side of the mean

Foster, Schulz and Starck (1961): Range from 12 to 28; mean 16 and modal (*i.e.* most common) value 13

Schleyer and Wichmann (1962): 15±7

Bonnichsen, Dimberg and Sjoberg (1964): 14 to 20

Shumate et al. (1967): Mean 17; range 10–21·8

Oliver (1982): range 9–27

Taking all of these results into account, it would seem that where a most probable rate of fall of blood alcohol has to be assumed, we should take 15mg/100 ml per hour, but that we cannot assume that the rate will not be as low as 10 (or even less in extreme cases) or as high as 25 (or even more in a few extreme cases).

These rates of elimination correspond, for a man of average weight (11 stones or 70 kilograms), to the disappearance of between approximately 5 and 13 grams of alcohol per hour, with a most probable figure in the neighbourhood of 7. This last figure is almost exactly the amount of alcohol contained in a single whisky (Chap. 1.).

In the feasibility study set up by the Home Office, following the publication in 1976 of the Blennerhassett report, to examine the use of substantive breath analysis (*Emerson et al.* 1980) it was necessary to take the rate of disappearance of alcohol from the blood into account because of the time interval between the taking of the blood specimens and the subsequent breath analyses. A rate of 15 mg/100 ml/hour was assumed.

Shumate et al. (*loc. cit.*), and also *Patel* (1969), point out that there is a characteristic rate of fall for each individual. This is in fact according to *Vessell et al.* (1971) innate and genetically determined; it is unaffected by, for example, the continuous administration of alcohol for several weeks before it is measured. For a given individual it has, however, been found to show a diurnal variation with a 24-hour cycle. (See *Kricka and Clark* pp. 44–45.) For a highly technical theoretical discussion of this topic see *Mullen* (1977).

Although a constant rate of disappearance of blood alcohol, which accords reasonably well with the experimental results, should be assumed in practice if any calculations have to be made, careful and reliable experimenters have found some evidence that the rate varies slightly with blood-alcohol level, age and degree of habituation to alcohol. A good many years ago, *Goldberg* of the Karolinska Institute in Stockholm, probably the leading authority in this field, showed that the rate tended to be slightly greater for high levels. More recently, it was found that the rate seems to be slightly greater in the old than in the young, and is considerably greater in alcoholics than in non-drinkers or occasional drinkers, (*Schweitzer* 1968; *Bonnichsen et al.* 1968). Bonnichsen, who was Director of the State Laboratory doing the blood-alcohol analyses for the whole of Sweden, is a most trustworthy authority.

There is a reasonable theoretical explanation for a greater rate at very high levels. Since diffusion into the breath and urine is a physico-chemical process of equilibration, the *concentrations* of alcohol in these two fluids will depend on that in the blood, and therefore the absolute quantities removed in that way per unit of time will be higher, the higher is the concentration in the blood. On the other hand, oxidation will remove the same absolute quantity per unit of time. Therefore, removal via the breath and urine will be proportionately the more effective the higher is the blood-alcohol level. *Lundquist and Wolthers* (1958) have suggested that at blood-alcohol levels of the order of 300mg/100ml, elimination via the breath and urine may represent as much as 15 per cent. of the total, as opposed to about 3 per cent. for a blood-alcohol level of 50mg/100ml.

At very low blood-alcohol levels the concentration of alcohol in the blood passing through the liver may also not be sufficient fully to saturate the oxidative capacity of the enzymes available, thereby reducing the absolute rate of destruction. This effect will however appear only at blood-alcohol levels too low to be of any significance in our present context. (See *e.g. Lester* 1961 and 1962.)

OTHER POSSIBLE EFFECTS ON THE BLOOD-ALCOHOL CURVE

Drugs

There is practically no experimental evidence that the administration of other drugs has any effect on the course of the blood-alcohol curve. For example, *Goldberg*, (Indiana 1965, p. 235) tried eleven different drugs in this respect, all with negative results. Insulin has been found to accelerate the metabolism of alcohol in dogs (*Newman et al.* 1959), but there has been little or no experimental confirmation of this effect in man—the administration of insulin to human subjects could produce a dangerous hypoglycaemia.

The possible effects of other drugs or compounds on the *effects* of alcohol—the level of intoxication—is however another matter. The effects of drugs in general will be discussed in a later chapter, but it will be convenient to mention here the question of whether any artificially accelerated sobering-up is possible. *Mattila* (Stockholm 1980, p. 909) tested a number of drugs of widely varying types in this respect, but was unable to find any clear evidence that any of them significantly counteracted the effects of alcohol. In particular, he was unable to confirm for caffeine the repute of strong black coffee in such a role. However, *Moskowitz and Burns* (Stockholm 1980, p. 969), of whom Moskowitz is one of the leading researchers in this field, are prepared to admit that caffeine may reduce impairment in some circumstances, and even commit themselves to the statement " . . . it can be said that several cups of strong coffee or tea may produce improvement in the performance of an alcohol-impaired driver."

Fructose: "soberers"

There is however one compound which has been extensively investigated in this context, namely *fructose* (laevulose, fruit sugar). On the whole, the experimental evidence appears to show (but with some conflicting results) that the ingestion of a sufficient quantity of this compound along with alcohol leads to a lower blood-alcohol level than would have been produced without it. This effect seems to have been first suggested in 1937 and confirmed in 1951 (*Stulfauth and Neumaier* 1951.) Further discussion will be found in, for example, *Elbel and Schleyer,* pp. 77–80; *Lester* (1961 and 1962); *Seppälä* et al. (1976–3); *Kricka and Clark* pp. 42–43. The effect was also discovered by *Lowenstein et al.* (1970); *Soterakis and Iber* (1975); *Schellmann et al.* (1979 and 1980); *Goldberg et al.* (1979). However, *Dundee et al.* (1971) and *Ylikahri et al.* (1976), were unable to confirm its reality. A possible explanation of these discrepant results is that the authors named had not seen or had disregarded some previously published Rumanian research (*Ghimicescu et al.* Freiburg 1969, p. I/9), in which it was found that two out of three test subjects showed the fructose effect on alcohol metabolism, whereas one third did not.

The effect, if real, is due to a complex biochemical interaction between the metabolic pathways of fructose and alcohol. (See

Kricka and Clark, loc. cit.) Different figures have been reported for the actual extent of the blood-alcohol reduction. *Lowenstein et al (loc. cit.)* found a reduction of as much as 43 per cent. but a lower figure is quoted by almost all other writers. *Patel* (1969) also found an increased rate of disappearance of alcohol from the blood—in the case of the subjects he tested from a mean of 17mg/100ml/hour (extremes 8–27) to a mean of 23·5 (extremes 10–32). Among the sugars which have been tested, only fructose has been found to have this effect; glucose is quite ineffective, and sucrose (ordinary cane or beet sugar) is effective only in so far as it is partially converted to fructose by hydrolysis in digestion.

This effect of fructose is produced only when it is administered along with the alcohol, and a dose large enough to be effective produces unpleasant side effects—nausea, severe abdominal pains and other symptoms. Over-indulgence in alcohol cannot be offset by the *subsequent* taking of any tolerable quantity of fructose.

A number of proprietary products have however been marketed in this country and on the Continent with the claim that, taken after drinking, they will speedily reduce the blood-alcohol level and act as "soberers." It has also been claimed for some that they will alleviate hangovers. Most if not all of these products have fructose as their active principle, in some cases with the addition of vitamin C. These products have included (this list does not pretend to be complete):
Activit; Alger; Alkohol Minus ("Almi"); Alsaver; Contra; Jatroneural; Laevoral C; Promill-X; Sangrita; Sobaro; Stop.

The claims made for the great majority of these products, whether as "soberers" or as hangover-alleviators, have not stood up to scientific testing. It would seem to be true in general for them what *Camps and Robinson* (1968) said of one: that they "are unlikely to be of value to the apparently healthy social drinker who wishes to drive home after an evening's entertainment without infringing the law." (See also: *Besserer and Springer* 1971; *Span et al.* 1977; *Bilzer and Kühnholz* 1979).

Muscular Activity

Some writers have claimed at one time that strenuous work does, others that it does not, increase the rate of alcohol metabolism. (See references cited by *Pawan* 1968.) An increased rate of respiration will of course *slightly* increase elimination (see p. 19), but there is no very convincing evidence that muscular activity increases the actual rate of metabolism *per se*. Pawan's own experiments, in which the subjects undertook really strenuous exercise (a 3-mile run or a 1,000-yard swim), produced no evidence of increased elimination. (See also *Elbel and Schleyer*, pp. 92–94; *Krauland, Mallach, Mellerowicz and Müller* 1965; *Krauland* 1966.)

Sleep: unconsciousness

The rate of alcohol elimination is unchanged during sleep or unconsciousness. (*Elbel and Schleyer*, pp. 92–94; *Apel* 1960.)

Vomiting

It is obvious that if vomiting occurs whilst there is still alcohol in the stomach, the alcohol ejected in the vomit cannot be absorbed and the blood-alcohol level will not therefore rise as high as if vomiting had not occurred. Vomiting, if it occurs before the peak has been reached, does appear to produce some small changes in the blood-alcohol curve, which can be ascribed to a changed rate of absorption of the alcohol remaining in the alimentary tract and not ejected with the vomit, but the evidence on this point is conflicting and unclear. There is no evidence that vomiting, whether spontaneous or induced, occurring after the peak—during the elimination phase—has any effect on the curve. It is of interest, incidentally, that the intravenous injection of alcohol can produce vomiting, which shows that it may be a reaction of the nervous system rather than a purely local effect. (*Elbel and Schleyer* pp. 97–99; *Wayne* 1962 Discussion; *Ditt* 1963; *Joachim, Friedrich and Ullmann* 1974).

Blood loss

The loss of up to 10 per cent. of the total blood in the body produces no change in the course of the blood-alcohol curve. (*Elbel and Schleyer*, pp. 102–103; *Ditt and Schulze* 1962.)

Other Physiological and Pathological Factors

Apart from the obvious facts that if no more drink is taken the blood-alcohol eventually falls to zero and a hangover eventually wears off, there is no obvious simple correlation between the magnitude of the former and the severity of the latter. There is a limited amount of experimental evidence that neither slight liver dysfunction (*Elbel and Schleyer* p. 55; *Kulpe and Mallach* 1961), nor anaemia (*Schleyer* 1966), nor diabetes (*Coldwell and Grant* 1963), nor head injuries (*Cooper, Schwar and Smith*, p. 130) have any effect on the blood-alcohol curve. The rate of alcohol metabolism in women has been found to vary slightly with the phase of the menstrual cycle (*Kricka and Clark* p. 44, citing a published source of 1974). To anticipate, however, later experiments (*Linnoila et. al.* 1980) failed to reveal any statistically significant connexion between the phase of the menstrual cycle and performance in tests of function such as reaction time or vigilance. (cf. Chap. 4)

The matters discussed in these preceding paragraphs are dealt with in some detail in *Cooper, Schwar and Smith*, pp. 126ff and 144ff.

"ENDOGENOUS" ALCOHOL

Traces of ethanol occurring as intermediate products of normal metabolism were at one time thought to be present in the body. However, it is now certain that these, if they occur at all, are much too minute to be of any forensic significance whatsoever. (See *Lester* 1961, modified by *Lester* 1961 and 1962; *Harger*, Indiana 1965, p. 182; *Harger and Forney* 1967; *Sprung et al.* 1981.)

INGESTION OF ALCOHOL BY INHALATION

It has occasionally been suggested that alcohol present in the body could have been inhaled as vapour—for example, by brewery workers, users of paints and varnishes containing ethanol as a solvent, etc.

The relationship between alcohol vapour in the lungs and alcohol in the blood will be discussed again below (pp. 116 *et seq.*). The earlier work on absorption by inhalation is summarised by *Elbel and Schleyer* pp. 11–12. The results of this are very inconclusive. It can however be asserted that blood-alcohol concentrations significant in the present context will never have been produced by the inhalation of alcohol vapour, since high concentrations of alcohol vapour are unbearably irritating to breathe, and the highest blood-alcohol level which could ever in normal circumstances be produced in this way seems to lie between 10 and 20mg/100ml. (*Elbel and Schleyer* p. 11; more recently confirmed by *Mason, J.K. and Blackmore* 1972.)

FURTHER READING

The names cited will be found arranged alphabetically in the list of scientific references on pp. 253 *et seq*.

Pawan, *Physical Exercise and Alcohol Metabolism in Man* (1968).

Dussault and Chappel, *Blood-alcohol levels after whisky and beer* (1974).

Batt and Couchman, *Blood Alcohol Levels after Drinking* (1977).

Cooper, Schwär and Smith, (1979). Chaps. 14 (absorption), 16 (metabolism) and 17 (elimination).

Flanagan et al. *Blood Alcohol and Social Drinking* (1979).

Kricka and Clark, (1979). Chap. 3 (absorption, excretion and metabolism of ethanol).

CHAPTER 3

DISTRIBUTION

Alcohol which has diffused into the bloodstream is carried by it to all the tissues of the body, and diffuses into them also. Eventually it is uniformly distributed thoughout the water in the body, and the concentration in any tissue is then proportional to the water content of that tissue; how quickly this state of equilibrium is reached in any particular tissue, however, depends upon the blood supply to it.

This question of distribution is important in the present context because chemical analyses for alcohol are not or cannot always be made on the blood itself, but on some other body fluid, yet it is always the blood-alcohol concentration which we seek to know. The ultimately important quantity is of course the level of alcohol in the brain. This however must obviously remain unknown in living persons, and our limited knowledge of the relationship between blood alcohol and brain alcohol is derived either from animal experiments, the results of which do not necessarily apply *in toto* to Man, or from analyses when the opportunity presents itself of samples from dead bodies, the results of which may be falsified by post-mortem changes and are in any case not necessarily applicable to the living. Experimental observations on the effects of various body-alcohol levels are always therefore related to blood-alcohol levels, whether these are determined directly or by analysis of some other body fluid.

"Blood-alcohol concentration" is not however even by itself a completely unambiguous term, since there is ample evidence that during the absorption phase the concentration differs in different parts of the circulation. (See, for example, *Payne et al.* 1966.) It has been shown both by animal and by human experiments that during this period the concentration in venous blood lags behind that in the arterial, with that in capillary blood occupying an intermediate position, possibly rather nearer to the arterial than to the venous concentration. (Arterial blood never of course reaches the forensic chemist for analysis in the present context; any blood which he receives will normally be venous taken by syringe from a vein, commonly in the arm. According to *Gostomzyk et al*. 1974, it is immaterial which arm, since both sides show identical concentrations.) The time required for the venous to catch up with the arterial concentration appears to be most usually between 30 minutes and 2 hours.

This differential during absorption is not hard to explain. The highest concentration of alcohol presumably occurs in blood flowing from the sites of absorption at the wall of the alimentary tract. This blood then, as explained in Chapter 2, passes into the general circulation, and any alcholol in it diffuses into the tissues, slowly into the muscles and rapidly into organs such as the brain or kidneys. The same blood returning in the veins after passing through the capillaries will therefore show a lower concentration. As diffusion into the muscles is a rather slow process compared with absorption from the alimentary tract, the arterial blood concentration will during this phase be rising faster than diffusion can maintain the equilibrium.

Once the peak has been passed, the blood-alcohol level then changes almost entirely through the (relatively slow) destruction in the liver, and as this is slow enough for diffusion into or from the muscles nearly to keep pace with it, a state of equilibrium is maintained thoughout the whole circulation—in fact, throughout the whole body. (Very precise experiments by *Payne* and his colleagues (*loc. cit.*) have, it is true, shown that during the elimination phase the venous alcohol concentration may be slightly higher than the arterial, which they explain as showing that elimination by excretion and metabolism is not in fact quite as rapid as diffusion back from the tissues into the blood. This difference is however quite small, and can legitimately be disregarded for our present purpose.) In short, there is general agreement that after not more than 2 hours from the end of drinking, circulation equilibrium can be assumed, and that from then on there will be for practical purposes a uniform blood-alcohol level which can be determined by the analysis of blood taken from any source.

As alcohol diffuses out of the bloodstream it naturally appears also in all the secretions, and it has been amply demonstrated that it can be detected in every accessible body fluid other than blood—sweat, saliva, urine, milk and expired breath, to name the most important. In Western Europe and North America breath is normally, or at least is rapidly becoming, the fluid of choice for analysis with, in this country, blood itself as the "fall-back" in cases where breath analysis is uncertain or impracticable, and urine as a permissible but less desirable alternative. In the U.S.S.R., however, breath or saliva are normally used, with blood when the driver has "administrative or other responsibility" (*Ivanov* and *Uljanov* 1983).

As far as Great Britain is concerned, the relative importance of the fluids used depends upon legal and historical considerations as well as purely scientific ones. Before the passing of the Road Traffic Act 1962 the fluid submitted for analysis was normally urine, since at that time alcohol analyses were merely corroborative and their results given in evidence at the discretion of the courts; the law took then no special cognizance of alcohol concentration in body fluids, and urine was used simply because it was convenient to collect and easy to analyse. The 1962 Act for the first time directed that courts "shall have regard" to such analytical results; however, as the Act mentioned no figure, the convenience of urine left it the normally preferred fluid. It was only after the prescription of a legal limiting concentration by the Road Safety Act 1967, which clearly favoured the analysis of blood directly, with urine as a permissible but discouraged second choice, that the analysis of blood specimens became the norm. This practice lasted until the present time, when the Transport Act 1981 incorporated many of the recommendations of the Blennerhassett Committee's report of 1976, and made breath analysis the normal practice, "demoting" blood and urine to subordinate roles.

The rest of this chapter deals with the relationship between alcohol levels in the various body-fluids taken for analysis. The actual methods used will be discussed in the Chapter 5.

ALCOHOL IN THE BREATH

It is important to recognise that the 1981 Act represents a fundamental change of attitude towards breath analysis. In the various earlier Acts from 1967 onwards, it was assumed (on the basis of *ad hoc* experimentation and a large body of published work—see for example *Harger, Forney and Baker* (1956); *Begg, Hill and Nickolls* (1962); *Fox et al.* (Indiana 1965, p. 128); and *Enticknap and Wright* (Indiana 1965, p. 161); and the references cited in the following paragraphs—that the blood-alcohol level could not be determined via breath analysis with an accuracy sufficient for the implementation of a fixed-limit law, and breath analysis was therefore relegated to the secondary position of forming a preliminary screening test. The 1981 Act lays down a breath-alcohol level which, on the basis of the best available evidence (discussed in some detail below) represents the nominated limiting blood-alcohol level as accurately as possible, and makes it an offence to have a breath-alcohol level greater than this; there is then no room for argument as to whether the blood-alcohol level is or is not above the legal limit.

The use of the ratio of breath-alcohol to blood-alcohol concentrations has the advantage of immediacy—one depends directly upon the other at the time of sampling. On the other hand, the determination of the true value of this ratio is complicated by several factors.

The detection of alcohol in the breath after drinking wine was reported as long ago as 1847 (*Bouchardat and Sandras*, cited by *M. F. Mason and Dubowski* 1976), and the quantitative measurement of breath alcohol as a means of determining blood-alcohol seems to have been first suggested over 50 years ago, possibly by *Demole* in 1914 (*Elbel and Schleyer* p. 40), but more certainly by *Bogen* (1927); since about 1930 the topic has been the subject of a great deal of research. *M.F. Mason and Dubowski* (*loc. cit.*) list 27 published papers dealing with it in the years 1930–1974, and there have also been several more recent research reports.

The method rests fundamentally on the assumption that alcohol from the blood circulating through the lungs diffuses into the breath in the alveoli,[1] and that under the right conditions an equilibrium is reached, so that the alcohol content of breath expired from the lungs reflects accurately the blood-alcohol concentration at the moment of expiration.

The first and most fundamental essential is therefore that the true ratio at equilibrium between the alcohol contents of breath and blood shall be accurately known. To a first approximation, this almost certainly lies somewhere between 2,000 and 2,500, this figure being the number of volumes of breath containing the same mass (weight) of alcohol (as vapour) as one volume of blood (as dissolved liquid). The published mean values of this ratio cited by *M.F. Mason and Dubowski* (*loc. cit.*) range in fact from 1,142 to 3,478. If one excludes (1) these extreme and almost certainly unreliable figures, (2) figures based on measurements made with equip-

---

[1] The alveoli are the several hundred million tiny sacs in the lungs of each one of us in which the respiratory passages terminate and through the walls of which there is interchange of gases and vapours between the blood and the breath. (Astonishingly, their total surface area in the average individual is something like one third of that of a doubles tennis court!)

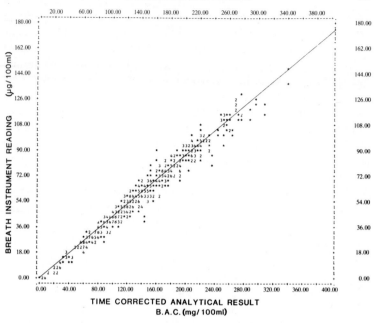

Figure 3: Correlation of Blood and Breath Alcohol Levels

This figure plots some of the results obtained in the 1981–2 field trials conducted by the Home Office of breath analysis to determine blood-alcohol levels. Each point represents the alcohol levels in one or more simultaneously taken pairs of blood and breath specimens. Blood-alcohol levels were determined by gas chromatography: breath-alcohol with a Lion Intoximeter 3000. The oblique line is where all of the points would have fallen if the blood/breath ratio was always exactly 2,300 to 1. "Time corrected" means that the results of the blood-alcohol analyses were adjusted to allow for the drop in blood alcohol between breath analysis and blood sampling. (*Crown copyright; courtesy of Controller, H.M. Stationery Office*)

ment calibrated on the basis of a ratio assumed *a priori*, and (3) one set of measurements on a dog, then the mean of the remaining 23 values is 2,166.

In practice a ratio of 2,100/1 was generally assumed, based on the careful work of *Liljestrand* and others in Scandinavia and of *Harger* and others in the United States; (*Liljestrand and Linde* 1930; *Forney, Harger, Hughes and Richards* 1964; *Harger, Forney and Barnes* 1950; *Harger* 1956, 1961, 1962 and Indiana 1965, p. 182; *Harger, Forney and Baker* 1956; *Harger and Forney* 1967, Freiburg 1969, Pt. II, p. 73), and instruments using breath-alcohol concentration as a measure of blood-alcohol (see pp. 89–95) were commonly calibrated on the basis of this figure. However, a review by *Wright, Jones and Jones* (1975) cast doubt on it, and the most recent and probably more accurate measurements put the mean ratio rather higher. *A.W. Jones* (Ph.D. thesis 1974, cited by *Alobaidi, Hill and Payne* 1976) gives 2,367; *Alobaidi et al.* themselves (*loc. cit.*) 2,475; *Dubowski* (1975) 2,280. It is now in fact generally agreed that 2,300 rather than Harger's 2,100 should be taken as the best ratio. This figure has also been amply corroborated by the careful, thorough and extensive field trials undertaken in preparation for the Transport Act 1981 (see *Emerson et al.* 1980; *Isaacs et al.* 1982), and it has been used in fixing the limiting legal level prescribed by that Act.

These descrepancies are almost certainly a consequence of, and highlight, the various factors which are possible sources of error. These are as follows:

1. The interchange of alcohol vapour is subject to a law of physics known as Henry's Law, which states that at a given temperature the mass of gas or vapour which dissolves in a given volume of solvent is proportional to the pressure. In the present instance this will be the vapour pressure of the alcohol dissolved in the blood, which depends on its concentration therein. (It has been shown by *M.F. Mason* (1974) that this relationship will not be affected by the ambient barometric pressure.) Any variation of temperature will however lead to error in a simple application of the Law. It can be assumed that the temperature inside the alveoli, where the initial interchange takes place, is the normal body temperature ($36 \cdot 8 \pm 0 \cdot 6°C$), but the temperature of the walls of the smaller respiratory passages, at which further blood/breath equilibration may occur, might be slightly lower, so that the action of Henry's Law at the intra-alveolar temperature can no longer be assumed.

Numerous measurements have been made of the temperature of expired breath as it leaves the body, and the results of these have given figures from as high as body temperature to as low as 31°C. *M.F. Mason and Dubowski* (*loc. cit.*) found 34–34·5°C for normal unforced expiration in healthy persons breathing in a comfortable ambient temperature, and calculated that there will be an approximately 6·5 per cent. variation in the breath/blood ratio for each 1°C of departure from body temperature. *Payne* (1975) gives 34°C and 5·8 per cent. per °C variation. It will be obvious that, whatever the precise figure, any measured value of the breath/blood ratio will be very sensitive to small variations in the temperature of the expired breath.

2. The state of the respiratory passages will obviously therefore be important. These are lined with mucus, and the rate and extent

of alcohol interchange may depend on the condition of this layer, which in turn will be affected by the absence or presence of any respiratory embarrassment or disease. According to *Wright, Jones and Jones (loc. cit.)*, in normal healthy persons the mucus layer will absorb more alcohol than it gives up, and lead therefore to a net diminution in the alcohol content of breath passing over it. (See also *Slemeyer*, Stockholm 1980, p. 456)

3. The manner in which the breath specimen is taken is therefore very important. (For a discussion of this, see *Slemeyer, loc. cit.*) In normal breathing, the first part of the breath expired will be a mixture of so-called "dead-space" air and air from the alveoli. Dead-space air is that filling the larger respiratory passages, which takes no part in the exchange of gases and vapours in the lungs and is simply forced in and out with each respiratory movement. Its normal volume is between 100 and 200 millilitres. In addition, the lungs can never be completely emptied; at the end of the most forced expiration possible they still contain 1–1·5 litres of so-called "residual air." The total volume of breath which can be used for analysis is then the total which can be expelled in one expiration (the so-called "vital capacity") minus the volume of the dead space. *Dubowski* (1975) gives the following figures (in millilitres) based on his own and previously published results.

Maximum exhalation during normal breathing:
> Men 1,180–4,550 (mean 2,951)
> Women 1,480–3,000 (mean 2,141)

Maximum possible exhalation using forced breathing:
> Men 2,245–6,550 (mean 4,502)
> Women 1,825–3,200 (mean 2,800)

Breath specimens for analysis collected during normal breathing could therefore have a volume of about 2,800ml in men and about 2,000 in women.

It will be clear from the foregoing that in taking a specimen of breath for analysis the object must be to obtain a sample of alveolar air. In the course of one exhalation, the alcohol content of the expired breath will rise from a low value (for the reasons discussed above) to, eventually, that of alveolar air, at which it will remain constant until the end of the exhalation (the so-called "alveolar plateau"). In practice there are two ways of ensuring that a meaningful specimen is collected. One, much used in the earlier researches, is to use *re-breathed* air—that is, air from a closed space into and out of which the test subject has breathed several times, so that his lungs and respiratory passages, and the collecting equipment, are all filled with identical air which has, or should have, the true alveolar-air alcohol content. This technique, however, although admirable for laboratory studies, is at the best inconvenient in routine breath analysis for law enforcement. The other way of collecting what is presumed to be alveolar air is to arrange for a forcible expiration by the subject, reject the first portion of exhaled breath and collect the remainder for analysis, assuming that the dead-space air will have been eliminated with the rejected portion. Even this may not however produce a wholly adequate specimen. For most commercial instruments the amount rejected varies with its design from a few hundred millilitres upwards, but several investigators recommend that at least 70 per cent. of the vital capacity, or at least 2 litres in the case of men, be discarded. (*See Dubowski* 1974; *M.F. Mason and Dubowski* 1976; *Jones and Jones* 1971.)

A recent paper from the prestigious Karolinska Institute in Stockholm (*Jones* 1982) shows however that there is still room for argument about and experimentation on how the manner in which the breath specimen is taken will affect its alcohol content. From experiments reported there it was found that: thirty seconds' holding of the breath, or five minutes' shallow breathing with the mouth closed, increased both the temperature of, and the alcohol concentration in, the expired breath by about 0·5°C and 15 per cent. respectively; twenty seconds' hyperventilation (rapid deep breathing) decreased these by about 1°C and 10 per cent. respectively. These results show, Jones suggests, that changes in the alcohol content of the expired breath are caused partly by changes in its temperature and partly by the length of time it spends in contact with the mucous membranes of the upper respiratory tract. The paper concludes by stressing the importance of breath testing being preceded by a period of normal breathing.

4. A possible source of error is condensation inside the breath-collecting equipment. If water vapour in the breath condenses as liquid water on its interior surfaces, this may take up alcohol vapour from any subsequent breath passing over it; this would of course reduce the alcohol of that "late" breath below its true figure.

5. Finally, serious error could arise, but should not if the point is borne in mind and the measurement properly conducted, from traces of alcoholic drink remaining in the mouth. Since even the weakest drink contains vastly more alcohol than is ever present in

blood (*cf.* p. 10), the presence of such traces would completely vitiate the result of any analysis of breath blown out through the mouth. This point was investigated by *Lins and Raudonat* (1962), who concluded that a wait of 20 minutes before sampling will ensure that any such mouth alcohol will have completely disappeared. More recently, *Dubowski* (*loc. cit.*) found that mouth alcohol became undetectable after 11 minutes, or 7–8 minutes if the mouth was rinsed out after drinking. It has, however, been suggested—how authoritatively the writers are unaware—that, exceptionally, traces of alcohol might linger longer than these times behind dental plates or in unfilled tooth cavities.

To summarise, the combined effect of these various factors is that there are three ways in which breath analysis may be used in enforcing a legally prescribed upper limiting blood figure.

1. It may be used for a preliminary screening test, as in this country after 1967, and a blood or urine specimen taken for accurate substantive analysis if the test indicates that its alcohol content is probably above the legal limit.

2. Breath may be analysed directly in one of the various instruments devised for the purpose (see pp. 90, 94), many or even most of which are calibrated to indicate the blood level on the assumption of a 2,100/1 ratio. This has been done for several years in several parts of North America and in Northern Ireland since 1968. The arrested driver may be given the right to demand a blood or urine analysis if he is not prepared to accept the result of the breath analysis.

3. An assumed blood/breath ratio may be written into the law, thereby making it an offence for the *breath* alcohol to exceed a prescribed figure, whether or not this is a true indication of the blood level at the moment of sampling/analysis. This is the position in New Zealand and in this country after the implementation of the Transport Act 1981, which, in fixing a legal breath limit (Pt. V, Sched. *8* (12)) assumes a blood/breath ratio of 2,300/1 and rounds off to 35 the resulting figure of 34·7 micrograms/100ml. The Act, however, still makes provision for a considerable margin of error in the assumed ratio, in that it confers on the arrested driver the right to demand a blood or urine analysis if the breath figure, though over 35, does not exceed 50 micrograms/100ml. However, see p. 114.

Before we leave breath, a point that is worth noting—though it is not a possible source of error—is that this type of analysis has nothing to do with the smell of "alcohol" on the breath after drinking. This smell is in fact not due to ethanol (ethyl alcohol) at all, but to the various other volatile compounds ("congeners") present in practically all drinks. (see p. 6) (This is the origin of the belief in vodka leaving a "clean" breath; vodka is practically pure alcohol in water without congeners.) Actually, modern gas-chromatographic methods of analysis are so sensitive that it would be possible by using them to discover by analysis of a body-fluid what sort of liquor a drinker had consumed. (See *Machata and Prokop* 1971; *Bonte, Decker and Busse* 1978.) It is possible to imagine circumstances in which this knowledge could be useful. The smell of "alcohol" may in fact persist after all ethanol has been eliminated from the body. In the same connection, it has been shown that the odorous substances present in bad or garlic-laden breath will not react as false "alcohol" in the methods used for breath analysis. (See *Elbel and Schleyer* p. 43; *Greenberg and Lester* 1954.)

ALCOHOL IN THE URINE

Although the relationship between blood- and urine-alcohol levels will rarely, one supposes, nowadays be of practical importance within our present context, some discussion of it must not be omitted. Although there are fewer obstacles to its accurate determination than in the case of breath alcohol, it is in one important respect more complex: it lacks the quality of *immediacy*, because the alcohol level in a specimen taken at any given moment depends, not on the blood-alcohol level at the time of sampling, but on the level during the whole period in which the urine was being secreted. The relationship depends upon two factors:

1. Urine consists for our present purpose entirely of water; its other consitituents are all in solution and may be disregarded. Blood on the other hand contains about 15–20 per cent. of suspended solids.

2. The blood-alcohol concentration is changing continuously, either up or down. Urine, on the other hand, although also continuously secreted by the kidneys from this ever-changing blood, is stored in the bladder and excreted in "batches" in each of which the alcohol concentration depends upon and reflects the average blood concentration whilst it was being secreted.

The effect of the first factor is that for blood and urine in diffusion equilibrium, (*i.e.* at the moment of secretion in the kidney),

$$\frac{\text{Urine–alcohol concentration}}{\text{Blood–alcohol concentration}} = \frac{\text{Water content of urine}}{\text{Water content of blood}}$$

$$= \frac{100 \text{ per cent.}}{83 \text{ per cent. (average)}}$$

$$= 1\cdot20.$$

This figure cannot of course be experimentally checked in Man, since the urine is not accessible at the moment of its secretion in the kidney. It has however been reasonably confirmed by animal experiments.

However, because of the second factor mentioned above, one would *a priori* not expect the same ratio to be found with samples taken under normal everyday circumstances. In general, a "batch" of urine which has been secreted during the absorption phase will show a lower concentration than that corresponding to the blood level at the moment the urine is passed, and conversely a batch secreted during the elimination phase will show a higher concentration. Also, because of the time-lag between the secretion and the passing of urine, the urine peak will occur later than the blood peak. The general form of the relationship between urine and blood alcohol levels is shown diagrammatically in figure 4. Experimentally, the urine peak has been found to occur up to an hour after the blood peak. (Figure 5. See also *Payne et al.* 1966.)

Such results seem to show that the bladder wall is not permeable by alcohol; if it was, a diffusion equilibrium would be established across it and the blood and urine concentrations would always be equivalent. This is prima facie surprising, since other body membranes are permeable by alcohol and since various diffusible substances, including alcohol, injected into the bladder can be detected subsequently in the blood. The truth appears to be that, although the bladder wall may be permeable by alcohol to some extent, it is so poorly supplied with blood vessels that the interchange across it of alcohol between the blood and the bladder contents is too slow to have any significant effect in this connection. (See *Weinig et al.* 1970.)

The earlier experimenters did not always realise clearly the necessity for making a distinction between absorption-phase and elimination-phase urine; in any case, the actual time of the blood peak was rarely known. However, since the absorption phase lasts a much shorter time than the elimination, most published results probably relate to elimination-phase urine, unless special

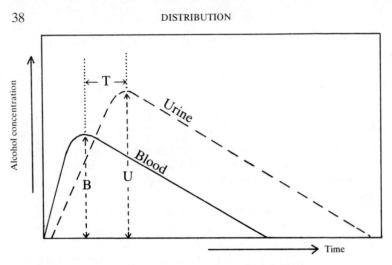

Figure 4. Blood Alcohol and Urine Alcohol: Theory

As explained in the text, the "peak" concentration of alcohol in the urine is higher than that in the blood, but is reached later. Normally, the urine peak is about one-third higher than the blood (*i.e.*, U/B = 4/3, approximately), and the time lag between the peaks (T) is around $\frac{1}{2}$-1 hour.

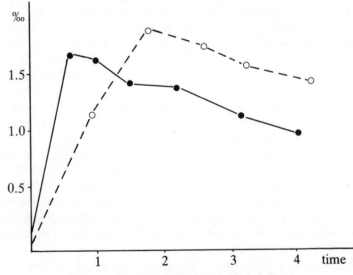

Figure 5. Blood Alcohol and Urine Alcohol: Practice

An actual pair of blood-alcohol and urine-alcohol curves, determined for a test subject weighing 175 lb. (80 kilograms) who had drunk 102 grams of alcohol as whisky during 32 minutes. The figures on the horizontal axis are hours, and those on the vertical axis blood alcohol as parts per thousand ($1 \cdot 0$ = 100 mg/100 ml).
Courtesy and Copyright, Professor R. Bonnichsen, Stockholm.

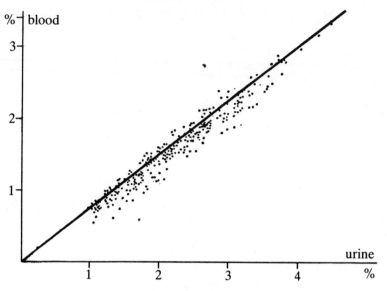

Figure 6. The Urine/Blood Ratio

Some Swedish results obtained in routine traffic-law enforcement are shown here. Each point represents a pair of simultaneous urine and blood specimens, and the sloping line the ratio 4/3. The blood specimens were capillary ones, and the urine specimens in each instance the second of two taken about 1 hour apart. Note how closely all the ratios approximate to 4/3.
Courtesy and Copyright, Professor R. Bonnichsen, Stockholm.

measures for prompt sampling after drinking were taken. In addition, there is a large body of experimental results available from the analyses of blood and urine samples taken simultaneously, or nearly simultaneously, from arrested motorists, and in these cases, because of the usual time lapses between drinking, arrest and examination, it is likely to be the rule rather than the exception for the sampling to take place during the elimination phase.

Obviously, therefore, for samples taken during the elimination phase, the urine/blood ratio will be somewhat greater than the theoretical figure of 1·20 derived above. *Elbel and Schleyer*, after considering all the experimental work which had been published up to about 1955, conclude (p. 39) that the most reliable value for the ratio in practice is 1·27. Most of the earlier authorities, however, preferred the marginally higher figure of 1·32–1·33 (see *Nickolls* 1956, pp. 335–340), and this is the figure which was approved by the British Medical Association (*The Drinking Driver*, 1965, p. 29). The analytical results used by *Drew et al.* in their now classic report on drinking and driving (1959) give a mean ratio of 1·25. Some other published results are:

Coldwell and Smith (1959, Canada): mean 1·24.
Lundquist (1961, Denmark): mean 1·35.
Bonnichsen et al. (1964, Sweden): approximately 1·3.
Morgan (1965, Northern Ireland): mean calculated from published results 1·36
Saury et al. (1966, France): mean 1·35. ·
Payne et al. (1967, England): mean 1·44.
Weinig et al. (1970, Germany) 1·3–1·4.

As already mentioned, however, a knowledge of the precise value of this ratio is now of little practical importance. There are two reasons for this. One is the probable rarity of the need to analyse urine specimens. The other is that all legislation including and since the Road Safety Act 1967 has adopted the British Medical Association's figure of 1·33 for the urine-blood ratio, and laid down that a urine-alcohol figure of 107mg/100ml shall be deemed to be equivalent to a blood figure of 80—an enactment which leaves no room for argument about whether or not the 107/80 equivalence is scientifically correct.

Should it ever be necessary to deduce a blood-alcohol concentration from the results of a urine-alcohol analysis, the only sensible course is to use the 1·0/1·33 (*i.e.* 0·75) conversion factor, with the proviso that the result of this arithmetic is only a most probable figure and cannot be scientifically proven in any given case; its use means that the calculated blood figure is very roughly as likely to be too low as too high. *Morgan* (1965, *loc. cit.*), using the data from 224 simultaneous blood and urine specimens taken in Northern Ireland cases, found that, starting with the urine figure, the assumption of a 4/3 urine/blood ratio would, within the limits of experimental error, have given the correct blood figure in 44·7 per cent. of his cases, too low a figure in 22·3 per cent. and too high a figure in 33 per cent. Rather earlier, *Froentjes* (Netherlands, 1962) had found a mean urine/blood ratio of about 3/2 in a series of nearly 10,000 cases. The discrepancy between this figure and the commonly accepted 4/3 has never been satisfactorily explained.

The methods of analysis used for the various body-fluids will be described in Chapter 5.

FURTHER READING (arranged chronologically)

The names cited will be found arranged alphabetically in the list of scientific references on pp. 253 *et seq*.

Nickolls, p. 335. Summary of early work on the blood/urine ratio. (1956).

Elbel and Schleyer, Full account of early work on the blood/urine ratio. (In German) (1956).

Begg, Hill and Nickolls, *A Statistically Planned Comparison of Blood and Breath Alcohol Ratios* (1962).

Forney, Harger, Hughes and Richards, *Alcohol Distribution in the Vascular System* (1964).

Payne, Hill and King, *Observations on the Distribution of Alcohol in Blood, Breath and Urine* (1966).

Payne, Foster, Hill and Wood, *Observations on Interpretation of Blood Alcohol Levels Derived from Analysis of Urine* (1967).

Harger and Forney, *The Temperature of Re-breathed Air, and the Arterial Blood/Re-breathed Air Alcohol Ratio* (1969).

Jones, Wright and Jones, *A Historical and Experimental Study of the Blood/Breath Alcohol Ratio* (1974).

Payne, *Measurement of Alcohol in Body Tissues* (Contribution to symposium on the pathology of alcoholism) (1975).

Wright, Jones and Jones, *Breath Alcohol Analysis and the Blood/Breath Ratio* (1975).

Dubowski, *Studies in Breath-Alcohol Analysis: Biological Factors* (1975).

Mason, M.F. and Dubowski, *Breath-Alcohol Analysis: Uses, Methods and Some Forensic Problems—Review and Opinion* (A wide-ranging and authoritative review of the subject) (1976).

Alobaidi, Hill and Payne, *Significance of Variations in Blood/Breath Partition of Alcohol* (1976).

Cooper, Schwar and Smith, Chap. 15 (Distribution of alcohol) (1979).

Kricka and Clark, p. 35–37. *Distribution of Ethanol in Body Fluids*, pp. 35–37 (1979).

Emerson, Holleyhead, Isaacs, Fuller and Hunt, *The Measurement of Breath Alcohol* (1980).

Jones, *How Breathing Technique can Influence the Results of Breath-Alcohol Analysis* (1982).

CHAPTER 4

EFFECTS OF ALCOHOL

The grosser effects of alcohol are too familiar to need description. However, contrary to a popularly held belief, it is not a stimulant: it is a depressant or narcotic. Its apparently stimulating effects are due to the fact that it acts first on the so-called "higher" centres of the brain which govern the inhibitions, so that a loosening of the check which these exercise makes the drinker more responsive to the stimulation of the company and circumstances in which social drinking is usually done. In addition, its slight anaesthetic effect may make him less aware of depression or fatigue.

For the average occasional or moderate drinker, the correspondence between blood-alcohol levels and effects is, *very* approximately:

Blood-Alcohol mg/100 ml	Effects
Under 50	No obvious effect, except perhaps a tendency to talkativeness and a subjective feeling of well-being.
50–100	First obvious effects begin to appear: slurred speech, bravado, some loss of co-ordination and of sensory perception.
100–150	More marked loss of co-ordination, hence erratic or staggering gait; poor sensory perception; possibly nausea and/or a desire to lie down.
150–200	Drunkenness and probably nausea.[1]
200–300	Probably coma ("passing out").
Over 300	Approaching the danger limit.
Over 450–500	Probably fatal (respiratory paralysis. Hence the stertorous breathing associated with "sleeping it off").

[1] It is noteworthy that during the exhaustive investigation of breath analysis carried out by the Home Office Central Research establishment in 1977–78 (following the Blennerhassett Committee's 1976 recommendations, and in preparation for the Transport Act 1981) none of the healthy volunteers used in testing was able to reach a blood-alcohol level over 160mg/100ml without becoming ill. (*Emerson et al.* 1980).

It must however be remembered that (1) persons, especially young persons, unused to drink will almost certainly show that succession of effects at lower blood-alcohol levels, and may well be markedly affected at levels below 100 or even below 50; (2) persons well habituated to drink will, correspondingly, show much less effect at any given level. In particular, real "soaks," and even more true alcoholics, may show few outward effects at levels at which the occasional drinker would be comatose, and there have been cases recorded of alcoholics appearing passably sober with levels around 300mg/100ml. (See, for example, *Patscheider* 1975). *Zwahlen* (1976), in summarising the results of a highly sophisticated series of experiments on alcohol and driving, states categorically that "in all experiments the effects of alcohol vary widely from one subject to another."

It has been suggested, probably correctly, that normal social drinking rarely leads to blood-alcohol levels above about 50mg/100ml. (See, for example, *Wright* 1963; *Milner* p. 73.) At the other extreme, most of the recorded fatal cases have shown figures over 400mg/100ml. A reliably established figure below about 350 probably indicates some complicating factor (such as heart disease) or a delayed death from secondary effects (giving time for some elimination to have occurred). However, death from acute alcoholic poisoning may occur quite quickly. In a series of six fatal cases reported from Northern Ireland (*Odesamni* 1978) the blood levels at death (ranging from 331 to 767mg/100ml) were higher than those in the urine (257–428). The seemingly reasonable explanation offered for this apparent anomaly is that the deceased died quickly of respiratory paralysis before the blood-alcohol levels had reached their peaks. While any fatal figure over 500 is sufficiently rare to be a matter of comment, survival of even higher figures is occasionally reported. There are, for example, reports of recovery after hospital treatment from levels of 620 (*Püschez* 1979) and 650 (*Polkis and Pearson* 1977) mg/100 ml. A report in *The Guardian* of May 22, 1976 of a pedestrian killed in a road accident who was apparently still on his feet with a level of 656, would seem to call for corroboration if it is not a misprint.

Broadly speaking, the effects of alcohol on driving performance can be studied in five ways:

1. By reasoning from the effects on other operations requiring attentiveness and good co-ordination.
2. By studying actual cases of alcohol-impaired driving, and cor-

relating the observed behaviour with the results of subsequent examination and the blood-alcohol levels (if determined).

3. By arranging actual vehicle-handling tests in safe conditions, and correlating performance with blood-alcohol levels and/or amounts of drink consumed.

4. By tests in vehicle simulators, and correlating performance as in (3).

5. By a statistical study of the correlation between blood-alcohol levels and the incidence of accidents.

The third and fourth of these modes of testing have the advantage compared with the fifth that the experimental conditions can be accurately standardised and controlled, but the disadvantage that the subjects know that they are being tested and may not therefore behave as they would in actual driving.

EFFECTS IN GENERAL

A great deal of research has been done in this field, often by psychologists, and some of its results are clearly and directly applicable to driving performance. Research up to about 1955 has been admirably summarised (in German) by *Elbel and Schleyer* pp. 133–163, from which many of the following details are taken. *Drew et al.* (1959) also give a short résumé of the subject on pp. 6–14 of their report, and a more recent account of it will be found in *Cooper, Schwar and Smith*, Chaps. 18 and 27.

It is clearly impossible to formulate any precise scale of measurement of the well-known effects of alcohol on *personality and behaviour*—the loud, babbling speech; the restlessness; the idiotic pranks; the irresponsibility; the loss of self-control. It is equally clear however that the appearance of just these last effects, in however small a degree, will transform a safe driver into a dangerous one. To quote *Elbel and Schleyer* (p. 133): " . . . they are probably a great deal more important as determinants of driving skill than any measurable impairment of mental capacity; in traffic they lead to situations in which the secondary effects of diminished sensory discrimination and precision of reaction become relevant, in that they weaken the driver's control of the situation. In short, the bad effect of alcohol on a driver is primarily conceptual rather than perceptual." Or, to quote *Loomis and West* (1958), "the severely intoxicated person is not the main public hazard as an automobile driver, but rather the person in a moderate state of intoxication who is not capable of reacting to an emergency situation with his normal efficiency." (See also *Crompton*, 1982.) That opinion should not, of course, be taken as implying that a severely intoxicated is less incapacitated than a moderately intoxicated driver, but rather that the latter is more likely to escape police attention until he has an accident. *Zwahlen* (1976), says of his own results (see p. 72) that they 'seem to indicate that alcohol restricts a driver's ability to respond with a high degree of consistency to a "quick-action" situation.'

Equally important is the drinker's diminished faculty for self-criticism and diminished ability to evaluate his own performance. In any sort of test requiring precise performance, keen perception and good co-ordination, it is quite usual for a test subject who has had some drink to think he is doing better than normal, when in fact he is doing worse. This effect, transferred to the road, means that the averagely competent driver affected by alcohol is apt sooner or later to find himself in an accident-generating situation from which he might or might not be able to extricate himself if he was completely sober, but—even more important—into which he would never have got in the first place if he had not been affected by drink.

There have been several studies of the effect of alcohol on the capacity to sustain attentiveness—a capacity of obvious importance in modern traffic conditions. The results of these agree to the extent that impairment may be detected at blood-alcohol levels above 30–50mg/100ml and that thereafter the capacity deteriorates steadily.

There have also been numerous tests of what may broadly be called *dexterity*—the capacity to perform some simple mechanical task. Such tests will evaluate simultaneously co-ordination and proneness to fatigue, and the "score" is based on the time required to perform the task and/or on the number of mistakes made. In such tests, with blood-alcohol levels in the range 70–150mg/100ml, the times required may be markedly increased and the number of mistakes made increased by several hundred per cent. In the most recent experiments of this type, however, to which we shall return on p. 71, the main effect of alcohol was found to be slower performance rather than more mistakes. (See, for example, *Price and Hicks* 1979.)

Sensory perception

Sight, hearing and touch have also been subjected to numerous tests, measuring both absolute sensitivity (that is, the threshold of perception) and sensitivity to small changes in the stimulus. In general, perceptible impairment at quite moderate blood-alcohol levels has been found. In the case of vision, general acuity, extent of vision, depth perception, accommodation (*i.e.* continuing ability to see after a sudden change from light to dark or vice versa) and resistance to dazzle or glare are all impaired, and the visual field is laterally reduced ("tunnel vision"). Moreover, it is pointed out by *Drew et al.* (1959) that "subjects are normally unaware of these changes in visual efficiency."

The effect of fairly large doses of alcohol (0·9–1·0 gram per kilogram body weight) on, specifically, twilight vision was studied by *Wilhelm, Lindner and Audrlicky* (1972). They found that, on average, the acuity of this was significantly reduced within 30 minutes, and that the effect was still detectable after an hour, or 2 hours if there was glare. They also found that the effect seemed to depend less on the absolute blood-alcohol level than on the rate of absorption.

Another effect on the eyes, though not specifically on vision, is the phenomenon of lateral nystagmus—a side-to-side involuntary movement of the eyes. This may of course occur from several causes, but medical opinion seems to be almost unanimous that it is of all clinical symptoms one of the most reliable as an index that alcohol has been consumed.

Finally, among general effects to be mentioned is that on the *reaction time*. This seems to have caught the popular imagination, and is commonly the first if not the only effect to be mentioned in casual discussion of drink and driving. In fact, of all the faculties affected by alcohol, reaction times are possibly the most complex and therefore show the most ambiguous results when they are measured. For example, *Elbel and Schleyer*, the German authorities, say (p. 152) that "reaction times are less affected by alcohol than any other parameter measured in psycho-technical measurements," while on the other hand *Rentoul, Smith and Beavers* (1962), of whom Dr. Rentoul was a very experienced Glasgow police surgeon, say: "There is no doubt that prolongation of visual motor reaction time is the most constant detectable sign of physical deterioration caused by alcohol." More recent work has tended on the whole to support Dr. Rentoul rather than the earlier authors cited by Elbel and Schleyer. For example, *Rose and Glass* (1970) found a detectable increase in reaction time at blood-alcohol levels below 75mg/100ml and a considerable increase in the range 80–125; this was true whether the reaction was a simple "go/no-go" one or involved an element of choice. *Joachim and Weyer* (1975) found that 80mg/100ml blood-alcohol, or deprivation of a night's sleep, produced comparable impairments in simple reflexes. *Lutze and Schacher* (1979) found a significant increase in reaction time in a group of 40 young and middle-aged drivers at blood-alcohol levels averaging 49mg/100ml.

The term "reaction time" is in fact ambiguous. Reaction times may be measured on either (1) pure reflexes (such as the knee jerk), which do not involve the higher centres of the brain, or (2) reactions requiring judgment or decision.

It would seem in fact to have been established that: pure reflexes ((1) above) may be slightly speeded up by small doses of alcohol, which can be accounted for by a reduced control of the lower nervous centres by the higher inhibitory ones; with more complex reactions, though there is some not very conclusive evidence of a slight speeding up immediately after a *small* dose of alcohol, the main effect is quite certainly a considerable increase in reaction time—increases ranging from 10 to 150 per cent. have been recorded for a range of blood-alcohol levels up to 150mg/100ml. Although every independent investigator has found reaction time to increase with increasing blood-alcohol levels, no simple correlation between percentage increase and level can be detected. This is hardly unexpected, since different investigators used quite different types of measuring equipment, measuring reactions of different degrees of complexity. *Zwahlen (loc. cit.)* found that, although all reaction times showed some increase with blood-alcohol levels of about, or slightly under, 100mg/100ml, this increase was not statistically significant for simple reactions, and was significant only for complex ones involving an element of choice.

As Elbel and Schleyer point out, it is the most complex reactions which are most relevant to actual traffic situations, where quick decisions between different possible courses of action may have to be made, and it does seem possible to draw the tentative conclusion from the figures they quote that, the more complex the reaction measured, the greater the increase in time required after a given dose of alcohol. They also state, quoting some earlier workers, that a very short interval between successive stimuli delays the response to each stimulus, which is very relevant to driving fast or in heavy traffic.

The most recent work on reaction times is discussed on pp. 71–73.

Effects: some additional points

Five other matters relating to the effects of alcohol in general which should be mentioned are: (1) the phase of the blood-alcohol curve; (2) the effects of fatigue and deprivation of sleep; (3) habituation; (4) the personality of the drinker; (5) the effect of hangovers.

(1) There is some evidence that a given blood-alcohol level produces more effect during the rising than during the falling phase of the curve—that is, there appears to be a sort of "micro-habituation," so that the drinker can to some extent adapt himself to the effects of the alcohol while it is still circulating in his system. This effect was first noticed by *Mellanby* as long ago as 1919, and has been named after him. Most of the earlier work on this subject was summarised by *Harger* (London 1962, p. 212); see also *Gerchow and Sachs* (1961), *Dennemark* (1962), and the experiments of *Taylor and Stephens* (Indiana 1965, p. 252) described on p. 54. These earlier studies have been criticised (*Moskowitz et al.* Melbourne 1977, p. 184) on the grounds that they used unnecessarily high blood-alcohol levels and did not allow sufficiently for the effect of practice: that is, subjects were tested sequentially, first during the rising then during the falling phases of the blood-alcohol curve produced by a single administration of alcohol, whereby practice gained during the first set of tests would of itself improve performance in the second, and to tend to mask the effect, if any, of the alcohol. The authors just named designed their own experiments to avoid this difficulty. They used as subjects groups of heavy and moderate drinkers, and made the rising and falling tests at quite separate times. The doses of alcohol given were adjusted to bring the moderate drinkers to levels of about 100mg/100ml at a rate of about 20mg/100ml/hour and the heavy drinkers to 150mg/100ml at a rate initially of about 20, rising to 25. Impairment was measured by behavioural performance (hand steadiness, body sway, etc.). In these conditions, they were able to confirm the reality of the effect—both groups of subjects performed worse while their blood-alcohol was rising. Two other findings possibly attributable to the same cause are: *Naeve et al.* (1974) found that the hasty finishing up of drinks produced a more marked clinically observable effect than the same quantity of alcohol drunk slowly throughout; *Lewrenz et al.* (1974) found in testing a group of students on a simulated Volkswagen (see p. 57) that *rapid* drinking

an empty stomach produced detectably impaired co-ordination at blood-alcohol levels as low as 20–30mg/100ml.

(2) It is a well-known fact that impairment of faculties and loss of alertness can be caused by fatigue or deprivation of sleep as well as by alcohol; the effects of these factors may be additive—that is, reinforce each other. *Grüner, Ludwig and Trabant* (1970) found that impairment due to a given moderate blood-alcohol level was more marked in the "small hours" (1·0–3·30 a.m.) than in morning daylight. The study by *Joachim and Weyer* (1975 *loc. cit.*) of the effect of fatigue on reaction time has already been mentioned. *Huntley and Centybear* (1974), using a special test vehicle wired up to record control-use rates, also found that loss of a night's sleep produced much the same effect as a blood-alcohol of about 100mg/100ml, in that both produced more frequent and more erratic use of the controls. They also found, however, that, though the effects reinforced each other, they were not strictly additive, in the sense that the proportional impairment by alcohol in sleep-deprived subjects was less than in rested ones.

(3) It is also well known and need not be elaborated here that alcohol considered as a drug is habit-forming in the sense that persons used to taking it can take more without undesirable effects than can persons not so used; this point has already been mentioned on p. 43. Without examining in detail the possible causes for this, it could be due either to a reduction in the concentration of alcohol reaching the brain, or to increased tolerance by the brain and central nervous system generally of a high cellular alcohol level, or to both these factors.

The effect of habituation on the blood-alcohol concentration has been extensively investigated experimentally, and many quite unjustified general conclusions have been drawn from inadequate or unreliable data. There have been reports of habituation speeding up absorption, slowing down absorption, producing a lower peak and producing a higher peak.

The most reliable earlier work produced, in most cases, no evidence of a greater rate of elimination in persons habituated to alcohol (see *e.g. Lester* Indiana 1965, p. 267). However, subsequent investigations by *Bonnichsen et al.* (1968), an authority who must be respected, produced evidence of a significantly greater rate of elimination in alcoholics. The explanation for the apparent discrepancy may be that Bonnichsen worked with alcoholics who were bad enough to be hospitalised for treatment—a class of person probably not available to most of the earlier workers. One may perhaps tentatively conclude that habituation tends to produce some increase in the rate of elimination of alcohol, but that unless it reaches the stage of actual alcoholism this effect is so small as to be masked by normal personal variability.

In fact, following the extremely reliable and authoritative work by *Goldberg* (Stockholm 1951, p. 85), habituation can be ascribed almost entirely to the second factor mentioned above—greater tolerance by the brain and central nervous system. Goldberg also points out, however, that, as habituated drinkers tend to drink more, the known slightly greater rate of elimination at very high blood-alcohol levels (*cf.* pp. 20–21) might also have some slight contributory effect.

(4) There have been a number of observations that the effects of alcohol vary according to the psychological type of the drinker. Most of these are of little significance in the present context, but it is of some interest that Drew (himself a professor of psychology) in his 1959 report (see p. 59 below) confirms earlier observations that extroverts and introverts react in different ways to alcohol, a finding which was later confirmed by *Huntley and Centybear* (*loc. cit.*). In general extroverts tended in Drew's experiments to drive after taking alcohol a little faster and much more erratically—to show a "couldn't-care-less" reaction—whereas introverts seemed to be anxious to demonstrate their unimpaired capabilities, by driving either faster (and usually rather worse) or with exaggerated caution. (Some of the drivers tested by *Coldwell et al.* 1958—see p. 54—also behaved in this last way when under the influence of alcohol.)

Although the experiments of *Andersson et al.* (1977—see p. 255) investigating the effects of smoking showed as already mentioned that it had no effect on the blood-alcohol curve, they did find with a small group of test subjects that it affected alcohol-impaired behaviour in that (perhaps not surprisingly) they showed rather less impairment when they were allowed to smoke as they desired.

(5) It is a matter of common observation that a "hungover" driver is a worse driver, but there has been scarcely any scientific investigation of this point. This is hardly surprising when one considers that such an investigation would require some sort of quantification of the driver's subjective feelings. However, *Seppälä et al.* (1976–2) have published some informed observations on the topic in connection with an investigation of the effect of fructose on alcohol elimination (see p. 22). They found that a hangover affected driving ability adversely by reducing the accuracy of reactions

involving an element of choice by the driver (see p. 46), especially when there had to be some information retrieval. They found no correlation between the subjective intensity of the hangover and its impairment of psychomotor performance.

THE CLINICAL EXAMINATION AND BEHAVIOUR OF ALCOHOL-IMPAIRED DRIVERS

Much useful information has been gathered, though often in a rather unsystematic manner, from the correlation of the results of clinical examinations and subsequently measured blood-alcohol levels. It may however be dismissed briefly here, since this sort of approach to the problem has now been overtaken by more recent and more systematic investigations.

Before the Road Safety Act 1967, there was no statutory obligation to call in a doctor at all, and some police forces did not at one time normally do so. However, because of the various illnesses and effects of injury which might, because of the similar symptoms produced, be mistaken for alcoholic intoxication, the prudent practice arose, and gradually became the norm, of calling in a doctor (often the local police surgeon) to examine the arrested person in order to discover whether there was any cause other than drinking which would account for his peculiar behaviour and/or impaired driving.

After the prescribed-level offence had been statutorily created (Road Safety Act 1967 and subsequent Acts), there was of course no need to prove impairment in a prosecution for that offence, and a clinical examination therefore became unnecessary. It may be presumed, however, that a doctor called in to take a blood specimen would make one if the accused consented and if his condition seemed to call for it.

Recommended practice for the clinical examination of arrested drivers before 1967 was authoritatively dealt with in publications by the British Medical Association, namely *Recognition of Intoxication* (1954 and 1958) and *The Drinking Driver* (1965). A supplement to the latter publication—*Alcohol, Drugs & Driving*—was issued by the Association in 1974, and dealt with the taking of blood specimens as required by the prescribed-level Acts, and with the procedure recommended when impairment by a drug other than alcohol was suspected. *Cooper, Schwar and Smith* give as their Chapter 19 (pp. 160–198) a detailed discussion of the theory and practice of clinical examination in the present context. *Hart-*

mann (pp. 110–115) also gives, for those who can read German, a detailed and illuminating account of the signs and symptoms of alcohol misuse up to and including true alcoholism. Readers are referred to these publications for information about medical examinations and the significance of their result.

A number of attempts have been made from the 1930s onwards to correlate the results of medical examination with blood-alcohol levels. The results of these showed a fair degree of agreement that observable intoxication (*i.e.* obvious drunkenness) would be produced in many persons by blood-alcohol levels in the range 75–150mg/100ml, and in all persons by levels above 150–180. (*cf.* the figures at the beginning of this chapter.) The last figure was generally quoted in most of the textbooks of forensic medicine as being that above which intoxication might be taken as certain.

It gradually became apparent, however, necessary though a clinical examination might be to detect injury or disease, that it was inadequate as a means of detecting a degree of intoxication short of drunkenness but sufficient to constitute a driving hazard. A committee of the American Medical Association appointed in 1936 reported in 1937 that " . . . 0·15 per cent. or more of alcohol by weight[2] in body fluids is associated with mental and/or physical inferiority . . . (and) much lower levels of alcohol are associated with definite impairment of judgment and particularly of self-criticism."

Later, the British Medical Association said (*Relation of Alcohol to Road Accidents* 1960, p. 33): "Relatively low concentrations of alcohol in the tissues cause a deterioration in driving performance and increase appreciably the likelihood of accident," and "clinical examination in the absence of biochemical tests is neither sufficiently sensitive nor reliable enough to detect deterioration in performance of this degree."

It may therefore be of interest to note at this point that in this country during the 1950s the *average* blood-alcohol level of motorists charged with driving under the influence of drink was about 220mg/100ml (approaching half the fatal level!—see p. 42) and that only about 10 per cent. of all drivers charged had levels under 150. (*Walls* 1958 and 1962; *Haisman et al.* 1963). Such levels would render most persons who are not alcoholics or problem drinkers

---

[2] That is, assuming that this means per cent. weight/weight, 150mg/100g. Since the specific gravity of blood is about 1·06, this is equivalent to 150mg/94ml or 159mg/100ml.

incapable of driving at all, and will be found only in the category which *Blennerhassett* (1976) calls "high-risk offenders." *Crompton* (1982), in contrast with the opinion of *Loomis and West* cited on p. 44, believes that chronic alcoholics cause more road accidents than occasional drinkers. Similar figures have, at various times and places, been reported from California (*Bradford* 1966), Ireland (*Hickey et al.* 1975), New Zealand (*McDonald et al.* 1982) and several other countries. *Little* (1972) made a statistical comparison of the effects of different limiting blood-alcohol levels in various parts of the United States, and found that, with legal limits of either 100 or 150mg/100ml the mean figure or arrested drivers lay between 150 and 200.

<h2 style="text-align:center">VEHICLE-HANDLING TESTS</h2>

Tests of this kind have the advantage of requiring the minimum of special equipment, and several were carried out in both Germany and the United States from the early 1930s onwards. These however have been superseded by later and more carefully designed tests of the same type.

The classic experiment of this type was the Swedish one carried out by Bjerver and Goldberg in 1950 (*Goldberg*, Stockholm 1951, p. 85). They were particularly concerned to test the effects of fairly low blood-alcohol levels, since by that time it was well recognised (at least in Sweden) that levels above about 100mg/100ml seriously impaired driving ability. A team of thirty-seven skilled drivers took part; they were divided into two series, one to test the effect of beer and the other the effect of spirits, and each series was again subdivided into drinking and non-drinking (control) groups. Everything was carefully arranged so that any differences between the performances of the drinking and non-drinking groups would not be biased by fatigue, inherent differences in driving skill, etc.

The tests consisted essentially of relatively simple starting, steering, reversing, turning and parking exercises. Each group made two complete runs, with about an hour in between, through all the tests, and immediately after the first run the drinking groups were given their alcohol. The blood-alcohol levels of the beer drinkers were 39 to 56mg/100ml (mean 46), and of the spirit drinkers 16 to 74mg/100ml (mean 49). Scoring was on the basis of the times required to perform each operation *correctly*.

Most of the control drivers did better, some markedly better, on their second runs, because of the practice gained in the first, and the mean improvement in the control scores was 20 per cent. The drinking drivers, on the other hand, performed on the average about as well in the second test as in the first, and their mean score was unchanged. This, because of the way the experiment was designed, could mean only that alcohol had impaired performance to roughly the same extent as practice would have improved it. The actual extents of impairment ranged from 3 to 72 per cent. (mean 28). Thus, the authors concluded, blood-alcohol levels between 40 and 50mg/100ml demonstrably impair performance by 25–30 per cent. Some further experiments and calculations showed that the threshold level (that is, that below which no impairment is detectable) seemed to lie around 40–50mg/100ml for normal straightforward driving, or as low as 20–30mg/100ml for emergency situations. On the other hand, some 20 years later, another group of investigators was unable to confirm by a series of double-blind tests any statistically significant impairment of performance at levels between 40 and 50mg/100ml. (*Staak et al.* 1972.) In view, however, of the mass of evidence subsequently obtained supporting Bjerver and Goldberg's figures, this may perhaps be considered a "maverick" result. (But see also *Zwahlen* 1976, p. 57 below.)

Some years later two similar and in some respects more ambitious trials were made in Canada. In the first, carried out by *Coldwell et al.* (1958) under the aegis of the Royal Canadian Mounted Police, 50 drivers were used, grouped into "light," "medium" and "heavy" drinkers on the basis of their normal weekly consumptions, which varied from 2 to 76 ounces of whisky. They were given whisky to produce blood-alcohol levels ranging from 40 to 160mg/100ml, but between 60 and 100 in over half of them. Scoring was by a combination of times required for correct performance and of recorded errors, plus observations by experienced passengers who assessed performances without talking to the drivers. Numbers of errors appeared to provide the best simple criterion of the effects of alcohol, and the passengers' evaluations the most sensitive index of impairment. The results were: one driver was impaired at 36mg/100ml; half were impaired at between 75 and 80; none were unimpaired at levels approaching 150; with heavy drinkers,although they performed better on the whole than light at similar blood-alcohol levels, 8 out of 10 were impaired at levels between 51 and 120.

The second trial (*Taylor and Stephens*, Indiana 1965, p. 252) used fewer drivers but rather more elaborate tests, again with skilled observers as passengers. The subjects had to drive round a 1·6–mile circuit and to avoid a multi-coloured ball suddenly appearing in their paths, which they knew to expect, but not when. Much emphasis was placed on the observers' reports, which assessed performances on a points system. Blood-alcohol levels were measured frequently with a Breathalyzer (see pp. 64 and 89). One driver showed impairment at only 10mg/100ml and obvious intoxication at 40. For the others, impairment was first detectable somewhere between 40 and 100, and intoxication between 80 and 160. An interesting observation (*cf*. para. 1, p. 55) was that, in more than half the subjects, the blood-alcohol level at which impairment was detectable was lower during the rising (absorption) than the falling (elimination) phases. The difference between these two "just-impaired" levels was 20–30mg/100ml.

In recent years (and since the first edition of this book was written) there have been no major further trials along the lines of those just described; their main results had been clearly established and did not need to be proved again. A few experimental results of interest have however been published. A trial with, specifically, experienced racing drivers (*Gerlach* 1973) showed that, at moderate blood-alcohol levels (40–113mg/100ml), their main impairment was a tendency to steer wrongly into curves on the track. An Australian series of experiments (*Lovibond*, Melbourne 1977, p. 168) measured what the report on them calls "handling perturbation"—that is, steering and car-handling errors—on a skid-prone surface at blood-alcohol levels of 30 and 60mg/100ml and at a speed kept as closely as possible at 50 kilometres/hour (31 m.p.h.). A small but statistically significant degree of impairment was detected at both blood-alcohol levels. In a Swedish series of experiments (*Laurell*, Melbourne 1977, p. 157) the test subjects, mostly students who were regular drivers and occasional moderate drinkers, were required to take, on a given signal, emergency avoiding action while driving at 50 kilometres/hour in a lane marked by movable plastic bollards. After they had been given enough alcohol to produce a blood level of 30 or 50mg/100ml, their performance was significantly impaired, even at the lower level. This result bears out the generally accepted view, already mentioned in the present chapter, that the deleterious effects of alcohol are at their worst when an emergency arises.

It has also been mentioned already that another effect of alcohol is that it increases the driver's willingness to take a chance—an attitude which is likely to lead eventually to an accident. The classic trial of this factor was reported by *Cohen et al.* in 1958. Cohen is or was an eminent professor of psychology. The test subjects were experienced Manchester bus drivers, whose normal drinking habits ranged from total abstinence to 20–30 pints (11·5–17 litres) of beer a week. (Few of them drank spirits regularly.) They were divided into three groups—a control, a group receiving 2, and a group receiving 6 fluid ounces (55–170ml) of whisky. Each driver was first asked to indicate the narrowest gap (marked by a pair of light posts) through which he *thought* he could always drive his bus, then to indicate the width of gap at which he was willing actually to try, and finally to make the attempt.

It was found that the alcohol impaired the drivers' actual performance only slightly (as would be expected in these fairly small dosages) but made it measurably more hazardous.[3] That is, the difference between the widths of the gap which the drivers believed they could always get through, and the gap which they in fact got through, was nearly twice as great in the 6-ounce as in the sober group. Three of the drivers who had had only the smaller dose were in fact willing to attempt a gap actually 14 inches narrower than their buses! Professor Cohen summarises his results by saying: "The effect of alcohol was not to make the drivers take more risk[4]—that is, to act at a lower level of subjective probability (which means to embark on a task with less certainty of success)—but to assign the same subjective probability to a more difficult task."

Professor Cohen's results have been criticised in matters of detail—for example, that he was not sufficiently careful to ensure that the difference between the control and the drinking groups was only in respect of the drink taken. One may also wish that he had secured more detailed reliable information than he did about the actual blood-alcohol levels of his drivers. Nevertheless, his experiment was a noteworthy pioneer one, and his results have been by and large accepted.

This topic of risk acceptance has been discussed in more recent papers by *Klebelsberg* (1973) and by *Zwahlen* (1976). The former is a German psychologist, the latter an American professor of

---

[3] Professor Cohen distinguishes between "risk-taking," which is embarking on a task without being certain of its success, and "incurring hazard," which is embarking on a task in which the performer will not always be successful.

[4] "Subjective probability" is defined as the gambler's estimate of, as opposed to the true chance of, an event occurring.

industrial and systems engineering. Klebelsberg's paper is wholly theoretical and unfortunately (though in English) largely incomprehensible; he defines risk taking thus: "risk-taking behaviour can be understood as the individual pattern of achievement and safety tendencies and depends on superimposed cognitive restructuring processes." Zwahlen's paper (which has been mentioned more than once in preceding pages of this chapter) describes both his measurement of reaction time (see p. 46) and his development of a "driver safety index" (DSI) based upon the three components: visual perception, driving skill and risk acceptance. The second component was quantified by an arrangement rather similar to Cohen's; the test subjects were required to drive at 20 m.p.h. through an adjustable gap, whereby performance was assessed on the basis of vehicle displacement from the gap centre line when the total clearance was 20 inches, and the third component by the subjects' estimates of whether they could drive through the gap widths presented to them. The DSI, calculated from the values found for the three factors already mentioned, was arranged to fill a scale running from 0 to 10, a high figure indicating a safe and cautious driver who, in Zwahlen's words,"is only willing to engage in a risk-taking activity when the subjective probability of failure is extremely small." When the subjects' blood-alcohol levels were raised to around or just over 100mg/100ml with vodka or whisky, their driving was, as expected, impaired and their DSIs tended to fall. In neither case, however, were the changes large enough to be statistically significant; in this respect Zwahlen's results do not wholly support Cohen's, in that the latter's subjects appeared to be more affected by the alcohol taken.

Dummy Car and Tracking Simulator Tests

Such tests are made by seating the subject in something corresponding to a car driving seat, and requiring him or her to make the appropriate responses to presented stimuli; these may be anything from agreed visual or audible symbols to "driving" along a "road" simulated by a film projected on a surface occupying the place of a normal windscreen. An important point made by *Rafaelsen et al.* (1973–2) about such tests is that it is necessary to distinguish between arrangements which, by demanding only predetermined mechanical responses, treat the subject as a mere robot, and those which call for an element of choice as to the appropriate reaction to each presented situation. (See also p. 47.)

Several pioneering investigations of this type were made in both the United States and Germany during the 1940s, but two much more comprehensive and thorough ones were carried out in the late 1950s, one in Seattle (Washington, U.S.A.) and one in this country. In the former (*Loomis and West* 1958), the test subject had to "stop" and "start" a dummy car with the usual controls at "traffic lights" and, by steering, to keep a model car centred on an irregularly moving black strip (the "road"). Scoring was on the basis of the recorded reaction times to the "traffic lights" and the time during which the "car" was off the road.

The 10 subjects were first given weekly practice runs until their performance showed little further improvement. Test runs were then made approximately 1, $2\frac{1}{2}$ and $4\frac{1}{2}$ hours after the initial drinking, and a blood sample taken for analysis after each run. A unique feature of these experiments was that, in addition to the initial drink, further drink was given as "maintenance doses" in order to maintain as far as possible a uniform blood-alcohol level during the whole period of the test. During the drinking-test periods the subjects had blood-alcohol levels ranging from 30 to 180mg/100ml.

The aggregated result was: some impairment could be detected at blood-alcohol levels of 30mg/100ml; on the average, performance had decreased to 85 per cent. of the control figure at blood-alcohol levels of 100 and to 70 per cent. of the control at 150. An interesting point was that performance fell off exponentially with increasing blood alcohol (*cf.* pp. 70–71).

The subjects were also asked to fill in a questionnaire about how they *thought* the alcohol had affected their driving. Although all of them admitted being aware of having taken alcohol, sizeable minorities believed that their driving performances had actually improved during the last two hours.

The British investigation, which was carried out under the aegis of the Medical Research Council by a team headed by Professor G.C. Drew (a psychologist), was probably the most elaborate and exhaustive of this kind that has been done. (*Drew et al.* 1959). It was specifically directed towards discovering the effect of quite small doses of alcohol. The subjects were given psychological personality tests as well as the actual "driving" ones. They had to "drive" along a winding country road projected on to a "windscreen." A most elaborate scoring system was devised, which took into account speed, driving errors and numbers of movements of the various controls. Each test lasted two hours—a period sufficient to ensure that subjects affected by alcohol could not "pull themselves together" for long enough to compensate for this effect on their performance.

There were 40 subjects, 35 men and 5 women, and each was given alcohol in doses of 0·20, 0·35, 0·50 and 0·65 gram per kilogram of body weight. Similarly flavoured placebo drinks containing no alcohol were also given, so that the subjects did not know at the time of driving whether they were taking alcohol or not. Each subject was tested after each dose and after the placebo—five tests per subject in all. This enabled each subject to be used as his or her own control. The *order* in which the tests were given was so arranged that: (1) it eliminated the effect on the results of any improvement due to practice; (2) as each order of tests was done by eight subjects, individual differences between the subjects within each group of eight could be fairly assessed. In one of the five-fold replications all of the five women subjects were used, in order to detect any sex differences. (None was found.)

Drinking lasted 10 minutes, and after a further 10 minutes the test began. Blood, urine and in some cases breath samples were taken during the course of the tests at 30, 60, 90 and 120 minutes after the end of drinking, and in some cases further samples were obtained up to 6 hours after drinking. The peak blood-alcohol levels naturally varied widely from subject to subject, as did the times after the end of drinking at which they occurred. Within these wide variations, however, the approximate mean peak levels and times were: 0·20 gram/kilogram dose—25mg/100ml and 33 minutes; 0·35 gram/kilogram dose—42 and 39 minutes; 0·50 gram/kilogram dose—64 and 41 minutes; 0·65 gram/kilogram dose—80 and 42 minutes. As would be expected from the considerations outlined on pp. 13–16, there was a slight tendency for peaks which occurred early to be also rather higher, and for women (who have more fat in their bodies) to have higher peaks than men for the same equivalent dose.

The results of the investigation were subjected to an exhaustive and elaborate analysis, which is described in full in the report (*Drew et al., loc. cit.*). Very shortly, the following were the main findings. Five of the subjects actually improved at the lower blood-alcohol levels, in that they "drove" more slowly, more consistently and with fewer errors. Others who also drove more slowly made more errors. Taking the results as a whole, however, impairment was detectable at concentrations as low as 20–30mg/100ml, and there was in fact no evidence of a threshold concentration below which there would be no effect. For a level of 80mg/100ml, the mean deterioration in performance amounted to 12 per cent. The connection which was found between personality and behaviour under the influence of alcohol has already been mentioned (p. 50).

The results of another trial designed on the same general lines as Drew's were published some years later by *Martin* (1971). A highly sophisticated simulator device enabled subject performance and the effects of this on the actual standard of driving to be independently assessed; it was found that impairment might manifest itself by the trial subject having (in Martin's words) "to work harder to maintain the same performance." Although some criticism was offered of the design of Drew's experiments—it was suggested, for example, that the spells of "driving" were too long, so that the "drivers" were affected by boredom and fatigue as well as by alcohol—Drew's conclusions were in general confirmed. Some subjects showed actual improvement at low levels (around 50mg/100ml) but all were impaired at 100.

Following publication of the Drew report, a committee of the British Medical Association, after carefully considering all of the evidence then available, published the opinion (*Relation of Alcohol to Road Accidents*, 1960, p. 33), which was widely quoted at the time and which was in fact very similar to the earlier American opinion mentioned on p. 52, that: "a concentration of 50 milligrammes of alcohol in 100 millilitres of blood while driving a motor vehicle is the highest that can be accepted as entirely consistent with the safety of other road users. . . . The committee is impressed by the rapidity with which deterioration occurs at blood levels in excess of 100mg/100ml. This is true even in the case of hardened drinkers and experienced drivers. The Committee cannot conceive of any circumstances in which it could be considered safe for a person to drive a motor vehicle on the public roads with an amount of alcohol in the blood greater than 150mg/100ml." It is of interest to compare that recommendation with the blood-alcohol levels found before the passing of the Road Safety Act in 1967 in motorists charged with driving under the influence of drink (p. 52). Not surprisingly, the recommendaton was at that time frequently cited in evidence in those cases—the majority—in which the accused's blood alcohol was well above 150mg/100ml.

BLOOD-ALCOHOL LEVELS AND ACCIDENT STATISTICS

The numerous investigations which can be classified under this heading range from what are little more than informed casual observations to painstaking and elaborate statistical analyses, and it it impossible here even to enumerate them all.

It had become obvious to informed observers many years ago that in nearly every country of the world whatever official statistics were available grossly under-estimated the part played by alcohol in causing accidents. There was however an obvious need for studies of the problem in which the element of guess-work, however well-informed, was eliminated as far as possible. Such studies, made in various countries, all showed in various ways an obvious correlation between drinking and accidents. *Klein et al.* (1971) boldly commit themselves to the statement that "for practical purposes a fatal crash (in the United States) can be considered synonomous to an alcohol crash until proved otherwise." No-one in this country seems to have been quite so forthright, but it could scarcely be mere coincidence that on Saturday nights, while the traffic flow between 10 p.m. and midnight was just over half that during the mid-day and afternoon hours, the number of accidents rose suddenly and sharply after 10 p.m. to approximately double the mid-day figure. (See for example, *Collister* 1962; *Jeffcoate* 1958; *Spriggs* 1958; see also p. 52.) *Hartmann* (p. 108) quotes an estimate that in the German-speaking wine-making districts of Central Europe up to 50 per cent. of drivers on the roads at night may be under the influence of alcohol.

Some useful information was provided by a study made by the Road Research Laboratory (*TRRL Reports* 1975) of the effect on the casualty figures of the imposition for the first time in this country (Road Safety Act 1967) of a legal limiting blood-alcohol level. Without going in detail into the statistics published in that report, it showed that the incontrovertible immediate result of the new legislation was an 11 per cent. reduction in total casualties. Although a reduction as large as this was not, unfortunately, maintained in succeeding years, and had fallen to 6 per cent. of the pre-Act figures by 1973, there was some reduction throughout the whole of the period 1967–73, even though motor traffic increased by 21 per cent. over the same period. These figures, and also statistics relating to the differential effects of times of drinking and ages of drivers, are considered in some detail in the *Blennerhassett* Report of 1976.

There can be no doubt, however, that the most fruitful approach of this type to the problem is one based on a correlation of the incidence of accidents with drivers' blood-alcohol levels. Reports and opinions from all over the world agree that these factors are highly correlated. In another report from the Road Research Laboratory (*Sabey and Codling* 1974), which examined the statistics for over 2,000 accidents, it appeared quite clearly that the groups in which a driver could be adjudged primarily at fault, or in which no other vehicle was involved, contained a much higher proportion of alcohol-affected drivers than did the driving population generally. In a series of 500 cases from north-west London, 42 per cent. of the fatally injured drivers had blood-alcohol levels over 80mg/100ml (*Sheehan and Bowen*, Stockholm 1980, p. 180). In 1981 about 29 per cent. of British drivers killed in road accidents were over the legal limit (*Department of Transport Press Notice No. 129 of 19/4/ 1983*). Of 113 accident victims received in Johannesburg General Hospital during two months in 1976, one third had blood alcohols over 80, and the incidence of injury and death among drinking drivers was twice that among non-drinking (*Myers et al.* 1977). The same writers cite an informed estimate from New Zealand that in 1970 alcohol played a part of 80 per cent. of all fatal accidents. In a group of 1,000 accident victims in Switzerland, alcohol was a contributing factor in 40 per cent. of drivers killed or seriously injured and in 30 per cent. of those involved in minor accidents (*Lutz and Leu* 1975). Similar correlations have been reported from New York City (*McCarroll and Haddon* 1962), New York State and Perth (Western Australia).

Even clearer evidence has come from the statistically more sophisticated studies of this correlation that have been made. The pioneer one of this type was that carried out by *Holcomb* in Illinois and published in 1938. He measured the blood-alcohol levels of 270 accident casualties and those of a random sample, during one week, of 1,750 non-accident drivers, and compared the numbers of safe and accident-involved drivers at different levels. He found that drivers with no alcohol in their blood formed 53·4 per cent. of the accident group and 97·9 per cent. of the non-accident group. The ratio of these two figures, namely $\frac{53\cdot4}{97\cdot9}$, is 0·55. The corresponding ratios for various ranges of blood-aclohol levels were:

Blood-Alcohol mg/100 ml	Ratio
0–60	1·9
70–100	3·3
110–140	8·7
Over 150	33·1

Although Holcomb's results have been criticised in that he was not sufficiently careful to ensure that his accident and non-accident groups were selected from exactly comparable traffic conditions, the inference to be drawn is inescapable.

No further investigation of this type was undertaken until after the war. Then *Smith and Popham* reported (Stockholm 1951, p. 150) an investigation in Toronto in which, from the case histories of a large number of accidents, they were able to find 582 in which the victim was quite clearly either to blame or not to blame. Comparing the "responsible" and the "blameless" groups, they found that the proportion of those having blood-alcohol levels over 50mg/100ml was eight times greater in the former than in the latter. (*cf.* the results of the Grand Rapids Survey below).

A later investigation, also from Toronto (*Lucas et al.* 1953), was carried out along the same lines as Holcomb's but with the additional precaution that the control (non-accident) group consisted of drivers passing the scene of each accident in cars of the same type and at about the same time of day. They obtained the following ratios (calculated in the same manner as Holcomb's):

Blood-Alcohol mg/100 ml	Ratio
0–50	0·85
50–100	1·31
100–150	2·10
Over 150	8·10

Similar results were obtained from an investigation in Czecho-slovakia (*Vamosi,* 1958 and 1960).

These investigations have however been dealt with briefly. The most exhaustive investigation of this type yet performed was the survey made in Grand Rapids (Michigan) in the early 1960s (*Borkenstein et al.* 1964), which is in a class by itself in respect of thorough and detailed preliminary planning and of the care and statistical sophistication used in the evaluation of the results. It was carefully considered in the White Paper, *Road Safety Legislation 1965–66* (Cmnd. 2859), which stated specifically that there was no reason to suppose that at a given blood-alcohol level the performance of British drivers would be affected differently from that of American drivers. There can thus be little doubt that the survey's results had considerable influence on the drafting of the Road Safety Act 1967.

The primary purpose of the investigation was, taking the four groups into which all drivers can be divided, namely:

(1) Non-drinking   — not involved in accident
(2) Non-drinking   — involved in accident
(3) Drinking   — not involved in accident
(4) Drinking   — involved in accident

to discover whether there was any significant difference between the incidence of accidents for the non-drinkers (classes (1) and (2)) and the drinkers (classes (3) and (4), and whether the proportions of drinking drivers were significantly different in the accident group (classes (2) and (4)) and the control group (classes (1) and (3)). In addition, however, a great deal of other valuable information was elicited.

Grande Rapids is a city in the peninsula between Lakes Michigan and Huron. A study of over three years' police records of where accidents occurred most frequently made possible the selection of a control group (classes (1) and (3) above) who were exposed to the same probability of accident involvement as drivers who had in fact been involved in accidents. The drivers who were stopped at random as controls were picked out by methods eliminating most rigidly any personal or other bias in their selection. In the event, during the 12 months in which the investigation was in progress, data were collected on 5,895 drivers involved in accidents, and 7,590 drivers not involved.

As it was extremely important to collect these data in such a way that the effects, if any, due to alcohol could be distinguished from those due to other driver variables such as sex, age, driving experience and so forth, a comprehensive questionnaire was designed. As far as possible, the following information was collected in every case: the details of the accident, if one had occurred; age; sex; estimated annual mileage; type of education; race or nationality; marital status; occupational status; details of the journey; frequency of drinking; where drinking is preferred; type of liquor preferred; when the last drink was taken; blood-alcohol levels as measured by breath analysis. (The breath samples were taken in blow-up plastic bags, which were taken back to the laboratory for the alcohol contents to be measured with a Breathalyzer). The forms used also contained an entry for the interviewer's assessment of the truth of the answers given. To overcome as far as possible the expected and not unnatural reluctance of drivers to answer probing personal questions, the interviewers were specially trained in the methods used by the investigators who collected the data for the Kinsey reports on American sex habits.

In the statistical evaluation of the results, much use was made of the χ^2 ("Chi-square") test. This is a mathematical test used by statisticians to discover whether, when two groups of numerical results of any sort have different mean values, this difference between the means represents a real difference between the groups, or is likely to have arisen by chance. In this case, no difference which was found was accepted as real unless the data on which it was based showed that the odds on its being so were at least 19 to 1.

The mass of data collected were considered under either *single-factor analysis* or *two-factor interactions*. To deal first with the former, the problem was to discover whether the two main groups of drivers (those involved in accidents and those not involved, which we shall call here groups A and NA respectively) showed any significant differences in respect of their various noted characteristics, taken individually—blood-alcohol levels, age, sex, driving experience, etc. Unless the Chi-square test showed a significant difference, it was assumed that it was *purely* a matter of chance whether a driver was involved in an accident or not.

This analysis showed that differences in every single one of the factors examined had some effect on liability to accident, but that the blood-alcohol level was by a large margin the most important in this respect; next, a long way behind, came age, followed by driving experience, with sex last.

Since no single factor was uniquely connected with the occurrence of accidents, any given accident might have been the effect of several together, and some attempt was made to elucidate their respective contributions by the analysis of *two-factor interactions*. This could not be applied to every possible interaction, since, taking into account the number or arbitrary divisions used for each factor (*e.g.* various ranges of blood-alcohol levels, age groups, etc.), the number of combinations to be examined would require data from millions rather than thousands of drivers. It was however shown quite clearly that, *within* each class (age group, drivers with similar driving experience, etc.), where sufficient data were available for the analysis, there was a highly significant correlation between accident liability and high blood-alcohol levels.

What is perhaps for our present purpose the most important

single result to emerge from this investigation may be given in the words of the report on it (*Borkenstein, loc. cit.* p. 125): "The effect of alcohol on accident experience in this study, using the test described, became statistically detectable at the 0·08 per cent. alcohol level class." (0·08 per cent. = 80mg/100ml. The "test described" is the Chi-square test. "Statistically detectable" means that the odds on its being a real and not a chance difference were at least 19 to 1; it does *not* mean that any difference detected at a lower blood-alcohol level could not be real also.)

Drivers with high blood-alcohol levels appeared more frequently in the accident than in the non-accident groups, as follows:

Blood-Alcohol mg/100 ml

50–100	—	1·5 times as frequently
100–150	—	4 times as frequently
Over 150	—	18 times as frequently

Figure 7 shows the relationship between various ranges of blood-alcohol levels and the incidence of accidents. In figure 8 the same date are presented in another way—namely as a relationship between blood-alcohol levels and the probability of being involved in an accident.

3,305 of the A group were also clearly, on the facts, solely responsible for the accidents in which they were involved. Within this sub-group, the following relationships were found (*cf.* the *Smith & Popham* experiment of 1951, mentioned above, p. 63).

It also emerged that there was a real tendency for drivers with high blood-alcohol levels to have more accidents in which no other

Blood-alcohol level	Formed following percentage of driving population (a)	Caused following percentage of accidents (b)	$\dfrac{b}{a}$
Positive (over 9 mg/100 ml)	11	20	1·8
Over 50	3	15	5·0
Over 100	1	10	10·0
Over 150	0·15	6	40·0

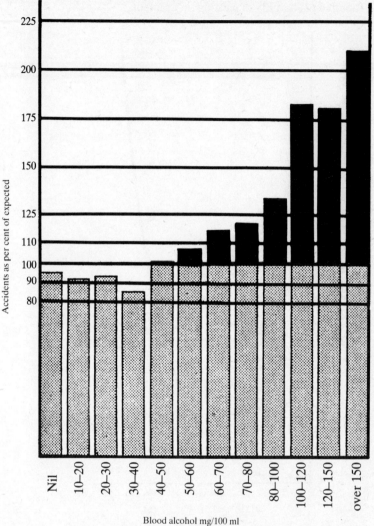

Figure 7. Blood-Alcohol Levels and Accidents—1

The data collected in the Grand Rapids survey can be assessed in several ways. One, which was used by the investigators themselves, is to compare the actual number of accidents occurring at each blood-alcohol level with the number that would have been expected within a group of that size *if there had been no connection between alcohol and accidents*. That comparison is illustrated here. The actual number of accidents for each blood-alcohol level is shown as a percentage of the expected number. If the actual and expected numbers had been the same, each column would of course have reached exactly to the 100 per cent. line.

The "Nil" column includes all cases with blood alcohols below 10. The reduced incidence of accidents for blood-alcohol levels in the range 10–40 is discussed in the text.

Relative probability of causing an accident

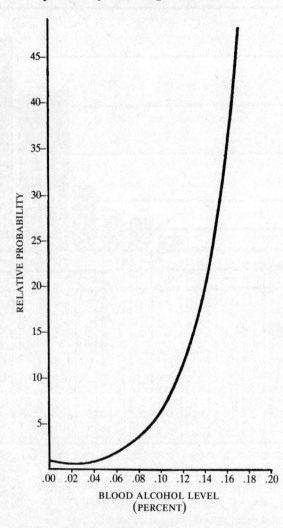

Figure 8. Blood-Alcohol Levels and Accidents—2

It is also possible to use the results of the Grand rapids survey to calculate the *probability* of an accident occurring at any given blood-alcohol level. (Note that 0.10 per cent. blood alcohol corresponds to 100 mg./100 ml.)

Chart taken from *The Role of the Drinking Driver in Traffic Accidents* (report on the Grand Rapids survey).

Figures 7 and 8 courtesy and copyright Professor Borkenstein, Indiana.

moving vehicle was involved, and for their accidents to be more serious ones as measured by the damage and/or injury caused.

It appeared from a study of the two-factor interactions that, at the lower blood-alcohol levels, the proportions of group A drivers within each class (*i.e.* age group, length of driving experience, etc.) varied widely, but that with levels above 80mg/100ml these differences tended to disappear. This result is of course not unexpected: as the blood-alcohol level increases, the relative importance of alcohol compared with the other accident-causing factors increases. Also, in the words of the report; "Apparently given sufficient alcohol, all drivers become about equally accident-involved."

There is one final point about the Grand Rapids investigation to be made. It appears from Figure 8 that there was a clear tendency for drivers with 10–40mg/100ml of alcohol in their blood to be *less* involved in accidents than drivers with no alcohol at all in their blood. This prima facie rather surprising result not unnaturally attracted considerable attention when the report of the investigation was published. It can be interpreted in two ways:

(1) Drivers with these low blood-alcohol levels are in fact safer than drivers who have no alcohol in their blood.

(2) Some unconsidered and unsuspected factor was affecting the results.

Interpretation (1), while supported by the minute care with which the whole investigation was planned and conducted, is hardly consistent with the numerous reliable investigations, many of them mentioned earlier in this chapter, which have shown detectable impairment at these low blood-alcohol levels. If we accept interpretation (2), two explanations (which need not be mutually exclusive) have been advanced (together with the purely speculative suggestion that these classes contained a proportion of over-tired drivers who had stopped to relax over a drink, and to whom the rest did more good than the drink did harm).

(1) *Harger and Forney* (1967) have pointed out that in most cases the driver's blood-alcohol level would be falling during the period between the accident and the taking of the breath sample and that therefore the levels at the times of the accidents would be higher then those measured. On the assumption of a delay of 15 minutes and a consequent drop in the blood-alcohol of 4mg/100ml, the consequent revision of the figures would move many drivers

into the next higher class of blood-alcohol levels. A re-calculation of the results on this basis makes the ratio

$$\frac{\text{percentage of accident drivers}}{\text{percentage of control drivers}}$$

approximately 1 for all blood-alcohol levels of 40 and below—that is, makes drivers with blood-alcohol levels up to and including 40 neither more nor less safe than completely sober ones.

(2) The explanation which is stated (*Goldberg and Havard* 1968) to have the support of the Grand Rapids investigators themselves is as follows. The alcohol-free group contained a large proportion of young inexperienced drivers who had a higher-than-average accident risk. The 20–40mg/100ml range included a large number of middle-aged, well-to-do and experienced drivers who had a lower-than-average accident risk which, even though it was increased by small doses of alcohol to a level above the average one for their group, remained lower than that of the driving population as a whole. The combined effect of these factors is to increase the accident-involvement index of the alcohol-free drivers and to decrease that of the 20–40 group of drivers.

It should also be noted that the blood-alcohol figures in the Grand Rapids survey were obtained by the analysis of breath samples taken in plastic bags. Experience in this country would tend to suggest that, if this led to any systematic error, it would be in the direction of giving low figures through loss of alcohol from the specimens. There is no evidence that this in fact happened, but if it did it would reinforce Harger and Forney's argument described in (1) above.

The Grand Rapids survey must be considered the definitive investigation of its type, and its results stand unchallenged. The results of later investigations along the same lines (see, for example, *McClean and Holubowycz,* Stockholm 1980, p. 113), although they may have shown small differences in points of detail, have merely served to confirm the essential validity of Borkenstein's approach to this subject.

Finally, before leaving the subject of alcohol and accident statistics, there are two points that should be mentioned. Firstly, in all investigations of the subject the liability to accident increases much faster than do the blood-alcohol levels, and the increase appears to be approximately *exponential*. Whether this applies right down to zero blood-alcohol levels does not appear to have been finally established, but *Ottis* (1963) claims that it does, and there certainly seems to be no clear evidence, if the tests applied are sufficiently discriminating, of a demonstrable threshold figure below which alcohol has no effect at all on driving.

Secondly, it is important not to confuse results from which predictions about the effects of alcohol on given individual drivers can be made, and results which predict only statistical probabilities. The Grand Rapids and similar investigations do *not* enable us to say that a particular driver must necessarily be impaired or more liable to accident with 80mg/100ml or more of alcohol in his blood. The results are therefore not inconsistent with the opinion of the British Medical Association quoted on p. 60.

RECENT WORK

It should be clear from the foregoing that most of the fundamental research into the effect of alcohol on driving was completed by, say, the late 1960s—that is, while the first edition of this book was still in preparation, so that there is comparatively little to add to what was written there.

Emphasis has been placed by several writers (for example: *Martin* 1971; *Perrine* 1976; *Rafaelsen,* 1973) on the importance, when conducting simulated-driving tests, of designing the apparatus so that results obtained under laboratory conditions are as far as possible directly applicable to actual driving. It is suggested that some apparently anomalous trial results may be traced to using equipment which cannot simulate the ever-changing complexities of modern traffic.

Another obvious current trend is the attempt to separate for consideration and evaluation the various factors which taken together constitute total driving skill. Most writers are agreed that the most fundamental division of these is into what may be called the perceptual/judgmental and the executive—that is, the evaluation of the driving situation at each moment and the taking of the action appropriate to it. There is also general agreement that the first factor is more liable to be affected by low or moderate blood-alcohol levels than the second, but that the degree of this impairment depends very much upon whether the activating stimulus is simple or complex. There is also evidence that the impairment affects the *speed* of the reaction rather than its correctness.

For example, *Lovibond* (Melbourne 1977, p. 168), says that (at least in simulator trials) "driving performance could be described in terms of two major factors or dimensions, a judgment/accuracy factor, and a handling/stability factor." *M.F. Mason and Dubowski* (1976), writing from the United States, put it that " . . . investigations support the conclusion that the most important functional defects caused by ethanol are those associated with perception and processing of information received by the special senses. Learned motor responses are relatively much less impaired." *Moskowitz* (1973), also writing from the United States, found that with blood-alcohol levels around 50–100mg/100ml, neither compensatory tracking nor visual search-and-recognition were, taken separately, much impaired, and is convinced that the true cause of alcohol impairment lies in the need to process information from more than one source simultaneously. "It is," he says, "the necessity for time-sharing the information-processing capacity of the brain between several information sources which imposes the greatest burden upon the driver," and he goes on to say that it is the higher brain functions which are most liable to be affected by quite low blood-alcohol levels. *Richter and Hobi* (1975), in discussing the arguments for lowering the Swiss legal limit from 80mg/100ml to, they suggest, as low as 30, stress the same point—that is, that the faculties most sensitive to alcohol are those most important to actual driving, namely complex perceptual mechanisms and states of divided attention. *Zwahlen* (1976), in the highly sophisticated approach to the problem to which reference has already been made, agrees fundamentally with the other writers just cited as to the true source of the deleterious effects of alcohol. In developing his "driver safety index," which has already been mentioned (p. 57), he utilises a quantity which he calls the driver's "safety distance" and which rests primarily on the difference between subjectively perceived distances and the actual safe margin of clearance. He supports his suggestions with a mass of statistical data.

As far as speed of reaction of concerned, *Moskowitz and Murray,* in a later paper (Toronto 1974, p. 399), express the opinion that the greatest effect is upon the time required for processing of information, and that the alcohol-impaired driver could perform this quite correctly if only he was given sufficient time. *Verhaegen et al.* (Toronto 1974, p. 405) produced some evidence supporting this contention; they tested groups of students of ages ranging from 18 to 28, and found that blood-alcohol levels over 60mg/

100ml (and even as low as 25 in older subjects) slowed up the decision-making process where swift responses were necessary. In the most recently published piece of research on this topic (*Antebi* 1982) the subjects had to choose which of four buttons to press in response to a randomly varied visual stimulus; with blood-alcohol levels in the range 30–55mg/100ml they did not make a statistically significant greater number of mistakes but they did take significantly longer to react. ("Statistically significant" is explained on pp. 65–66, 106).

Further Reading

The names and dates refer to the alphabetically arranged list of scientific references on pp. 253 *et seq*. The details given there should enable each item cited below to be found.

General, including Reaction Times:

Elbel and Schleyer pp. 133–163 (in German) (1956).

British Medical Association, *The Drinking Driver* (1965) supplemented by *Alcohol, Drugs and Driving* (1974).

Moskowitz and Murray, *The Effect of Alcohol on Human Information Processing Rate* (1974).

Zwahlen, *The Effect of Alcohol on Driving Skills and Reaction Times* (1976).

Moskowitz, Daily and Henderson, *The Mellanby Effect in Moderate and Heavy Drinkers* (1977).

Cooper, Schwar and Smith (1979); Chap. 18 (Effect of Alcohol) and Chap. 19 (Clinical Examination).

Clayton, *Effects of Alcohol on Driving Skills* (1980).

Driving and Simulator Tests:

Cohen, Dearnly and Hansel, *Risk Taken in Driving under the Influence of Alcohol* (1958).

Drew, Colquhoun and Long, *Effect of Small Doses of Alcohol on a Skill Resembling Driving* (1959).

Laurell, *Effects of Small Doses of Alcohol on Driver Performance in Emergency Traffic Situations* (1977).

Lovibond, *The Effects of Alcohol on Skilled Performance* (1977).

Statistical:

Borkenstein *et al.*, *The Role of the Drinking Driver in Traffic Accidents* (1964).

TRRL Reports, *Supplementary Report No. 134* (Effect of new legislation on accident rate.) (1975).

Department of the Environment, *Report of Departmental Committee on Drinking and Driving.* (Usually referred to as "The Blennerhassett Report.) (1976).

Sabey, Barbara E., *A review of drinking and drug-taking in road accidents in Great Britain* (Transport and Road Research Laboratory Supplementary Report 441) (1978).

CHAPTER 5

SAMPLING AND ANALYSIS

Until the implementation of the drink/driving provisions of the Transport Act 1981, the substantive analysis producing a result which was in one way or another used in evidence always had to be made in a laboratory of a body-fluid specimen taken from the arrested driver and conveyed there. That was true whether the analytical result was merely corroborative, as under all pre-1967 legislation, or whether it proved an offence after an on-the-spot check with a so-called breathalyser (properly: Alcotest) had suggested that one had been committed. It is not the least of the changes introduced by the 1981 Act that, in most cases, no laboratory analysis of each specimen will be required and that there will be no transmission of specimens from one place to another: the specimen is the breath from the suspected driver which he blows into the instrument at the police station to which he is taken. However, before we consider breath analysis, which will presumably become the normal practice, it will be convenient to deal briefly with the collection, transportation and analysis of blood or urine specimens, a procedure which will still be necessary in certain circumstances.

It is here assumed that the option open from April 16, 1984 to *all* drivers who show a breath-alcohol figure above the legal limit of having a blood or urine specimen analysed, (*Home Office News Release* of March 26, 1984) will prove eventually to be a temporary measure.

BLOOD

Sampling

Blood specimens were, from a time soon after the implementation of the Road Safety Act 1967, and still are when a blood analysis is demanded (see pp. 216 *et seq.*), normally taken intravenously by syringe and immediately transferred to a small phial capped with a septum penetrable by the syringe needle. When the 1967 Act was drafted it was envisaged that arrested drivers would

75

object strongly to the surgical assault of venepunture and that specimens would normally be collected by skin puncture with a "stabber" provided with the collecting kit. This practice was however soon abandoned: it had various disadvantages, including the difficulty of collecting an adequate specimen and the fact that it was by no means painless.

The Road Safety Act 1967 authorises the taking by a doctor with consent of the accused of a specimen of his blood. This must mean sufficient blood to enable the purposes of the Act to be carried out. The Act itself gives no guidance on quantity. It is arguable however, that the Act permits only one extraction, and the legality of a second specimen, if the first through inexperience or lack of skill or foresight proved insufficient, is certainly open to question and has not yet been considered by the courts.

Division of the specimen into three parts has been recommended—one part for the official analysis, one for the accused and one spare; however, this is not directly enacted in the statutory provisions of the Road Traffic Act 1962, s.2, which merely provides that where the accused at the time of providing the specimen asks to be supplied with such a specimen, evidence of the analysis is not to be admissible unless the accused received either a part of the original specimen or a second specimen taken on the same occasion. The Act, however, goes on to require that the constable requesting a person to supply blood or urine specimens must offer to provide him with a specimen for his own use. In this way he is made aware of his right to request a part of the specimen.

The provisions of s.3 of the Road Safety Act 1967 under which the blood samples are required for laboratory testing in connection with the impairment offence are similar but make no provision for an offer by the police of a specimen for the defence, though this is obviously an excellent procedure to adopt.

Skin contamination

The skin will normally be cleaned before venepuncture. It is clearly essential that this shall not lead to contamination of the specimen by ethanol, and most desirable that no other volatile compound shall be used. Organic liquids such as ether or *iso*-propanol, sometimes used in other circumstances as skin sterilisants, may contain small amounts of ethanol, and should not therefore be used. Some proprietary antiseptic creams appear to be satisfactory in this respect. Clearly however soap and water is the safest from this point of view.

If specimens are collected in non-disposable syringes which require prior sterilisation, it is obviously essential that no alcohol, and highly desirable for the reason just given, that no other volatile liquid be used for this purpose. Commonsense would seem to make this warning unnecessary, but cases have occurred which show that it is not.

Clotting

Immediately after the blood is collected, small amounts of sodium fluoride and potassium oxalate are dissolved in it; if these salts are already present in the phial when the blood is introduced, their quantity should be sufficient to ensure concentrations of 1·5 per cent. fluoride and 0·5 per cent. oxalate in a 2·5ml specimen of blood. This mixture of salts prevents both coagulation of the specimen and the growth of bacteria in it. Clotting (coagulation) of blood specimens before they reached an analyst was formerly a problem he encountered from time to time; it made his work much more difficult and necessitated the development of a small clot-breaking device. It arose largely because, although the small capped plastic cups in which the blood was originally collected and transmitted contained an anti-coagulant, it was difficult to ensure that this was properly dissolved after filling a cup. At one time much research was carried out, particularly in Germany, to determine the correct alcohol ratios of clot and serum to whole blood. The results of this are not now, however, of any significance in British law enforcement, because the ratios are not known with sufficient accuracy to be usable in enforcing a fixed-limit law, and the difficulty should never arise with the much larger blood containers now used.

Transmission and storage

Finally the specimens are despatched in suitably sealed packages to the laboratory. The sealing and labelling must be adequate to prevent any tampering with the specimens and to ensure as far as is humanly possible that they will be identifiable without risk of confusion.

Although forensic science laboratories make a point of analysing blood specimens as soon as possible after receipt (say, within a week at most) they have found that the alcohol content of a properly preserved and stored specimen will normally remain unchanged for a period that may be measured in weeks or even months. This is obviously important, because it may very occasionally be necessary to repeat an analysis at some later date. Proper preservation and storage means in practice: the presence of sufficient preservative to prevent any bacterial action; secure closure of the container; a container not too large for the volume of its contents; adequate refrigeration.

However, for one reason or another specimens may not always be so treated, and it is therefore important to understand and be familiar with what may happen if they are not.

1. An imperfectly sealed container may permit evaporation. This is not likely to occur with the rubber-septum-sealed phials now used, but could sometimes occur with the plastic cups used formerly; indeed, *Brown et al.* (1973) found it to occur in about 5 per cent. of the cups they were using in a research project. Loss in this way will obviously be prevented by secure closure and reduced by refrigeration.

2. There have for a long time been reports of the possibility of alcohol being lost by bacterial action. (See, for example, *Elbel and Schleyer* p. 119; *Krauland et al.*, 1960; *Gehm and Schmidt* 1962; *Schwerd et al.*, 1967; *Blackmore* 1968.) This can be minimised by refrigeration and prevented by making sure that the specimen contains enough of an effective bactericide. Sodium fluoride is as already mentioned above the most commonly used one. There have been conflicting reports of the minimum concentration of this necessary for its effective action to be ensured—*Blackmore (loc. cit.)* recommends at least one per cent., while *Brown et al. (loc. cit.)* found half of that sufficient. However, as already mentioned on p. 77, quantities sufficient to ensure a margin of safety are used in practice.

3. Alcohol may be lost for a reason unsuspected until about ten years ago. It has long been appreciated that the blood container should not have a large air space above its contents, especially if there is any likelihood of its being out of refrigeration for any length of time. However, the too ready assumption that this could lead to a loss of alcohol by evaporation into this space is easily demolished by an elementary knowledge of physical chemistry and a little simple arithmetic; in anything but the most improbable circumstances the maximum possible evaporation of alcohol into the space would not reduce significantly the concentration in the liquid specimen. It is now known that the loss in such cases occurs by the oxidation of the alcohol to acetaldehyde in a reaction catalysed by

haemoglobin (the red pigment of blood). (*Brown et al., loc. cit.*; *Smalldon* 1973; *Smalldon and Brown* 1973.) The oxygen for this reaction may come from both the oxidised haemoglobin in the specimen and the air above it. This reaction is not prevented by the presence of sodium fluoride; it is however very temperature-dependent and is therefore greatly inhibited by storage at refrigerator temperatures. It can also be inhibited by the presence of certain compounds such as sodium azide or nitrite.

The loss of alcohol from any of these causes, though undesirable, would clearly not lead to injustice to the defendant; this however would occur if alcohol is being produced for any reason in a stored specimen. According to *Osterhaus and Johannsmeier* (1966) and *Blackmore* (*loc. cit.*) this is readily caused by bacterial action in post-mortem specimens, but, fortunately, hardly ever in specimens from the living. In any case, bacterial action of this kind is also prevented by the presence of sufficient sodium fluoride, giving another reason for the regular use of this additive. Blackmore also points out that bacterially produced alcohol is generally accompanied by certain other characteristic compounds which can be detected by gas chromatography. However, in spite of the efficacy of this precaution, there must always be an element of doubt when one attempts to establish ante-mortem blood-alcohol levels by the analysis of post-mortem specimens. Obviously, the more promptly such specimens are taken and analysed the better.

Bailey et al. of the New Zealand Department of Scientific and Industrial Research have also (1982) made a thorough investigation into the storage of blood samples containing alcohol. They agree with Smalldon *et al.* that the loss of alcohol by oxidation is inhibited by the presence of sodium azide but not by that of fluoride, and can thereby be reduced to about 1mg/100ml/month.

URINE

The recently re-enacted s.8 of the Road Traffic Act 1972 specifically authorises the taking in certain circumstances of a specimen of blood or urine instead of breath. The decision whether this shall be done is left (medical advice having been taken if necessary) to the discretion of the police officer. Apart from the taking of urine to be tested for drugs (see Chap. 8), it would seem to have been retained in the Act (contrary to the recommendation of *Blenner-hassett* 1976) mainly to meet the contingency that breath cannot for one reason or another be supplied and that the taking of blood proves impracticable or is medically contra-indicated (for example, if there is no accessible vein or if the driver is a haemophiliac).

It was made a statutory requirement in both the Road Traffic Act 1972 and the Transport Act 1981 that the urine analysed shall be the second of two specimens passed, of which the first has been discarded. Although this procedure was always medically urged even before it was obligatory, at one period it was neglected and fell into disuse. Its purpose is simply to ensure that the urine analysed shall have been secreted into an empty bladder, thereby reflecting as closely as possible the alcohol concentration in the blood during its secretion, and not the average concentration during the whole period since the bladder was last emptied (which might even have occurred before drinking began).

For whatever reason it is taken, the collection of a urine specimen is clearly a simpler matter than that of a blood one. It is sufficient that it shall have been taken in a clean container and transmitted in a sealed bottle containing enough of a suitable preservative. (A clean dry container is sometimes prescribed. This, though possibly desirable, is not important: if the container has been rinsed in clean water and well drained, the dilution of a, say, 200–250ml specimen of urine by the water adhering to the sides of the container will be of no significance.) Some discreet supervision in the collection of specimens may however be desirable. At least one case is recorded of a defendant (who was also a magistrate!) who, professing extreme modesty, asked to provide his specimen in privacy and produced some well-diluted urine from the lavatory pan into which he had just urinated. There is also no way of subsequently detecting the substitution of one urine specimen for another.

The preservation of urine specimens is important chiefly because, if they contain any sugar, (as they may if taken from diabetics and in certain circumstances from healthy persons) then contamination by stray yeast spores could lead to the production of alcohol by the fermentation of this sugar. Sodium fluoride has been found to be an adequate and suitable preservative.

In the analysis of urine specimens for alcohol, therefore, a number of subsidiary tests will be made. These may include: (1) a test for the presence of the preservative; if no preservative is present, then (2) sugar may be tested for, and (3) a further test is made to ensure that alcohol has not been, or is not being, produced by the fermentation of sugar by (a) centrifuging and searching the sediment microscopically for yeast cells, and/or (b) leaving the specimen for some days at room or incubator temperatures, followed by re-analysis to see whether the alcohol content has increased. Yeasts will not grow in properly preserved urine specimens, but if it is ever found that alcohol is in fact being produced by fermentation, then of course the evidential value of the specimen is nil. Contamination of urine by bacteria (as opposed to yeasts) is unlikely to lead to the production of ethanol (*Blackmore, loc. cit.*).

As a footnote to this section, one of the present writers in the early days of urine tests received for analysis a specimen of urine contained in a gin bottle bearing its original label. He had no reason to suppose that there had not been at least an honest attempt to wash out the bottle properly, but he could not help feeling that a more suitable container might have been found!

Defence Specimens

It was formerly obligatory to offer a sample (or a portion of a large specimen) of blood or urine to the accused, so that he could if he wished have it independently analysed. This is now clearly impossible when a breath analysis is made. If however the circumstances occur in which a body-fluid analysis is demanded (see pp. 75 and 216), the accused has the right to ask for a specimen for independent analysis. He should therefore be offered his choice of container, and should be given it in a sealed package with the police officer's signature across every join and covered with transparent sticky tape so as to make tampering impossible.

The Royal Society of Chemistry, 30 Russell Square, London W.C.1., publishes a list of private analysts prepared to undertake this work. Many police forces also provide information on this point.

It may be expected that, as long as no-one has made a definite mistake, a reputable defence analyst will get the same result within the limits of experimental error, (a matter discussed in the following chapter) as the forensic science laboratory does. If a much lower result is reported, it may transpire that the specimen was left too long unrefrigerated before analysis. (See (3), p. 78).

However, human nature being what it is, and since it is a simple matter to replace an unsealed specimen of urine with an alcohol-free one, or to dilute it with water (as in the case of the modest magistrate mentioned in the previous section), adequate sealing of urine specimens is especially important. If a reputable and competent independent analyst reports a figure much lower than that found by the prosecution, and if it transpires that the defendant himself conveyed his specimen, unsealed, to the analyst the inference is obvious.

Blood specimens are reasonably safe from undetected tampering, but it is still important that they be adequately sealed.

BLOOD AND URINE: ANALYSIS

It should perhaps initially be noted that, though various Acts have authorised or enjoined the determination of alcohol in a specimen of a body fluid, none has anywhere laid down how this shall be done. The choice of method has always very sensibly been left to the skill and experience of the chemists involved; to do otherwise would impose an unacceptable constraint on their professional expertise and prevent them taking immediate advantage of the discovery of a method of analysis proved to be better than the official one. If in practice they all use the same method, that is simply because at any given time a certain method or group of methods has been found the most suitable.

Nearly all of the original methods for the analysis of blood or urine, including those used in this country before 1967, were purely chemical and depended upon separation by distillation of the alcohol from a measured volume of the specimen and its oxidation by a suitable reagent, the volume of reagent required for this being a measure of the alcohol content of the specimen. The reagent was most commonly a solution of a soluble bichromate acidified with sulphuric acid; it will be referred to in the remainder of this chapter as *acid bichromate*. Of the numerous methods utilising this reaction, and differing only in detail, the best known were the original *Widmark*, the *Southgate and Carter*, the *Cavett*, the *Kozelka and Hine*, and the *Nickolls* methods. Some of these were micro methods using 0·1–0·2ml of specimen per analysis; others required 1–2ml. They were all sufficiently accurate and convenient for their purpose, but some were too time-consuming for the routine analysis of large numbers of specimens, and others were not sufficiently specific for ethanol, so that a supplementary test for its identification was necessary. (This last disadvantage was however more theoretical than real; no other volatile oxidisable compound is liable to occur in a significant amount in the blood of a conscious person in normal health. See p. 87.)

The only other method at all widely used (though more abroad than in this country) was the ADH one. This is a micro-method utilising the reaction catalysed by the ADH enzyme mentioned on p. 19. In skilled hands it is extremely accurate and, like all enzyme reactions, highly specific. The enzyme does to some extent react with propanol and butanol—two other alcohols which are closely related to ethanol but which do not occur in human blood—but does *not* react with methanol, which may occur in minute amounts in the blood of "meths" drinkers. (See p. 87.)

For a prescribed-level law, however, as introduced by the Road Safety Act 1967, it was necessary to find a method which was, besides being very accurate, completely specific for ethanol, usable with very small amounts of specimen, and not too time-consuming so as to be suitable for the routine analysis of large numbers of specimens. It is common knowledge that a gas-chromatographic method was devised within the forensic science service which met completely all of these requirements (*Curry, Walker* and *Simpson* 1966). A similar solution to the same problem was also developed on the Continent; see, for example, *Machata* (1967). Gas chromatography is also used in the U.S.S.R. (*Ivanov* and *Uljanov*, both 1983).

The basic principle of gas chromatography is shown in Figure 9. As shown there diagrammatically, the movement of the pen governed by the recorder produces a series of peaks on a moving strip of paper; the position of each peak identifies the compound producing it and the area under the peak is a measure of the amount of this. However, since this area also depends slightly upon the operating conditions, in order to utilise peak area for accurate quantitative analysis it is necessary to add to the sample injected into the column a fixed but not necessarily known amount of an *internal standard*—that is, a compound other than ethanol which, with a given column-packing material and type of detector, produces a similar peak at a slightly different position. (In practice, *n*-propanol, another alcohol resembling ethanol but never as mentioned above found in human blood, is used for this.) The peak areas depend on the numbers of electrical impulses coming from the detector to produce them, and for each peak the number is counted and printed out by an *integrator*.

The actual analytical procedure is then as follows. The column is kept heated all the time to a temperature well above the boiling points of both ethanol and the internal standard. A minute amount of the specimen is withdrawn from its container and diluted with

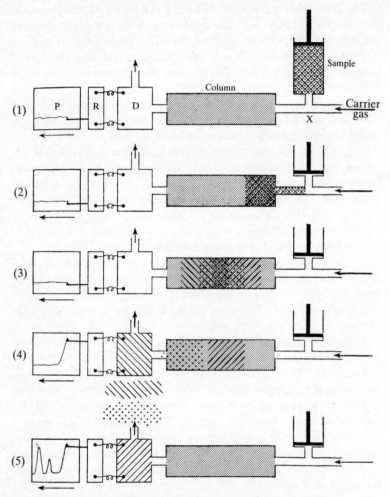

Figure 9. Gas Chromatography

The sample to be analysed is injected (1, 2) at X into the stream of carrier gas entering the column. The various constituents of the sample (*e.g.,* ethanol and the internal standard in blood-alcohol analysis by this method) are carried through the column at different rates (3) because they are adsorbed to different extents by the column packing. Hence, if the column is long enough, they emerge separately at different times (4). The detector D, which is sensitive to changes in the composition of the issuing gas, feeds electrical impulses corresponding to these into the recorder R, where they are amplified and converted to pen motions on a moving paper strip P(5).

The magnitude of the signals from the detector is also proportional to the amount of each component issuing from the column, and in blood-alcohol analysis the amplified signals are also fed into an integrator which prints out a number expressing that magnitude.

an aqueous solution of the internal standard; these operations are performed together automatically by one instrument. The dilution ratio need not be precisely known but *must* be invariable. Another minute amount (which again need not be exactly known) of the diluted specimen is then introduced into the carrier-gas stream as it enters the column. Originally this was done using the liquid and a micro-syringe. Nowadays the *head space* method is used. This makes use of Henry's Law (p. 32): at a given temperature the concentration of alcohol vapour in the closed space above the liquid depends solely on the alcohol concentration in this. A batch of diluted-specimen containers is therefore kept accurately thermostated, and a small volume of head-space gas withdrawn automatically from each and injected into the carrier-gas stream.

An ethanol solution of very accurately known concentration is put through the same whole procedure at frequent intervals; from the result of this, a factor is derived which applies to the immediately succeeding batch of specimens analysed. The final step is a calculation, using this factor and the ratio of the peak areas, which gives the alcohol content of the original specimen.

The New Zealand Department of Scientific and Industrial Research, which uses a similar method of blood analysis, has gone a stage further here, and computerised this part of the process (*Stone et al.* 1982—Pt. I).

The concentration of the calibrating alcohol solution is the ultimate standard upon which the correctness of the analysis depends, which is why neither the actual values of the initial dilution ratio nor the volume of diluted specimen need be accurately known. The most careful precautions are therefore taken to ensure the accuracy of the reputed concentrations of these solutions. From a "master" solution prepared by the Laboratory of the Government Chemist, the Home Office Central Research Establishment prepares, by diluting it, working standards which are distributed to all the forensic science laboratories, where they are further checked by the authorised analysts using a rather elaborate protocol. Finally, a checked standard is included with each batch of specimens analysed.

BREATH: BACKGROUND

It has already been stressed that in routine use breath analysis will not involve the transportation of specimens from the place of sampling to that of analysis. The immediate, reliably correct functioning of the analytical instrument is therefore of first importance, and the accuracy of the result depends primarily on its correct calibration. We shall deal in the next chapter with the matter of calibration; in this we shall merely describe the methods of measurement.

The reader should perhaps be reminded that an on-the-spot check with a comparatively crude breath-alcohol measuring device as a preliminary to an accurate analysis being made, as has been the practice since 1967, is no longer obligatory under the provisions introduced by the Transport Act 1981; a police officer investigating whether a drink/driving offence has been committed may at his discretion, without a roadside check having been made, require a driver to go to a police station for an immediate definitive breath analysis. It will undoubtedly, however, remain normal practice to begin with an on-the-spot check. A number of new instruments for this are now available; they will be briefly described on pp. 95–96.

Before we describe the instruments used for definitive breath analysis since the 1981 Act was fully implemented, there are some preliminary matters to be dealt with. In the first place there are a number of criteria which must be met by any breath-analysis instrument which is to be used in police stations by trained but not scientifically educated personnel, and several others which it is highly desirable should be met. These are, not necessarily in order of importance:

1. The analytical result must be both accurate and repeatable;

2. The instrument should if possible not respond to any other volatile substances likely to be present in breath. (This criterion is further discussed below.);

3. The instrument should automatically reject at the beginning of blowing a sufficient volume of breath to make it acceptably certain that the portion actually analysed is alveolar air (see pp. 30–34);

4. To meet the provisions of the Transport Act 1981, the instrument should be graduated to indicate directly the breath-alcohol concentration in micrograms/100 ml, rather than the derived blood-alcohol concentration, as in most if not all instruments hitherto used;

5. It must by possible to make an on-the-spot calibration check both immediately before and immediately after an analysis;

6. The design of the instrument should incorporate the maximum possible degree of automation;

7. The instrument should be easy to use, with no hard-to-remember precautions being necessary, and it should not be put out of action by any easily-made operator mistake;

8. The instrument should be robust enough to stand up to accidental knocks etc.;

9. If the instrument is not working properly, that fact should be immediately obvious;

10. If the instrument needs an electricity supply, it is an advantage if this can be from either the mains or a battery;

11. The instrument should, it is highly desirable, deliver a printed-out record embodying as much information as possible—certainly the blood-alcohol figure with the time and date, and preferably the names of the tested driver and the police-officer operator;

12. Any electronic circuitry in the instrument should be shielded from possible interference by nearby electrical equipment;

13. Reliable servicing facilities should be readily available.

The second of the above criteria—specificity for ethanol—is less restrictive than might at first be imagined. In theory, there are many compounds which could by themselves give a false "ethanol" reading. Traces of methanol (methyl alcohol) will be found in amounts up to perhaps 3mg/100ml in the bloodstreams of "meths" drinkers (*Kricka and Clark* pp. 63–66); it is both more toxic and more slowly eliminated than ethanol (*Cooper, Schwar and Smith* p. 380). In practice, however,there is only one volatile compound which is liable to occur to a measurable extent in the blood and breath of a conscious person able to go through the motions of driving—namely acetone. Small amounts are found in the plasmas of most diabetics and traces in some healthy persons on low-calorie diets. Amounts over 5mg/100ml have been found in the former (*M. F. Mason and Hutson*, Toronto 1974, p. 533), but at such levels the subjects were quite ill and could not have driven, and most diabetics showed under 0·5mg/100ml. Healthy persons ranged from none detectable to just under 0·3mg/100ml, but showed in most cases less than 0·1mg/100ml. The plasma-breath ratio appears to lie somewhere between 310 and 330. Such small amounts could not, of course, by themselves lead to a significant "alcohol" reading, but they could perhaps just "push" a true alcohol figure from just below to just above the legal limit. Any method of breath-alcohol analysis used in law enforcement must

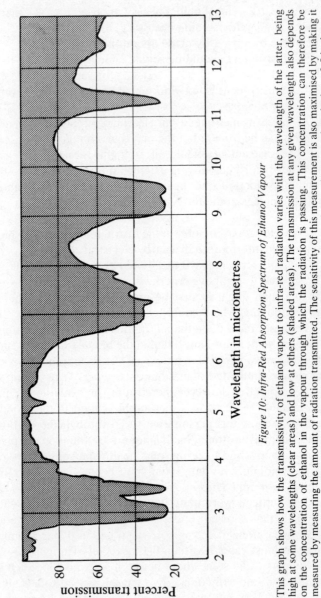

Figure 10: Infra-Red Absorption Spectrum of Ethanol Vapour

This graph shows how the transmissivity of ethanol vapour to infra-red radiation varies with the wavelength of the latter, being high at some wavelengths (clear areas) and low at others (shaded areas). The transmission at any given wavelength also depends on the concentration of ethanol in the vapour through which the radiation is passing. This concentration can therefore be measured by measuring the amount of radiation transmitted. The sensitivity of this measurement is also maximised by making it at a wavelength of high absorption, such as, for example, 3 or 7·25 micrometres; in practice a wavelength about 3·5 is chosen. See pp. 90–93).

therefore make allowance for the possible presence of traces of acetone. The various methods by which this is done will be described in their appropriate places.

There are several ways in which the alcohol content of breath may be determined. Five of these in current use (though not all in this country) are:

I. **Oxidation of the alcohol vapour** by a suitable reaction. This was the method used several decades ago by R. N. Harger in his pioneer *Drunkometer* (see *Borkenstein* 1960). More recent devices are simpler in design, and all use acid bichromate as the oxidant. The most successful of these is the now well-tried *Breathalyzer* invented by Professor Borkenstein of Indiana University about 30 years ago and long used successfully by many North American police forces. (*Borkenstein loc. cit.*; *Smith and Lucas* 1963). This instrument has since its first appearance been improved in various ways, and the most recent version, the Smith and Wesson *Breathalyzer* 1000, was one of the instruments used in the first field trial (see below, p. 94) preceding the passing of the Transport Act 1981 (*Emerson et al.* 1980). Its mode of operation is, briefly: when the subject blows into it, it automatically discards the first 400ml or so of exhaled breath; an accurately measured volume between 50 and 60ml of breath (assumed to be alveolar, though the volume discarded seems rather small for this to be ensured—see p. 33) is then collected and bubbled through a known volume of acid bichromate of known concentration, and the extent of the colour change from yellow/orange to green, which is a measure of the alcohol content of the breath, is monitored photoelectrically. All the surfaces with which the breath comes in contact are kept warm to avoid condensation within the instrument.

The Breathalyzer makes no specific provision for the possible presence of acetone in the expired breath, but, as this reacts much more slowly than ethanol with acid bichromate at the operating temperature, its presence would be indicated by the response of the instrument being slower and taking longer to reach its end point.

It is frequently cited as a disadvantage of the Breathalyzer that its use entails the opening of ampoules of a corrosive acid solution which, if spilt, could injure persons or damage materials. It is only fair to say, however, that this criticism is rarely if ever heard from persons thoroughly familiar with the instrument and accustomed to using it.

This method of breath analysis differs in two respects from most others in routine use: (1) since it makes quantitative use of a chemical reaction, the accurate measurement of a volume of breath is an essential part of the process, as opposed to the measurement of a physical property of an indeterminate volume of breath, as in most other methods; (2) the apparatus was designed on the assumption that the breath specimens analysed might be collected in plastic bags at the scene and analysed elsewhere. (This was the method of sampling used in the Grand Rapids survey described on pp. 63–69.) Although there was no evidence that this practice would not be reliable in skilled hands, it was considered unsuitable for use in this country in the enforcement of a fixed-limit law, on account of the possibility of alcohol being lost because of bag defects or through being trapped in condensed moisture in a bag allowed to get too cold.

The same oxidation reaction has also been used in a fairly sophisticated device produced by Professor Kitigawa of Tokyo with the collaboration in this country of Dr. B. M. Wright (*Kitigawa and Wright* 1962). In this the acid bichromate oxidant was contained in a column of granules through which the subject had to blow, and in that respect the device resembled, but claimed to be more accurate than, the familiar Alcotest (p. 95). It never "caught on" in this country.

II. **Measurement at a suitable wavelength of the absorption of infra-red radiation**. Every organic compound—a category which includes ethanol (alcohol)—absorbs such radiation at specific wavelengths each of which is due to one of the various frequencies with which different parts of the molecular structure of the compound resonate. The precise location of these wavelengths, and the intensity of the absorption at each one, constitute an unique identifying characteristic—the *infra-red absorption spectrum*. The determination of such spectra is widely used nowadays for identification: the spectrum of ethanol is shown in Figure 10. For our present purpose, however, what is utilised is rather the intensity of the absorption at some particular wavelength, preferably one at which ethanol absorbs rather strongly, such as, for example, the peak wavelength appearing at 3·39 micrometres[1] in Figure 10. The degree of absorption at this depends upon, and can therefore be used as a measure of, the ethanol content of a specimen of exhaled breath which the infra-red radiation is made to traverse. The principle of the method is shown in Figure 11.

[1] 1 micrometre (also known as "micron") = 1 millionth of a metre = 1/1,000 of a millimetre.

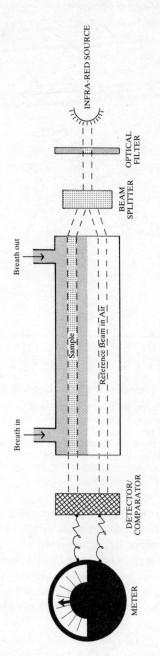

Figure 11: Principle of Infra-Red Breath-Alcohol Measurement

As explained in the test and in the caption to Figure 10, the concentration of alcohol in a vapour (*e.g.* the breath) can be determined by measuring ists absorption of infra-red radiation at a suitable wavelength. The basis of an arrangement for doing so is illustrated here. Radiation from a convenient source is limited by a filter to a selected wavelength band and then split into two identical beams; one of these passes through the breath specimen, the other as a reference beam through air. Both beams then fall on a detector/comparator, which measures and records (not shown here) the difference in intensity between them, this difference depending on and being a measure of the alcohol concentration in the breath. *Note:* The arrangement shown here is purely diagramatic and explanatory and does not illustrate the precise constructional details of any actual instrument.

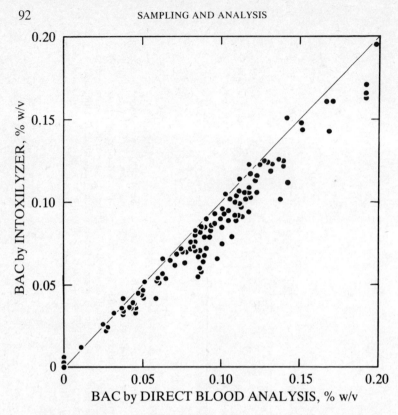

Figure 12: Blood-Alcohol Determination by Breath-Alcohol Measurement

This is a graph of some figures from the United States. Each plotted point represents measurements on simultaneously taken blood (horizontal axis) and breath
(vertical axis) specimens. Tfhe direct blood analyses were made using automated
head-space gas chromatography, those via the breath by using an Intoxilyser. If
correlation between the two methods of analysis had been perfect, all the points
would have fallen on the sloping line. Compare figure 3, p. 31. (*Courtesy and copyright of Professor Kurt M. Dubowski, Oklahoma*).

This method was developed some time ago as a laboratory
research technique (see, for example, *Alobaidi et al*. 1976), but for
law enforcement the equipment has necessarily had to be scaled
down in size and somewhat simplified. That having been achieved,
this has become one of the most successful methods of accurate
rapid breath-alcohol measurement, and is in fact used in both the
instruments approved for the implementation of the 1981 Act and
described below.

One caveat which is important here is that these instruments
must not be expected to perform a task for which they are not

designed: they do not *identify* ethanol by tracing its complete absorption spectrum; they *determine* it quantitatively simply by measuring the absorption at (usually) one single wavelength. This procedure does not by itself eliminate the effects of the presence of acetone, but modern instruments do this automatically, as will be described below. A recent American publication (*Erwin et al.* 1982) discusses at considerable length how this limitation can be exploited to confuse the issue by the defence in a drink/driving case.

III. **Gas chromatography**, as used for blood and urine after 1967. The principle has been described in Figure 9 and on p. 83. The equipment used in the laboratory is too bulky and complex to be used in a police station, but it has proved possible to scale it down to about the size of a portable typewriter. Its operation requires the ancillary provision of a cylinder of compressed carrier gas, which will require renewal from time to time and the safe stowage of which may present a minor problem. On the other hand, since each compound leaving the column is recorded under properly arranged operating conditions as a separate peak, the method is almost uniquely specific for ethanol, and the presence in particular of acetone does not necessitate any special provision being made to prevent it being registered as ethanol. An American instrument of this type was used, as described on p. 94 below, in the first field trial undertaken in preparation for the Transport Act 1981.

IV. **The use of a fuel cell**. This is a device which converts *directly*, with no intermediate stages, the energy of a chemical reaction into electricity. (Much of its development is a spin-off from space technology.) A cell suitable for the present purpose consists of two platinum or platinised electrodes separated by an acid electrolyte; any trace of alcohol vapour introduced into the cell is oxidised at one electrode, thereby producing a voltage difference across the cell which is proportional to, and can be used as a measure of, the alcohol concentration. The whole electrode system will also eventually require replacement, but should function for at least a year before this is necessary. The device must be calibrated before each measurement, but will then give a reading in half a minute or less. By a suitable choice of electrode design and construction it can be made almost completely specific for ethanol, and in particular insensitive to acetone.

V. **An application of semi-conductors**. These, as the name implies, are materials which are intermediate in properties between conductors (*e.g.* metals) and insulators (*e.g.* glass), and which under the right conditions can be made to conduct electricity; they are much used in modern electronic circuitry. If one of them is incorporated in a suitable circuit, exposure of its surface to the vapours of certain compounds, including ethanol, alters its conductivity by a measurable amount depending on the concentration of the vapour. It is not in general possible to make this effect specific for ethanol, and if necessary special provision must be made to eliminate the effect of any acetone present.

It is here assumed that the option open from April 16, 1984 to all drivers in England and Wales who show a breath figure above the legal limit of having a blood or urine specimen analysed (*Home Office News Release* of March 26, 1984) will prove eventually to be a temporary measure.

BREATH: PRACTICE

The provisions for breath analysis in the new drink/driving law introduced by the 1981 Act rest scientifically on two lengthy and exhaustive series of laboratory tests and field trials. These used at one stage or another all of the methods of analysis outlined above, and showed quite clearly that the analysis of breath (as recommended by *Blennerhassett* 1976) was a valid alternative, and indeed in several respects preferable, to that of blood or urine. The first series of trials, carried out in 1977–78 and reported on by *Emerson et al.* (1980) was basically a feasibility study. A number of breath-analysis instruments were submitted for evaluation, and after laboratory tests three different types of these were used for trials so designed that every participating police force tried one of each type. They were: *The C.M.I. Intoxilyzer* 4011A, an American instrument using infra-red absorption (see p. 90); the *Intoximeters Inc. Gas Chromatograph Intoximeter Mk. IV*, another American instrument whose principle of operation is described by its name; the *Smith and Wesson Breathalyzer* 1000, which is described on pp. 89–90. It is now common knowledge that the relevant parts of the Transport Act 1981 were based on this study.

In the period between the start of these trials and the passage of the 1981 Act improved analytical instruments became available, the improvements being mainly a greater degree of automation made possible by the incorporation of micro-processors in the designs. For the implementation of the Act, therefore, new instruments better than those tested in 1977–78 could be employed. A further series of laboratory tests and field trials (similarly arranged to the earlier ones) using this "second generation" of instruments was therefore conducted in 1981–82. The three instruments used in this series were: (1) the *Camic Breath Analyser* (British); (2) the *Lion Intoximeter* 3000 (American design, British manufacture); (3) the *Lion Auto-Alcolmeter* (British). The first two of these instruments both used infra-red absorption; the third used a fuel cell (see p. 93).

Not surprisingly, the choice of criteria by which breath-analysing instruments are adjudged for approval is as much an administrative as a legislative matter. The law is also silent on how many different types of equipment should be approved. It would not seem to matter very much how many types of screening device are used, but it would equally seem undesirable to have many different types of substantive device in use, since this could lead to arguments about their relative accuracies, and to difficulties with servicing and the supply of spares. On the other hand, it appears to be official policy not to rely exclusively on one type of instrument, in order to avoid creating a monopoly or over-taxing the resources of one manufacturer.

At the time of writing, in fact, four screening and two substantive instruments have been approved—the latter after the exhaustive 1981–82 field trial (*Isaacs et al.* 1982). The four approved screening instruments are of two types. Firstly, there are comparatively simple and cheap, but not very accurate, tube-and-bag devices utilising the yellow-green colour change of an acid bichromate reagent (see p. 82). One of these is the Draeger *Alcotest* familiar since 1967 (and commonly miscalled the "breathalyser"); the other is the newer but otherwise similar Lion *Alcolyser*. In both these devices the reagent is carried in solid granules filling a glass tube through which the subject has to blow until he has fully inflated an inelastic plastic bag about 1 litre capacity. The alcohol content of the breath is indicated by the distance over which the colour of the reagent is changed, and the tube bears a mark at the point to which the change will reach when the breath-alcohol level is up to whatever limit has been legislatively fixed.

The other screening devices are considerably more sophisticated. The Draeger *Alert* uses a semi-conductor (p. 93) the conductance of which, when it is electrically heated to about 350°C by a rechargeable battery, is increased proportionately to the ambient concentration of ethanol vapour. This is therefore sensed as a voltage change across the detector, and produces a reading almost immediately. By the incorporation of a built-in pressure switch and timer, breath is not collected for measurement until a certain minimum volume (about 1·5 litres) has been expired, thereby ensuring that the measurement is made on alveolar air. The instrument is accurate to ±10 per cent. of the ethanol concentration. It will need re-calibration at intervals which may be as long as 7–8 weeks, although a weekly check is advisable; the battery should be recharged after 30 tests or a month's storage.

The fourth screening device, the Lion *Alcolmeter S-L2*, utilises a fuel cell (p. 93), and is in fact a scaled-down and somewhat simplified form of a larger and more accurate non-portable instrument. After the rejection of a sufficient preliminary volume of breath, 1·5ml of alveolar air is used per test. The instrument uses a 9-volt replaceable battery, which is good for at least 500 tests. Each reading takes about 40 seconds, after which a wait of several minutes, to allow traces of alcohol to be cleared from the cell, is necessary before another test is made. The accuracy is comparable to that of the Alert, and 5 micrograms alcohol per 100ml breath can be detected. The fuel cell may show a slight variation in sensitivity, so that a monthly calibration check should be performed: normally, however, the instrument should be stable for 2–3 months. Acetone is not detected. (For an exhaustive test of the device, see *Jones A. W.*, 1978.)

Both the Alert and the Alcolmeter S-L2 are small enough to be easily portable, and both give one of three readings—"pass," "warning" (when the breath alcohol is over half or approaching the legal limit) and "fail." The difference between the tube-and-bag and the other screening devices is, in a nutshell: the former are less accurate, and are very much cheaper initially and require no batteries, but of course use a fresh tube for each test; the latter are more accurate and much more expensive initially, but require only the occasional renewal or recharging of batteries, and may well be cheaper in the long run if many tests are carried out.

The accuracy attainable with these screening devices is discussed in greater detail in the next chapter.

The two approved substantive instruments are the Camic *Breath Analyser* and the Lion *Intoximeter 3000*, which have been mentioned already on p. 95. Both measure alcohol by the infra-red absorption of its vapour (see p. 91), but the arrangements by which they do this are slightly different. The Camic instrument measures and compares the absorptions of sample and reference beams passing through cells 10 centimetres long, which are kept warm to avoid condensation within them. The instrument normally works off the mains, but can be adapted for battery operation. The measurement is made at a wavelength of 3·45 micrometres to determine any alcohol vapour present, the transmitted wavelength being very narrowly confined within ±0·17 micrometre of 3·45 by means of an interference filter. In this way the effect of any acetone present is eliminated. When the instrument has been set to a zero reading, and a deep *continuous* breath blown into it, it automatically rejects the first 1½–2 litres of breath, thereby ensuring that the measurement is made on alveolar air. The final meter reading depends through suitable circuitry upon the extent to which any alcohol present in the breath has upset the zero setting.

The routine of measurement is then as follows: after an initial calibration check of the instrument with the simulator (see below), the user is told by two light signals when to start and to stop blowing into it; then, after a short wait, a second breath sample is delivered and measured, a second and final calibration check follows, and the instrument prints out the necessary particulars— name, date, alcohol reading, etc. The complete test routine takes less than five minutes. If either calibration check or both are not correct, or if sufficient breath is not delivered, the whole test is automatically aborted.

The other substantive instrument, the Intoximeter 3000, resembles the Camic one in so far as sufficient breath is automatically rejected at the start of a test to ensure that alveolar air is being measured, and alcohol plus acetone, if any, are measured together by their common infra-red absorption—in this case at a wavelength (isolated by an interference filter) of 3·39 micrometres. However, the Intoximeter uses a different method of correcting for acetone: it measures it with a semi-conductor sensor (p. 93) which is several times as sensitive to acetone as to alcohol and uses this result to correct the combined alcohol/acetone figure. The sample is contained in one half of a "twin-tunnel" cell with sapphire end windows, the other half being filled with air through which the reference beam passes. Again, the cell is warmed to avoid condensation. A rotating "chopper" (a component which may be likened to miniature helicopter with very wide blades) allows the sample and reference beams to fall on the detector in very rapid alternation, and any difference between them is converted electronically (with the correction mentioned above) to a meter reading.

The routine of measurement with either the Camic or the Intoximeter machine is very similar—two measurements "sandwiched" between an initial and final calibration check. Both instruments automatically "purge" themselves before starting and between each measurement to ensure that no trace of alcohol from a previous measurement can remain. The test sequence takes a few minutes and the result is printed out. The test sequence is aborted if a satisfactory breath sample is not delivered or if either calibration check figure are outside the acceptable range. The most obvious difference between the two instruments from the user's point of view is that with the Camic the whole sequence is started by pushing a single button but some information must be entered on the printout by hand, whereas the Intoximeter 3000 has a keyboard like a typewriter's on which much more information can be printed out.

The obligatory calibration check before and after each test provides the answer to the inevitable question: namely, when was the instrument last calibrated, and what assurance can be given that it was reading correctly at the time of the breath measurement? Engineers approved by the British Calibration Service will check each instrument every six months, and also carry out an annual complete service (*Home Office Drink/Driving Fact Sheet* of April 19, 1983 on breath-testing machines). The degree of accuracy sought and attainable will be discussed in the next chapter.

The *simulator* with which the calibration of each instrument is checked is simply a sealable glass jar with a stirrer and warmer, carefully thermostated, and containing a dilute aqueous solution of alcohol of such a concentration that air bubbled through it at a selected temperature will, obeying Henry's Law (pp. 32 and 85), emerge containing a precise and predictable concentration of alcohol vapour. In practice, a solution concentration of 0·893g/l and a temperature of 34°C (approximately the temperature of expired breath—see pp. 32 and 34) produce the desired vapour concentration of 35 micrograms/100 ml. (The permissible limits for these figures, and the maintenance of the necessary accuracy, are discussed in the next chapter.) The solution must of course be replaced from time to time, since, alcohol being more volatile than water, each checking operation removes marginally more alcohol than water from it. It should in fact be changed at least once a week or after every 35 measurements, whichever is the sooner.

Isaacs et al. (1982) found in their extensive trials that renewal twice weekly was in practice more than sufficient to prevent detectable error.

It has however been authoritatively suggested (*National Physical Laboratory Report* 1983) that it may eventually be advantageous to use for breath simulation, instead of air blown through a dilute alcohol solution, a suitable compressed gas already containing the correct proportion of alcohol vapour. This could be contained in a cylinder holding several months' supply and would not require checking and renewal.

The two substantive instruments are used only in police stations by officers trained in their operation and able to satisfy their Chief Constables of their own fitness for the task. They will have received their training from instructors (288 of them, as of April 1983) who have themselves been trained in a short but intensive course conducted by a team of forensic scientists, police officers and Home Office senior instructors (*Home Office Drink/Driving Fact Sheet* (Training) of April 19, 1983).

FURTHER READING

Further information on some of the matters discussed in this chapter will be found in the following sources. Identifications by names and dates only refer to the list of scientific references beginning on p. 253.

The medical examination of, and the collection of blood samples from, suspected drivers are discussed in:

The Drinking Driver and *Alcohol, Drugs and Driving* (British Medical Association, London, 1965 and 1974, respectively).

The Practical Police Surgeon, (Sweet & Maxwell, London, 1969) and

Cooper, Schwär and Smith (1979); Chap. 19 ("Clinical Examination").

Hartmann, (1980) pp. 108–115 (In German).

There is unfortunately no single authoritative source giving full details of all the various methods used in the analysis of body fluids for alcohol. However, development in this field has been so rapid that any publication more than a year or two old is likely to be slightly out-of-date in some respect. All of the various drink/driving conferences listed on p. 254 *et seq.* had sections specifically on analytical methods (but note the warning just given!) and no doubt this will be true of future conferences in this field.

Good brief descriptions of the various recent and current methods of blood and breath analysis will be found in:

Denney (1979) and (more condensed) (Denney (1980).

The original chemical methods of blood and urine analysis are described in:

Nickolls (1956), 340–345 and *Analyst,* **85**, 840. The gas-chromatographic method used (sometimes with slight modifications) in this country since 1967 is described in Curry *et al.* (1966).

"Breath-Alcohol Analysis: Uses, Methods and some Forensic Problems—Review and Opinion" (Mason and Dubowski 1976) is wide-ranging, comprehensive and authoritative, but inevitably no longer completely up-to-date in all particulars.

Analysis using fuel cells, and its particular application in the Alcolmeter, are discussed in Jones, Jones and Williams (1977).

The analytical use of semi-conductors is described in *U.S. Patents* 3,676,820 of July 11, 1972 and 3,732,519 of May 8, 1973.

Useful information will be found in the descriptive and instructional literature issued by the manufacturers of the various analytical instruments, namely:

Alcotest and *Alert*	Draeger Safety, Draeger House, Sunnyside Road, Chesham, Bucks. HP5 2AR.
Camic Breath Analyser	Camic Ltd., 35 Upper Camden Street, North Shields, Tyne & Wear.
Alcolyser *Alcolmeter S-L2* *Intoximeter 3000*	Lion Laboratories Ltd. Ty Verlon Industrial Estate, Barry, South Glam. CF6 3BE.

Simulators: "Breath-Alcohol Simulators: Scientific Basis and Actual performance" (Dubowski, 1979) is detailed and rigorous.

CHAPTER 6

ANALYSIS: ACCURACY

The matters dealt with in this chapter are probably unfamiliar to many readers, but some understanding of them is highly desirable in dealing with a law which makes conviction depend upon the accuracy with which a quantity—in this case, the level of alcohol in a body fluid—is measured.

There is of course no such thing as an *absolutely* accurate analysis, or any other sort of measurement. Any measurement or analysis is subject to *error*, and the important thing is to recognise this fact and to know how large the error is likely to be.

The error of a measurement is the cumulative result of the inherent, inevitable, and individually insignificant small variations in the operations used in making it. The word "error" has therefore no pejorative significance in this context. The error must be distinguished from a *mistake*, which is due to carelessness and is avoidable. For example, if two cars made the same journey and recorded the distance as 25 and 25·5 miles respectively, that variation is within the permissible error of mileometers. But if one driver recorded the distance as 25 miles and the other as 35 miles, at least one of them has obviously made a mistake. The absolute error of a measurement will depend upon:

(1) The method of measurement or analysis used.

(2) The skill of the operator.

(3) The expenditure of time and trouble which the circumstances justify.

For the carpenter building a roof, for example, a rule graduated to (say) eighths of an inch is quite adequate, whereas the engineer requires a micrometer with which he can measure to the nearest thousandth of an inch, or even less in modern precision engineering. (These figures are cited without apology to the purist who would insist upon nothing but metric units being used.)

For most purposes, however, it is more useful to know the *proportional* rather than the absolute error—what percentage of the quantity measured does the error represent? (In this respect, the measurements of a ten-foot beam to the nearest quarter-inch, and of the diameter of a half-inch rod to the nearest thousandth of an inch, are of almost exactly the same accuracy.) The proportional error will also depend upon a fourth factor additional to the three mentioned above, namely:

(4) the size of the object being measured or sample being analysed. For any appropriate method of measurement, the larger the sample, the more accurately can it be measured. For example, in weighing out an ingredient on kitchen scales, the operation is more accurate by this criterion if the recorded weight is 2lb. (1 kilogram) than if it is 2oz. (50 grams).

In evaluating methods of analysis, two characteristics which it is important to distinguish clearly are *accuracy* and *precision*. The accuracy of a method is determined by how closely its results approach the true ones. The precision of a method is determined by the smallest difference in the quantity being measured which can be detected. It is therefore, with a competent analyst, equivalent to the extent to which successive measurements of the same quantity will yield identical results—that is, *reproducibility*. Precision or reproducibility is therefore a somewhat complex concept, since it depends both on the smallest difference which the method used is capable of detecting, and on the skill of the operator.

The distinction between accuracy and precision is easily made clear with the example just given—the operation of weighing. Kitchen scales are commonly graduated in ounces (25-gram steps) and bathroom scales in pounds (half-kilogram steps). The attainable *precision* of the operation is therefore to the nearest ounce with the former and the nearest pound with the latter. The *accuracy* in either case however depends on whether the scales are correctly zeroed and *calibrated*, and this must be independently checked—there is nothing in the scales themselves to tell us whether the indicated weights are correct within these limits of precision. We shall have more to say about calibration later in this chapter.

It is also obvious that the maximum precision inherent in the design and construction of the apparatus imposes an upper limit on the attainable accuracy, and that it is therefore useless to aim at a greater. This point is important when a method of analysis involves several sequential operations. Just as a good cook does not weigh some of her ingredients on bathroom and others on kitchen scales, so the analyst knows that the attainable accuracy of his result depends upon the precision of the least precise operation used in arriving at it, and that he would be wasting his time by working to a much greater precision in the other operation. (It is not unknown for this mistake to be made by laboratory workers who ought to know better!)

When blood and urine analyses were made by purely chemical methods, the analytical operations involved the measuring out of small volumes of the liquid to be analysed and of the reagents used. The final operation was normally a *titration*—the addition of a reagent until the reaction was completed, followed by the measurement to the nearest drop of the volume required for this. As this volume was commonly around 10ml, and as there are about 20 average drops in one ml, this meant that: (1) the precision was about 1 part in 200—that is, 0·5 per cent.—and we could express the volume as, say, $10 \pm 0·05$ml; (2) it was pointless to seek to improve the overall precision by measuring the other volumes more precisely (which it was quite easy to do).

There are four possible sources of inaccuracy in an analysis:

(1) The precision of the least precise stage imposes an ultimate limit upon the accuracy.

(2) There may be systematic errors in the method. It is the business of the analyst to detect these, and either to find a way of eliminating them, or to make an allowance for them.

(3) There may be an undetected fault in the equipment. Again, it is the business of the analyst to make sure that there is not, as far as is humanly possible.

(4) The analyst is human, and his skill, however great, is not infinite. He may make

(a) simple mistakes, such as misreading a number on a scale; or errors of two kinds:

(b) personal systematic errors, such as would be caused by, for example, a persistent tendency to read a scale too high or too low;

(c) errors imposed by the limits of precision with which he personally can make a measurement. If he measures the same thing several times, he will probably not get the same answer every time, in which case his answers cannot all be quite correct and none may be. (For example, if he is measuring something of which the true magnitude is 50, he might get 49·8, 50·2, and 50·1.)

Therefore, if we are to make our analyses as accurate as possible, various precautions must be observed. Quite generally, these may include:

A. A detailed study of the method of analysis, from which we may learn about (1) and (2) above.

B. The analysis of reference samples of known composition. This will enable us to detect and eliminate errors due to (2), (3), (4a) and (4b) above, and to evaluate the limit of accuracy imposed by (4c).

C. Repetition of the same analysis by the same analyst. (It is practically unheard of for any analyst ever to give a result unless he has made the analysis at least twice.) This detects errors due to (4a) above, and minimises errors due to (4c).

D. Repetition of the same analysis by two or more independent analysts. This detects errors due to (4a), minimises errors due to (4c) and, except in the very unlikely event of several analysts making the same personal systematic errors, detects errors due to (4b).

The figure $10\pm0\cdot05$ cited in a previous paragraph embodies the concept of *experimental error*—the amount by which a measurement may be inaccurate because of the inherent and unavoidable errors discussed at the beginning of this chapter. Such information is useful and may tell us all that we need to know. However, it is clearly better to know as exactly as possible by how much the measurement is likely to differ from the true value. This can be achieved, but to do so we must adopt more sophisticated criteria, and must in fact borrow from statistics the concept of the *standard deviation*.

Suppose that we make a number of measurements of the same quantity, and assume that there is no *systematic* source of error in our equipment or due to ourselves. Then the inevitable errors in our measurements will be randomly distributed above and below the true value, and the average of our measurements will be as near to the true value as we can get. The standard deviation also tells us, however, the extent to which the individual measurements differ from the mean—presumed true—value. (We are here and in the following paragraphs assuming "mean" and "average" to be synonymous.)

The standard deviation is, in words, the square root of the average of the squares of the deviations of the individual results from their mean. That rather complicated definition (which is not mathematically quite correct, but will suffice for our present purpose) is probably best elucidated by an example. Suppose that 2 analysts, A and B, each make 10 measurements of the same thing, and suppose that they get the following two series of results:

Analyst A: 148, 151, 153, 149, 144, 148, 156, 153, 146, 152.
Analyst B: 147, 158, 165, 152, 139, 150, 153, 148, 132, 156.

The average or arithmetical mean of both these sets of figures is exactly 150. It is obvious however merely from looking at their results that A is a more reliable analyst than B, in that his individual results are mostly much closer to their mean value than B's are. We would therefore place more reliance on a single measurement made by A than on one made by B.

Let us now calculate the standard deviations according to the verbal formula given above. For A, the deviations of his individual results from their mean are:

$$-2, +1, +3, -1, -6, -2, +6, +3, -4, +2$$

and the squares of these numbers are:

$$4, 1, 9, 1, 36, 4, 36, 9, 16, 4$$

The mean of these squares (*i.e.* their sum divided by the number of measurements, which is 10) is 12·0, and the square root of 12·0 is approximately 3·46. The standard deviation of A's results is then 3·46.

A similar calculation given the standard deviation of B's results as 9·67, which is nearly three times as great as A's. These two figures then give us a measure of the extent to which the two analysts' individual results differ from the presumed true value, and therefore, in one sense, of their reliability as analysts.

It should be noted that the standard deviation can, strictly speaking, be calculated only for results which show a so-called *normal* distribution. This cannot be described precisely in non-mathematical terms, but, roughly, it is the distribution characteristic of measurements showing only random unsystematic errors, with results distributed symmetrically round the mean value and deviations from this value getting progressively fewer as they get larger.

The standard deviation is sometimes referred to as "sigma," from the Greek letter σ by which statisticians designate it. It is also sometimes referred to as the "root mean square," from the way in which it is calculated. In spite of the labour entailed by that calculation, the standard deviation is, because of its important mathematical properties, much more useful as a statistic than the easily calculated *mean deviation*, which is simply the mean of all the deviations (disregarding their signs) from the overall mean. The property of most concern to us here is: if the mean and the sigma of a large number of measurements are calculated, then 68 per cent. (about two-thirds) of all the measurements will lie within one sigma on either side of the mean, 95·5 per cent. (21 out of 22) will lie within 2 sigmas, and 99·73 per cent. (369 out of 370) within 3 sigmas. This means, put in another way: taking a single measurement, the approximate odds are 2 to 1 that it lies within one sigma of the mean (presumed correct) value, 21 to 1 that it lies within 2 sigmas, and 369 to 1 that it lies within 3 sigmas. There is nothing arbitrary or mysterious about all that; it is simply a "built-in" consequence of the arithmetic used in calculating the standard deviation.

Since the standard deviation depends upon the "scatter" of a series of results round their mean, it can clearly be used as a measure of this. However, when the results in question are measurements of some quantity, their standard deviation must, to be meaningful, be related to the magnitude of that quantity. (For example, though mice and men may show a similar variability in their body-weights, the standard deviation of a group of the former will probably be measured in grams, of the latter in kilograms.) To express the extent of the scatter, therefore, the standard deviation must be related to the size of the mean measured in the same units. This is done by calculating the *coefficient of variation*, which is the standard deviation expressed as a percentage of the mean, and is therefore simply a pure number.

When the term "confidence limit" is used in connection with a measurement or series of measurements, it relates to these properties. Since only approximately 5 per cent. of a series of measurements of a quantity will deviate from their mean by more than 2 standard deviations (see above), this range is often quoted as the "95 per cent. confidence limit" for a particular measurement or series of measurements. The importance of this particular figure lies in the fact that, according to a convention generally agreed among statisticians, a statistical result is accepted as *significant* (*i.e.* genuine and meaningful) if there is a 95 per cent. probability that it is not merely the result of random variations in the measurements. (*cf.* for example, the results of the Grand Rapids survey described in Chap. 4.)

It must lastly be noted that the standard deviation is a property simply of a particular series of measurements; it is not a property either of the method used to make them or of the operator who made them. However, if an operator practised in a certain method finds that his results for the analysis by that method of a known quantity regularly show a certain standard deviation, then it is a legitimate extension of the meaning to use that standard deviation to predict the degree of accuracy of his results for an unknown quantity.

We started this chapter by pointing out that there is no such thing as an *absolutely* accurate measurement, and that its accuracy must depend upon the precision with which it is made. Whatever the degree of this, however, accuracy depends also upon another critical factor—correct *calibration*. All measurement depends in the last resort on comparison of the magnitude we are measuring with the graduations of a measuring instrument which we assume to be free from error. We measure the length of a piece of wood, for example, by comparing it with a yard or metre rule which we accept as correctly graduated. At some stage this rule must have been calibrated—that is, authenticated by comparing it with a more rigorous standard. This principle applies to all measurements—length, volume, temperature or whatever. It is obviously impossible to check every metre rule we use against the standard metre kept in a thermostated air-conditioned cellar in Paris, but for any measurement to be trustworthy there must always be an unbroken chain of comparisons back from the instrument immediately in use through ever more rigorously checked standards to the universally accepted ultimate standard of whatever quantity we are measuring. Then, provided that we are satisfied that no-one has made a mistake in this "traceability chain," we accept our instrument as having been correctly calibrated—that is, accurately graduated to within whatever degree of precision is warranted by the methods of comparison and the care used in applying them. Further than this we cannot go—we can only be satisfied "beyond reasonable doubt."

Blood and urine analysis

The relative importance of the various factors considered above depends upon what is being analysed, and how. Before 1967, when analysis of blood or urine by purely chemical methods was the norm (see p. 82), correct calibration of the equipment used (volume-graduated glassware), though obviously crucial, could be done once and for all and thereafter taken for granted; the most important factor affecting accuracy was the skill of the analyst. After 1967, body-fluids were (and still are, in the event of a blood or urine analysis being demanded) normally analysed by gas chromatography. In this, as already explained (p. 85), the equipment is checked by periodically putting through the analytical process alcohol solutions of precisely known concentration. This constitutes the calibration, and the concentration of the calibrating solution is the critically important parameter upon which the accuracy of the whole process depends. These solutions were (and are) normally made up centrally by the Government Chemist's Laboratory and the Home Office Central Research Establishment; each authorised analyst (see below) also prepares his own standards for further checks.

When signed certificates of analysis were or are issued, the signatories must be authorised analysts. The possessor of this qualification, which was first introduced by the Road Traffic Act 1962, is currently defined by s.10(9) of the Road Traffic Act 1972, as "any person possessing [certain qualifications prescribed by regulations made under the Food and Drugs Act 1955 or the Food and Drugs (Scotland) Act 1957], and any other person authorised by the Secretary of State to make analyses for the purposes of this section." In practice most authorised analysts in the Forensic Science Service were and are qualified under the last clause of that description: laboratory directors recommend(ed) to the Home Secretary for qualification members of their staffs who had proved themselves able regularly to produce replicate results showing a standard deviation of 2mg/100ml or less.

The practice in the forensic science laboratories was and is then as follows. A standard deviation of 2mg/100ml is assumed. Determinations of 6 standards must agree to within 1·5mg/100ml or less. Each body-fluid specimen is analysed by two independent analysts using entirely separate sets of equipment, and their results must agree to within 2mg/100ml or less. From the mean of these determinations 6 per cent. of its value (that is at least three standard deviations) is deducted if it is over 100mg/100ml, or 6mg/100ml if it is less than 100, and the alcohol content of the fluid is finally reported as being "not less than" whatever figure is so arrived at. It can be shown that the chance of this figure being too high is several millions to one against.

In New Zealand, where a similar method of blood analysis is used (cf. p. 85), 6mg/100ml is deducted from all results whatever their magnitude. The accuracy of their figures is discussed in some detail by Stone et al. 1982 Pt. 2).

Elaborate precautions are also taken against other possible

sources of error. A careful analyst will avoid specimens getting muddled up by checking their identity at each stage. The results should be entered at the time and once and for all on the appropriate form, so as to make copying errors impossible. Strictly observed sealing and handling practices will ensure against the accidental contamination of the specimen by extraneous alcohol. Any malfunctioning of the analytical equipment will be made apparent by the results from independent sets not agreeing.

Breath analysis

Obviously rather different considerations apply when we are using the new methods of breath analysis. As already discussed in the previous chapter, the instruments approved for roadside screening tests are of two types: relatively primitive throw-away tube-and-bag devices utilising the colour change of a reagent (*Alcotest* and *Alcolyser*), which are simple and cheap but not very accurate, and more accurate, but also more complex and expensive devices (*Alert* and *Alcolmeter SL-2*). The first type are accurate only to within about ±20 per cent.—that is, something like 20 per cent. of "fail" readings turn out to have blood-alcohol levels below 80mg/100ml, and, the evidence suggests, about the same proportion of "pass" readings would have levels above 80 if analysed. Screening devices of the second type are claimed to be accurate to within ±10 per cent.

Inaccuracy in a screening device cannot by itself lead to injustice, because its indication is not evidence. Obviously, however, the more accurate the device the better: false positives waste police and laboratory time and will exasperate drivers who have been stopped and had a body-fluid analysed—unnecessarily as it turns out; false negatives mean that drivers who should have been prosecuted are escaping, which is unfair to the law-abiding majority and a potential hazard to other road users.

The effect of changing from a less to a more accurate screening device is illustrated by the example of one police force in the south of England which in 1981 made such a change. The following figures from the laboratory which served the force in question (*Neylan* 1982) compare the number of cases actually submitted for analysis with that which would have been expected on the assumption that the force had not made the change and had maintained its previous proportion of the total cases in the area served by the laboratory.

The significance of these figures is that, when the more accurate

TABLE 3

	Number actually submitted		Expected		Number actually submitted compared with expected	
	Number	Per cent.	Number	Per cent.	Number	Per cent.
Below limit	382	13·5	626	22·1	244 fewer	8·6
Just above limit	746	26·4	521	18·4	225 more	8·0

screening instrument was used, 244 (8·6 per cent.) cases below the limit were not submitted for analysis unnecessarily, and 225 (8·0 per cent.) cases just above the limit (in fact, within the range 81–115mg/100ml), which would otherwise have escaped, were detected.

The desirable is however not necessarily the essential. For the substantive breath-analysis instruments, on the other hand, the maximum possible accuracy is clearly of paramount importance. In the first (1977–78) field trial the results with the original three types of instrument tested, using simulator solutions corresponding to various blood-alcohol levels between 50 and 400 (350 in one case) mg/100ml, showed coeffecients of variation (p. 106) never above 2·5 and in most cases between 1·0 and 2·0 (*Emerson et al.* 1980, tables 18, 19 and 20). The accuracy of these results was even greater than the manufacturers of the instruments claimed for them; it must be realised, however, that the measurements were made by trained scientists working under optimal laboratory conditions. In the second (1981–82) field trial, where the conditions of testing were those of actual cases, a greater variability could be expected. Here the two approved types of instrument produced readings between 34·55 and 35·11 on checking with 35 micrograms/100ml simulated breath; standard deviations were between 1·27 and 1·62 and coefficients of variation between 3·67 and 4·69 (*Isaacs et al.* 1982).

In both trials there was some evidence that the instruments might produce less accurate readings at very high breath-alcohol levels—those corresponding to blood-alcohol levels above, say, 200mg/100ml. These are the sort of levels found with alcoholics and what *Blennerhassett* (1976) calls "high-risk offenders." As already mentioned (p. 42) it was found impossible to test this point with volunteer subjects, since none of these could stand blood-alcohol levels above 160mg/100ml. These very high levels are however so far above the legal limit that it seems virtually impossible that any slight inaccuracy in measuring them could lead to injustice.

There are several factors to be considered in assessing and maintaining the accuracy of breath-alcohol measurements used in law enforcement. Quite generally, the errors which must be guarded against might arise through an unrepresentative breath sample reaching the instrument, or through a malfunction or incorrect calibration of it. The first of these might be due to (a) the measurement being made on non-alveolar breath, or (b) alcohol reaching the analysed breath from retained mouth alcohol or from "burping" immediately before or during the measurement. As explained on pp. 96–98, both the approved instruments automatically reject before making the measurement a volume of breath believed to be sufficient to ensure that only true alveolar breath is analysed. It is conceivable that the rejected volume might be insufficient if the blower's respiratory capacity is exceptionally large, but in that case the reading would be too low, which could not prejudice him. The possibility of alcohol from the mouth is excluded by the required 20 minutes' delay before analysis, and the possibility of alcohol from either source by making two measurements at an interval of several minutes and, if they show a difference, using, as the law prescribes, the lower reading.

With both the approved substantive instruments a malfunction is excluded as completely as is humanly possible by their design and mode of operation. If the relevant instructions are strictly followed, they reject automatically measurements which have been made without satisfactory checking of calibration or which are in any way suspect.

Their calibration and its checking remain as the most crucial part of the whole operation. They have been studied in detail by a special panel of the British Calibration Service (BCS Technical Panel 9). The 15 members of this included representatives from all parties with a legitimate interest in the subject—scientists from the Home Office Forensic Science Service, the National Physical Laboratory and the Laboratory of the Government Chemist; public analysts; solicitors; Home Office administrators; and several others. The panel's report (*NPL Report BCS 2—BCS Scheme for Evidential Breath Testing*) appeared in January 1983. It will be referred to in the remainder of this chapter simply as the *NPL Report*. It is much too long and detailed to be summarised here, and the reader is referred to the original for its particulars. It deals with: acceptance checks of the equipment used; the preparation and analysis of simulator solutions; their certification; the equipment, organisation and operation of laboratories seeking approval as certifying ones; the qualification and designation of approved signatories.

The parameters the accurate control of which is absolutely essential are the alcohol content of the simulator solution and its temperature. The solution should contain 89·33mg/100ml of ethanol, the permissible margin of error here being ±1·38mg. It is manufactured industrially in batches, and these are checked by a laboratory approved by the British Calibration Service (BCS) against a master standard prepared by the Laboratory of the Government Chemist. The solution is finally issued to the police users in sealed and identifiably labelled containers, which should be used in order of issue. The "traceability chain" (p. 107) is therefore:

Laboratory of the Government Chemist → BCS-approved laboratory → police user

The NPL Report recommends, but does not make mandatory, two methods of analysis of the solution: a chemical and a gas-chromatographic one. The reported analytical result, which, as mentioned above, is acceptable if it lies between 87·95 and 90·71mg/100ml of ethanol, should be based on the analysis of 30 samples from each batch, and the standard deviation (p. 104) of the individual results should be quoted. The alcohol content of the simulated breath should remain constant within ± 2 micrograms/100ml over 7 days. For the initial calibration, it is recommended that two simulators in series should be used in order to ensure positively that the correct vapour concentration enters the measuring instrument, and (Appendix A) that this calibration should be done at simulated breath-alcohol concentrations of zero, 35 and 50 micrograms/100ml, together with one other between 35 and 75. Although properly sealed sterile ethanol solutions should remain unchanged more or less indefinitely, one further precaution is taken: the possibility of bacterial degradation is ruled out by the addition to each batch of solution of 0·25 per cent. of copper sulphate as a preservative. The traceability chain for the simulator thermometers is:

NPL standard → BCS–approved laboratory → operational simulator

The thermometers should be capable of being read to the nearest 0·02°C, should register correctly to within 0·05°C at 34°C, and should be re-calibrated at least every two years. Calibration checks on the heater control system should be made over five on/off cycles of the thermostat, and readings should be taken when the heater is in the "off" position.

The importance of exact temperature control will be realised when it is pointed out that an error of 1°C would produce a change in the alcohol content of the "breath" as large as, or slightly over, 6 per cent. (*Emerson et al.* 1980). It must also of course be remembered that no thermostat can keep a temperature *exactly* on the chosen setting all the time; the temperature must rise or fall by some finite amount (depending on the design and construction of the thermostat) before the correcting mechanism comes into action. If, for example, this finite amount is 0·2°C and if the thermostat is set for n°C, then the closest limits within which the temperature can be maintained are n±0·2°C.

The simulator jars should be refilled with fresh solution at least weekly, preferably at a fixed time, and more often if there is the slightest evidence or suspicion that the alcohol content of the solution might have fallen below the lower permissible limit. Then, to sum up, if all the equipment is correctly calibrated, properly maintained and correctly used, the simulated "breath" will contain between 34·0 and 35·9 micrograms of ethanol per 100ml. The *NPL Report* suggests (paragraphs 18 and 29) that the confidence level (p. 106) for the concentration being within the prescribed limits should be as high as 99·9999 per cent.—that is, the chance of error here should be as low as 1 in 1 million.

For routine use, *Home Office Circular No. 46/1983* specifies the more regularly attainable limits of ±3 micrograms—that is, the check reading must fall within the range 32–38 micrograms/100ml. Then, to provide against the possibility of injustice through the check figure falling only just within the permitted limits, the police will not, according to the Circular, prosecute for a reading of less than 40 micrograms/100ml. (Compare the enforcement of the 30 m.p.h. speed limit).

Although they do not have the same mathematical basis, these operational safeguards correspond in purpose and effect to the deductions made in reporting the results of blood analyses (p. 108), and like them are an operational practice not legally prescribed. They must therefore be distinguished from the already mentioned legally enacted provision (Transport Act 1981, Sched. 8) that a driver whose lower breath–alcohol reading is, though above 35, not above 50 micrograms/100ml. may demand that a specimen of blood or urine shall be used in place of breath. Although this provision constitutes a further safeguard against instrumental malfunction, its primary purpose would seem rather to be provision for cases near the prescribed limit by allowing the subject to have a specimen for independent analysis; since there is no way of storing breath, the option of providing a blood or urine sample is retained for a limited breath range.

Although the Act implies but does not specifically mention any blood/breath ratio, it is generally realised that the 35 micrograms/ 100ml breath figure, to exceed which is an offence, is based on the accepted blood level of 80mg/100ml and a value of 2,300/1 for that ratio (see p. 32). The 35 breath figure would however correspond to a lower blood level if the blood/breath ratio was in the case of an individual aggrieved driver less than 2,300/1. Anyone whose breath level was just over 35 might therefore claim that, although he had technically committed an offence, he was being oppressively penalised because at the time of being tested his blood/breath ratio happened to be unusually low. The enacted figure of 50 micrograms/100 ml meets this particular objection, in that it corresponds to a blood/breath ratio of about 1,600, which is below the lowest figure, namely 1,750, found in the pre-legislative trials.

NOTE: At the time of going to press the contents of much of this chapter, and especially of the preceding paragraph, must be substantially modified. In consequence of a press campaign seeking to cast doubt on the accuracy of the Lion Intoximeter 3000 and suggesting that wrongful convictions could therefore arise from its use, the Home Office decided that, for an experimental period of six months starting at 00.01 hours on April 16, 1984, the option of a blood or urine analysis, hitherto limited to those drivers whose breath figures lay between 35 and 50 micrograms/100ml, shall in England and Wales be extended to *all* drivers whose breath figure exceeds 35 micrograms/100ml (Home Office, *News Release* of March 26, 1984. See also p. 75). In Scotland, where the Lion Intoximeter is not in use (police forces there having selected the alternative Camic breath analyser), it has been decided that no such administrative relaxation shall be allowed, and the statutory procedure will be followed.

FURTHER READING

The classic text on the statistical evaluation of the significance and accuracy of experimental results is Sir Ronald Fisher's *Statistical*

Methods for Research Workers (originally published by Oliver and Boyd, Edinburgh; 14th ed. (1970) now published by the Hafner Press, New York, a division of the Macmillan Publishing Co., Inc.). An excellent book for the scientific layman is *Facts from Figures* by M. J. Moroney (Penguin Books Ltd.).

The following papers may also be helpful:

J. P. Payne, *The Quality of Measurement* (1970).

Stone, Norris, Muirhead and Singers, *Accuracy of Blood-Alcohol Analysis by Gas Chromatography* (1982).

K. M. Dubowski, *Breath-Alcohol Simulators: Scientific Basis and Actual Performance* (1979, Pt. I).

N.B. As this book goes to press a paper very relevant to the discussion in the above Chapters 5 and 6 was published, and should be noticed, though it cannot be treated in our text: J. A. Dossett (1984) 81 *Law Society Gazette* 2840.

CHAPTER 7

BACK CALCULATIONS AND CONVERSION OF BLOOD ALCOHOL TO DRINK TAKEN

In dealing with this topic we are treading on dangerous ground, since the necessary calculations involve so many approximations and unverifiable assumptions that their results are liable to be barely meaningful. However, if the precaution is taken of keeping extrapolation to the minimum necessary, occasions may arise when the best possible estimate of the blood-alcohol level at some period before the taking of the specimen analysed may be desirable or even necessary. Indeed, one such occurred, as described on pp. 20 and 117, during the "run-up" to the Transport Act 1981. There may also be circumstances in which some sort of estimate, based on the analysed blood-alcohol level, of the quantity of liquor consumed to produce it may provide useful information.

Back calculations

As far as pre-1981 prescribed-level cases are concerned the law of this country specifically laid down that the level of alcohol in the blood or other body fluid given in evidence, and which by exceeding the legal limit produced the offence, should be taken to be that present in the analysed specimen (Road Traffic Act 1972, s.(1) and (10)) and was deemed by the very definition of the offence to be that present at the time of driving. In the case of the prescribed-level offence as re-defined following the Transport Act 1981 there is a specific provision requiring the assumption to be made (except in limited circumstances) that the breath, blood or urine alcohol level at the time of the offence shall be not less than in the analysed specimen (Road Traffic Act 1972, s.10(2) as amended). In either, the certificate of analysis, if unchallenged, proves this level. In prescribed-level cases it is therefore inappropriate to consider a hypothetical figure relating to the actual time of driving and based on back calculation from the figure found by analysis. In pre-1981 impairment cases however there was still room for considering whether there could be some variation between the blood-alcohol level at the time of sampling and the level at the time of driving, but this is now removed by the statutory presumption referred to above. In such cases, of course, the blood-alcohol level would not be conclusive but would simply be an item of evidence which might or might not be indicative of impairment of the driver. Except in the limited circumstances in which the statutory presumption is not operative there will therefore be few occasions on which back calculation will be required.

The British suspicion of such calculations is not universal. German courts, it would seem, accept or even welcome such evidence. *Zink* and others have published (1975, 1976, 1977, 1980 and 1981) some careful and detailed investigations of the subject. From a computerised analysis of 1,486 blood-alcohol curves they derive an equation which, they claim, can be used to calculate within a 99 per cent. confidence limit (see p. 106) the blood-alcohol level at a given time prior to sampling.

Assuming that all the information is available, a calculation of this kind will be based on: the alcohol concentration in the specimen analysed; the time at which the specimen was taken; the time when the liquour was consumed; the consequent probable time of the "peak"; an assumed rate of fall of the blood alcohol during the elimination phase. The result will then give the estimated blood-alcohol concentration at the relevant time. What particular rate of elimination is assumed will, of course, depend on why the calculation is being made—that is, whether its purpose is to determine the most probable blood-alcohol level, or to establish limits within which the level may be assumed to lie. The rates of fall which may be assumed are discussed on pp. 19–21.

One area in which back calculations assumed importance in this country was however in the extensive trials leading up to the legalisation of substantive breath analysis by the Transport Act 1981; in these the alcohol levels in the blood and breath of arrested drivers were compared. As already mentioned (p. 20), in these experiments a considerable time, during which the blood-alcohol level would almost certainly be falling, normally elapsed between the taking of a blood specimen and the breath analysis. It was therefore necessary to adjust the blood figure to be compared to that probably present at the time of the breath analysis; for this purpose a rate of fall of 15mg/100ml/hour was assumed.

Conversion of blood alcohol to quantity of drink taken

Calculation from blood-alcohol levels to liquor consumed must be based on the assumption that the blood-alcohol was at its "peak" and that the simple Widmark equation given on p. 13 applies. This assumption may well not be true, but any attempt to make an allowance for the resulting error is so completely a matter of guesswork that it is quite impermissible. Tables based on such a calculation were at one time published by the British Medical Association (*Recognition of Intoxication,* 1958). Figures either calculated by the analyst himself or taken from these tables were then often given in evidence at the request or even on the insistence of the courts, the members of which usually found a figure of x pints of beer or y single whiskies more meaningful than a blood-alcohol level.

These quantities of liquor were in fact the quantities which contained the same amounts of alcohol as could be assumed, given the conditions described, for the various blood-alcohol levels to be present in the whole body of the accused, so that at least these amounts of alcohol must have been drunk. Unfortunately, it proved almost impossible to persuade courts that the quanitities were not estimates of the volumes of liquor *actually* consumed. However, as we have already pointed out, the quantities actually drunk must usually be greater than this, and sometimes very much greater. (See, for example, *Rentoul et al.* 1962).

Such figures were admittedly of some value in prosecutions under the old impairment laws when the calculated quantities were perhaps three or four times what the accused admitted to having drunk. However, although defendants naturally tended to underestimate their consumptions, such very large discrepancies were unusual.

In short, figures taken from the B.M.A. tables or based on similar calculations were quite unrealistic and generally misleading. Consequently, the B.M.A. have, in recognition of this fact, long abandoned such tables in all their publications on drink and driving.

If calculations are to be made, it is best to rely on the simple Widmark equation, remembering that the results cannot be other than approximate and are subject to possibly quite large errors. The equation has already been given, (p. 13), namely

$$a = c \times p \times r$$

If we take c as the blood-alcohol level found by analysis, p as either the known body weight of the drinker or as the average for his/her sex (men, 11 stones or 70kg; women, 9 stones or approximately 55kg) and for r, the Widmark factor, assume conservative values of 0·6 for men and 0·5 for women, then "*a*" is calculable as a weight of alcohol; it only remains then to further calculate, from Table 1 on p. 6, the volume of any specified type of liquor containing this weight of alcohol. Then, obviously, assuming that the calculation of "*a*" is valid, not less than this can have been drunk.

We have already pointed out that in the particular case of beer the blood-alcohol level is almost invariably much lower than that calculated from the amount of alcohol ingested. Therefore, if the liquor taken was beer, it is reasonable to increase by 50 per cent. the quantity as given by the calculation outlined in the previous paragraph—or, which amounts to the same thing, to use for men a Widmark factor of 0·9 instead of 0·6. (Women need not be considered here, since cases of women driving after drinking large quantities of beer are virtually unknown, at least in Britain).

The following table gives for various determined blood-alcohol levels the nominal weights of alcohol which may be assumed to be present in the bodies of (1) men after drinking beer; (2) men after drinking any other liquor; (3) women. The weight given there may then be used in conjunction with the figures given in the last two columns of Table 1 on p. 6 to calculate the minimum volumes drunk of any given type of liquor.

TABLE 4

Blood-Alcohol Concentration in mg/100 ml. (c)	Weight of Alcohol in Grams (a)		
	MEN (p=70kg)		WOMEN (p=55 kg)
	Beer (r=0·9)	Other Liquors (r=0·6)	(r=0·5)
50	31	21	14
60	38	25	16
70	44	29	19
80	50	34	22
90	57	38	25
100	63	42	27
110	69	46	30
120	75	50	33
130	82	55	36
140	88	59	38
150	94	63	41
160	101	67	44
170	107	71	47
180	113	75	49

TABLE 4—cont.

Blood-Alcohol Concentration in mg/100 ml. (c)	Weight of Alcohol in Grams (a)		
	MEN (p=70kg)		WOMEN (p=55 kg)
	Beer (r=0·9)	Other Liquors (r=0·6)	(r=0·5)
190	120	80	52
200	126	84	55
210	132	88	58
220	138	92	60
230	145	96	63
240	151	101	66
250	158	105	69
260	164	109	71
270	170	113	74
280	176	118	77
290	183	122	80
300	189	126	82

Cooper, Schwär and Smith also publish (pp. 251–256) a set of tables giving weights of alcohol calculated in this way for various assumed values of "*p*," "*c*" and "*r*." One must not however forget that the apparent precision of such figures may be quite misleading.

In making any such calculations, the following points should be borne in mind.

(1) The blood-alcohol level reached after the consumption of any given weight of alcohol will depend on the *weight* of the drinker—the smaller the body throughout which the alcohol is distributed, the less water it contains, and the higher therefore the alcohol concentration in this water. However, it is not worth while attempting to allow for this if the drinker's weight is anywhere near the average, since the variation due to incalculable personal factors is sufficient to make the apparent precision of a small correction completely spurious. (See, for example, *McCallum and Scroggie* 1963). It should also be remembered that fat does not absorb alcohol (p. 14), so that the "equivalent" body-weight of a drinker who is heavy because he/she is fat will be less than his/her actual weight.

(2) Calculations of this kind are based on the assumption that all the alcohol is ingested within a fairly short time (say, 1 hour or less). If the drinking is spread over a longer period, then more will quite certainly have been drunk than calculation shows.

(3) These calculations may well give an approximately correct figure for fairly strong drink taken within a short time on an empty stomach. In other circumstances however the figure will probably be too low, and *in any circumstances the results, depending as they do on unknown and incalculable personal factors, cannot be accepted as trustworthy. It would be extremely dangerous to attempt to use such calculations to discover how much can be drunk before a given blood-alcohol level is exceeded.*

The "hip-flask" defence

There is however one area in which the connection between the quantity of drink taken and the alcohol level in a body fluid must sometimes unavoidably be considered: this embraces cases in which, when a body-fluid alcohol over the limit has been found, drink is alleged to have been taken after driving but before arrest and sampling. It may then be claimed that a high figure found on analysis was wholly or partly due to the additional drink, and that but for it the body-fluid alcohol would have been within the legal limit. In a typical case of this sort a driver who has had a drink or two has an accident of some sort near his destination on his way home, leaves his car and rushes into his house, and has a stiff drink by way of restorative before the police arrive. When a breath or blood analysis is made, his body-fluid alcohol is found to be above the limit: was it so during driving, or is the excess wholly due to the drink taken after the driver arrived home?

This defence (colloquially "the hip-flask defence") was held to be incompetent in England because post-driving drinking simply invalidated the certificate of analysis. In Scotland, the accused was allowed to prove the effect of the additional drinking if he could, but the recent Transport Act amendments have permitted a statutory form of this defence applicable throughout the United Kingdom (see p. 238 *et seq.*).

If such a defence is offered, such estimate as is possible will have to be made of the contribution of the additional drink to the body-alcohol level. The data or assumed figures which may be used in such a case are:

The nature and sizes of drinks taken before and after driving;

The times of drinking;

The time at which a body-fluid specimen is taken, and the analysed alcohol content of this specimen;

The assumed rate of elimination by the drinker, and such

information as is available about his/her size, weight and body-habit.

Then, given as much of this information as possible, the body-fluid alcohol level may be calculated in the manner described on pp. 118–119 and compared with that found by analysis, and/or the quantity of liquor allegedly taken may be compared with that calculated as described in the earlier part of this chapter. Discrepancies shown by these results may be instructive and may be helpful to a court when properly explained by a competent witness. By way of illustration we may perhaps cite two actual cases in which one of the present writers was recently involved.

Case I: At about 7.45 p.m. on a summer evening the driver S, a shopkeeper, on his way home collided with a stationary car parked almost outside his house. He attributed the accident to his having been distracted by a parcel having fallen to the floor and prevented the proper operation of the brake and clutch pedals. He had had, he said, three single whiskies on his way home between 6.45 p.m. and 7.40 p.m. and a good deal to drink at a wedding on the previous day. Immediately after the collision he entered his house and was given by his wife a quantity of whisky which they both estimated at $3\frac{1}{2}$fl.oz. Breath tests at about 8.15 p.m. and 8.45 p.m. were positive, and a blood specimen taken at 8.48 p.m. contained 106mg/100ml of alcohol. S was charged with driving with excess alcohol in his bloodstream. In testing the possibility that S's blood-alcohol level was less than 80mg/100ml at the time of the collision, it was assumed that: (1) alcohol taken at the wedding on the previous day would have been entirely eliminated; (2) the whisky taken at 7.45 p.m., being strong drink taken on an empty stomach, would probably have produced an early peak (see pp. 14–15) of 70–80mg/100ml at around 8.0–8.30 p.m.; (3) this level would have begun to decline by 8.48 p.m.; (4) the time interval between the probable peak and the taking of the blood specimen was so short that it would have been an unrealistic pseudo-refinement to attempt making any allowance for it. On the basis of these assumptions, the whisky taken at 7.45 p.m. would probably have produced a blood-alcohol level of about 75–80mg/100ml at 8.48 p.m., in which case S's blood-alcohol level at the time of the collision would have been only about 30 (106 minus, say, 75); this agrees well with S's own account of his evening. He was acquitted on a drink/driving charge.

Case II: The driver L admitted having had rather a lot to drink on the previous day, but denied having had any on the day of the following incident. He was returning home in the dusk of a winter evening, and at about 5.15 p.m. collided with a pedestrian who, he said, emerged without warning from between two stationary buses. He panicked, left his car and walked home, arriving about 6.30 p.m. He appeared to be in a state of shock, and his wife at once gave him a large whisky the volume of which, according to her recollection of the tumbler used and how full it was, would have been not less than 100 or more than 130 ml (4–5½ "singles"). The blood-alcohol peak from this drink would probably in the circumstances have been reached about 7 p.m. Breath tests about 7.15 p.m. and again about 8 p.m. indicated a blood-alcohol level above the limit, and a blood specimen was taken at 8.45 p.m., by which time the blood level would be falling; the specimen showed 90mg/100ml on analysis. L was therefore charged both with failing to stop after an accident and with a blood-alcohol level above the permitted figure.

Any calculation based on these figures must take two areas of uncertainty into account—the rate of elimination of alcohol from L's blood stream, and the precise quantity of liquor drunk at 6.30 p.m. Taking the rate as not less than 10mg/100ml/hour, and not more than 25, with a most probable figure of 15 (p. 20), the range of possible values of the blood alcohol at 8.45 p.m. from the drink taken at 6.30 p.m. is shown here in tabular form (with all figures rounded off to the nearest 5).

	Smaller drink	Larger drink
At peak (probably about 7 p.m.)	65	85
At 8.45 p.m. (time of taking of blood specimen), assuming following rates of elimination in mg/100 ml/hour: 10	50	70
15	40–45	60–65
25	25–30	45–50

That part of the analytically determined blood level which is derived from drink taken before L arrived home will be represented by the difference between 90 and the figure selected from the above table. It will be seen that:

(1) Even assuming the larger drink and the smallest rate of elimination, the drink consumed by L after his arrival home can hardly by itself have produced a blood-alcohol level of 90 unless (a) L's body weight was much less than average, (b) the quantity of drink consumed was under-estimated, or (c) L was not strictly truthful in his account of drink taken on the way home.

(2) Even assuming the circumstances most unfavourable to L (smaller drink and highest rate of elimination), less than 65mg/100ml (that is, 90 minus 25) was derived from the drink taken on the way home and his blood level at that time was therefore *ipso facto* less than 80. He was acquitted of the drink-driving charge.

FURTHER READING

Cooper, Schwär and Smith, *Blood Alcohol Calculations*, Chap. 23 (1979). (A thorough and detailed discussion of the subject of this chapter and kindred matters).

Zink and Reinhardt (1975, 1976, 1977, 1980 and 1981) (in German).

N.B. As this book was going to press a more general discussion of the "hip-flask" offence was published: J. K. Mason (1984) 128 *Solicitor's Journal* 539.

CHAPTER 8

DRUGS AND DRIVING

As we have pointed out elsewhere, the offence introduced by the Road Safety Act 1967, re-stated in sections 6 to 12 of the Road Traffic Act 1972 and now re-enacted by the Transport Act 1981, is concerned only with the level of alcohol in the blood. Any prosecution for driving whilst under the influence of drugs or a combination of drugs and alcohol must therefore be brought as an impairment offence, as sometime set out in the Road Traffic Act 1960, and now re-enacted by the Transport Act 1981 as part of the re-stated drink/driving code contained in sections 6 to 12 of the Road Traffic Act 1972. It will in consequence be necessary to prove that driving ability was actually impaired and that the impairment was caused by a drug or drugs.

Since ethanol is also scientifically speaking a drug, it is perhaps unfortunate that the law has always put "alcohol" and "drugs" in separate categories. However, the practical distinction is clear enough: "alcohol" needs no further definition, whereas a "drug" in the present context is most commonly a pharmaceutical product taken for the relief of some specific ailment or complaint and usually medically prescribed, or, it could be, a pharmacologically active substance taken (often illegally) to relieve stress or "for kicks." The World Health Organisation's Expert Committee on Drug Dependence has defined a drug quite generally as "any substance that, when taken into a living organism, may modify one or more of its functions." Another (legal) definition will be found on p. 167.

There can be no doubt that there are numerous drugs the consumption of which, even by themselves but especially if taken together with some alcohol, can affect driving just as adversely as too much alcohol does. *Clarke* (1982) has also pointed out that, just as in the case of alcohol, this may occur at blood-drug levels too low to produce any gross obvious outward symptoms. It is not clear when this effect of drugs was first generally realised, but *Milner* (p. 25) cites the late 1950s, when traffic violators who were being arrested in Indiana because they appeared to be drunk were found to have little or no alcohol in their blood and to be in fact affected by tranquillisers they had been taking. However, apart from the simple fact that drugs can impair, the legal and scientific problems differ from those with alcohol in three major respects.

1. With drugs it is, as mentioned above, necessary to prove impairment before a charge can be brought. Although the drug manufacturers keep documented blood-level figures for the "minimum effective" and "toxic" doses (*Clarke, loc. cit.*), there is no well established and generally accepted body of data on which a law for drugs corresponding to the prescribed-level one for alcohol could be based. This is true even taking into account the almost unmanageable mass of information which recent research in the field has produced (a mass which is in sharp contrast to the paucity of information available when the first edition of this book was in preparation). As recently as 1976 *Linnoila* (Helsinki), one of the most active researchers in this field, writing in a special issue of the journal *Accident Analysis and Prevention*, stated categorically that with drugs no correlation between tissue concentration and performance, as there is with alcohol, is possible. *Moscowitz* (1976), writing editorially from California in the same issue, put it: "The review papers reveal the sparseness of relevant data regarding the nature and extent of behavioural side-effects of many drugs." *Lundberg et al.* (1979), also writing from California, describe a meticulously careful comparative series of tests of impaired drivers with and without drugs detectable in their bloodstreams, but come to the same conclusion: namely that much further study is required before blood-drug levels can be laid down from which impairment can be predicted.

However, the problem is probably not as intractable as it may seem. Careful collation of the existing data would almost certainly provide the beginning of a solution, and in fact some progress here can now be discerned. *Forney* (1979), in his report of the Sub-committee on Human Factors of the United States National Safety Council's Committee on Alcohol and Drugs, proposes as a measure of unacceptable driving impairment the effect of a blood-alcohol level of 100mg/100ml, and goes on to suggest that for most central-nervous-system depressants it would be agreeable to most toxicologists and physicians to specify a dose or body-fluid concentration which is associated with a similar degree of impairment. In a recent European contribution to the topic from Heidelberg (*Aderjan and Schmidt* Stockholm 1980, p. 996) much information is given on the effects, plasma levels and recovery times for the class of drugs of which diazepam (*Valium*) is the best known.

2. The analysis of a body-fluid for drugs involves the additional step of identifying the drug(s) present before its/their amount present can be determined. Moreover, as most drugs are much more potent than alcohol, the amount present in the body of a living person affected by any of them will be very much smaller. For both these reasons the problems of analysis are more difficult. There is also no way, as there is for alcohol, of using a simple roadside screening test.

3. Compared with the number of alcohol analyses made, the number for drugs is exceedingly small. This is in part an effect of the factors mentioned in the preceding paragraph. As has been pointed out by a number of authors (see, for example, *Milner* p. 70), the lack of any quick screening test must greatly reduce the number of specimens submitted for laboratory analysis. At the time of writing, such drug analyses performed in this country in the Home Office forensic science laboratories formed everywhere well under 1 per cent. of those made for alcohol: the actual figures for 1981 varied from fewer than 12 such cases in a laboratory doing nearly 7,000 bloods to 45 such cases in over 7,000 bloods. In London, not surprisingly, the proportion of drug analyses made in drink-and-driving cases is rather greater: in 1981 there were 261 (203 blood, 58 urine) drug analyses made in a total of 14,364 cases submitted, a proportion of about 1·8 per cent. (*Williams, R.L.* 1982). Allowing for the fact that drugs were not in fact detected in all of both the provincial and the metropolitan cases examined for them, these figures are not very different from those reported in the mid-1960s from Sweden, where drugs were detected in slightly under one-half per cent. of a series of over 50,000 cases (*Bonnichsen et al.* 1967). It is of course possible that the full implementation of the Transport Act 1981 will eventually cause more drug analysis to be made in this country, since it contains for the first time a provision (Sched. 8, s.8) that in certain circumstances a blood or urine specimen may be demanded as well as a breath one, in order that drugs may be tested for. Some (for example *Clarke* 1982) maintain that a wide use of this provision would make an important contribution to road safety.

The smallness of the present numbers of drug tests must not however obscure the fact that the quantities of drugs prescribed and consumed are enormous. According to *Moffat* (1980), over

290,000,000 prescriptions were dispensed in England alone during 1976, of which a large number, possibly even the majority, were for drugs that might affect driving. *Osselton et al.* (1980) cite an estimate by *Havard* that in Great Britain there are currently 500,000 drivers who take psychotropic (that is, potentially mind-affecting) drugs as well as alcohol. The number of prescriptions for drugs of this type issued annually in the United States has been variously given as: tranquillisers, mid–1970s, 100,000,000 (*Linnoila* 1976); "sleeping pills" (mainly tranquillisers), 1980, 70,000,000 (*Chorlton* 1983). It has been estimated (cited *Hartmann* p. 125) that in the mid–1970s there were 60,000 regular, possibly addicted, users in West Germany. Statistics of this kind are becoming commonplace. They do, however, emphasise—though the emphasis is insufficiently heeded—the danger which may arise from taking together with alcohol what may be no more than a normal dose of a quite legitimately prescribed drug, or of taking a combination of drugs which may interact unpredictably with each other. *Milner* (p. 2) aptly calls this "polypharmacy." He cites, for example, (p. 24) a case in which two heavy drinkers died during treatment with an anti-depressant drug; post-mortem analysis of their bloods showed only therapeutic levels of the drug and only moderate levels of alcohol (100 and 150mg/100ml).

In this way a safe driver may innocently become a dangerous one. It has been repeatedly stressed by writers who ought to know (for example, Dr. A. J.A. Havard, Secretary of the British Medical Association) that only a minority of prescribing doctors give their patients adequate warnings about the possible effects of the prescribed drugs on driving and the particular danger of combining them with alcohol (*Havard* 1973, 1976; also *Silverstone* 1974). Moreover, the patients often disregard obvious precautions such as: waiting to discover what side effects there may be; not taking more than the prescribed dose; not mixing it with alcohol; not continuing to drive if feeling unwell.

It is of course virtually impossible to discover just how many drivers become potentially dangerous in this way. There are few reliable data about the numbers of drug-using drivers and the amounts they consume. In any case, it has been suggested by *Linnoila* (*loc. cit.*) that drug users may not be a representative sample of the whole driving population, since their drug use may be a sign of personal and social problems that might make them worse drivers anyway. In the Swedish investigation already cited (*Bonnischsen et al., loc. cit.*), notwithstanding the small number of specimens in which drugs were actually detected, about 12 per cent. of the drivers admitted that they had taken a drug or drugs, with or without alcohol. *Clarke* (1982) believes that certainly 15 and possibly more than 25 per cent. of all drivers on the road have taken long-acting drugs shortly enough before driving to be still possibly affected by them. *Kibrick and Smart* (1970), of the Addiction Research Foundation in Toronto, conclude in a review of the earlier studies in this field that nearly half the general population drive after drug use at least once a year and that 11–15 per cent. of accident drivers have taken a psychotropic drug before their accidents.

In an investigation described by *Sabey* (1978), a group collected over a ten-year period of 1,216 drivers (1,060 men and 156 women) who had been involved in accidents were questioned about what drugs they may have taken, and the results compared with those from a larger control group of car-park users. Sabey is at pains to emphasise that the methods of sampling and the way in which her figures were derived rule out any sophisticated statistical treatment, and certainly they do not at first glance show any striking connection between drug-taking and accidents: of the accident victims 11 per cent. of the men and 26 per cent. of the women admitted taking some drug before driving, the corresponding percentages for the control group being 8 and 15 respectively. However it is of interest that, whereas among the victims the most frequently occurring class of drug was for both sexes tranquillisers (which are fairly potent substances), the commonest class among the control group, for both sexes and by a large margin, was analgesics—presumably the relatively harmless aspirin or paracetamol.

In the connection, however, *Kibrick and Smart* (*loc. cit.*) point out that questioning the drivers themselves, while it is bound to furnish some information, is not a reliable method of obtaining it, since the replies are frequently untruthful. A more trustworthy source of information is the analysis of body-fluids. In Bonnichsen's Swedish investigation cited above the drugs most frequently detected were barbiturates and tranquillisers. *Alha et al.* (1977) record that, of 100 randomly selected blood specimens from suspected alcohol-impaired drivers in Finland, alcohol was present in 76, and some other drug as well in 25 of these 76. *Van Ooijen* (Stockholm 1980, p. 342), reported that in Rotterdam the number of drivers using drugs as well as alcohol rose from 8·8 to 16·5 per cent. during the decade 1965–75. *Gelbke et al.* (1978), reporting from Heidelberg, made a detailed study of the occurrence of the common tranquilliser diazepam *(Valium)* in specimens of this kind; regarding their results as positive only when the drug was present above a "cut-off" concentration of 20 micrograms per ml, they found it to be present in 46 out of 2,050 specimens (that is, 2·25 per cent.). This, though a low figure, can be considered a significant one. A rather different picture emerges, however, from an American study by *Terhune and Fell* (1981), who studied a series of 497 drivers injured in accidents and hospitalised. Their findings may be summarised as follows:

		per cent. of total
Total samples analysed	497	
Alcohol or other drug detected	188	38
Alcohol alone	125	25·5
Alcohol over 100 mg/100 ml	97	19·5
Two or more substances detected	52	10·5
Cannabis	47	9·5
Tranquillisers (usually diazepam)	37	7·5
Sedative or hypnotic	14	3
Other drugs (cocaine, anticonvulsant, analgesic)	22	4·5

When more than one substance was detected, one of these was most commonly alcohol; that is, there were few cases of drugs other than alcohol being taken together.

In spite of what Kibrick and Smart (1970) say, the dead of course cannot lie. Of the numerous determinations that have been made of the presence of drugs in the bloods of fatally injured drivers, two examples, both from the United States, may be cited. *Turk et al.* (1974) found in North Carolina that, of the 61 per cent. of solitary drivers killed in accidents who had blood-alcohol levels between 30 and 220mg/100ml, 5 per cent. had another drug in addition. *Garriott et al.* (1977), after examining 207 cases during eighteen months of fatally injured drivers in Dallas, found alcohol alone in the bloods of 52 per cent. drugs alone in 9 per cent. and alcohol plus a drug in another 9 per cent. Of the drivers in the latter survey, alcohol and/or a drug was present in 76 per cent. of those demonstrably at fault in the accident, but in only 41 per cent. of those not at fault. *Milner* (1972), writing from Australia but having made a survey of world literature on the subject, states bluntly in the last sentence of his book that "drugs other than alcohol probably play the major role in causing 5 to 10 per cent. of traffic accidents and 10 to 15 per cent. of all road deaths."

As the law stands at present, a request to the laboratory to analyse a specimen of blood, urine or saliva for drugs would probably be made only in the following circumstances: (1) there was evidence of impaired driving, but the breath test for alcohol proved entirely negative; (2) the breath test showed a blood-alcohol level under 80, but there was clinical evidence of gross impairment such as would normally be associated with a much higher blood-alcohol level; (3) the driver admitted having taken some drug, or sought to explain his behaviour by alleging an unusually large effect of a small amount of drink; (4) there was evidence of possibly impairing drugs being found in the vehicle.

CLASSIFICATION AND NOMENCLATURE OF DRUGS

The drugs with which we are here concerned may be broadly divided into: (1) prescribed or legitimately taken drugs which may of themselves impair driving, especially if misused, or exaggerate the effects of alcohol; (2) illicit drugs such as Cannabis or LSD.

Legitimate drugs:

There is a very large number of these. As their nomenclature can be confusing to the uninitiated, this will be briefly explained before their classification is described.

Briefly, each drug which is a single chemical compound (that is, almost all modern synthetic drugs) has or may have three names: (1) a full chemical name, which is constructed accordingly to agreed rules and is for the chemist a complete specification of the chemical structure, but which is unintelligible to others and is usually too long to be readily memorisable; (2) an approved shorter pharmaceutical name, often based on the chemical name but fundamentally arbitary; (3) in most cases, a proprietary name (or several proprietary names) by which the drug is marketed and which is commonly the name by which it is best known in everyday speech.

To take only one example, the drug known pharmaceutically as diazepam is, chemically, 7–chloro–2, 3–dihydro–1–methyl–5–phenyl–1H–1, 4–benzodiazepan–2–one and is available in several proprietary brands, of which the best known in this country is *Valium*.

There are several possible modes of classification of these drugs, including the Department of Health and Social Security's official one, but it will be convenient here to follow the well-established authority of *Martindale's Extra Pharmacopoeia* (1977, 1984) and classify according to function, with some sub-classes based on chemical structure. Note that in the following lists only a few of the best-known drugs are cited, and that proprietary names are in italics and have capitals. (A useful cross-checking table of pharmaceutical and proprietary names will be found in *Cooper, Schwär and Smith* p. 372).

The duration of action of a drug is usually expressed as its *half-life*—that is, the time required for its tissue concentration to fall to half its highest level. The half-lives of psycho-active drugs vary widely; for some it may be over 24 hours from a single dose (*Clarke* 1982).

Tranquillisers: Freely prescribed—too freely, many believe—for relief of anxiety, stress, tension, etc. Commonly divided into *major* and *minor* according to potency, with further sub-division (neglected here) based on chemical structure. May produce vertigo, confusion, drowsiness, blurred vision and other side-effects. A few examples are:

chlordiazepoxide	(*Librium* and others)
chlormezanone	(*Trancopal* and others)
chlorpromazine	(*Largactil, Thorazine* and about 15 others)
chlorprothixine	(*Taractan* and others)
diazepam	(*Valium, Atensine, Tensium*)
haloperidol	(*Haldol, Serenace*)
meprobamate	(*Equanil, Miltown, Mepavlon* and others)
thoridiazine	(*Melleril* and others)
trifluoperazine	(*Amylozine, Stelarid, Stelaxine* and about 12 others)

Anti-depressants: Given, as the name implies, for the relief of depression. Rather resemble tranquillisers in their effects and possible side-effects; also dizziness. Are sub-divided into mono-amine oxidase inhibitors (the type that must not be taken with certain foods such as cheese) and tricyclic anti-depressants ("tricyclic" refers to chemical structure). An example of the first type is

phenelzine	(*Nardil*)

and examples of the second are

amitriptyline   (*Amizol, Triptafen* and about 15 others)
imipramine   (*Tofranil* and about 15 others)
nortriptyline   (*Aventyl, Motival* and about 10 others)

Anti-histamines: Are used against allergic conditions—urticaria, hay fever, motion sickness, etc. May produce drowsiness, disturbed vision, lack of concentration, unco-ordination, etc. A few examples are:

chlorcyclizine   (*Histofax*)
dimenhydrinate   (*Dramamine*)
diphenhydramine   (*Benadryl, Histergan*)
mepyramine   (*Anthisan* and others)
promezathine   (*Phenergan, Avomine*)
tripellenamine   (*Pyribenzamine*)

Analgesics: For the relief of pain. Include both mild analgesics such as aspirin and paracetemol, which may in themselves be considered harmless, and narcotics such as

codeine   methadone
morphine and its derivatives (*e.g.* heroin)
pethidine (*Meperidine* in the United States)
various others most of which are notoriously habit-forming.

Hypnotics and sedatives: Used for general sedation and as "sleeping pills." Include:

(1) barbiturates, which are usually classified according to the duration of their action and of which the best-known are:
phenobarbitone (*Luminal*)   cyclobarbitone   (*Phanodorm*)
amylobarbitone (*Amytal*)   hexobarbitone   (*Evipan, Evidorm*)
butobarbitone   (*Soneryl*)   quinalbarbitone (*Seconal*)

The effects resemble those of alcohol. Very liable to addictive misuse. Tolerance is easily acquired. In American usage, names ending in "-al" instead of "-one" are used.

(2) others: the commonest are:
carbromal   glutethamide   (*Doriden*)
methaqualone (a constituent of *Mandrax*)
nitrazepam (*Mogadon*) methadone

Anaesthetics: After administration of a general anesthetic for minor surgery (that is, where the patient is not confined to bed) traces of it causing some degree of "hangover" may persist in the body for 24 or even (some authorities maintain) 48 hours, during which period it is unwise to drive. It has even been recommended (*Hartmann* p. 121) that after minor local anaesthesia (*e.g.* in dentistry) the patient should not drive for an hour.

Stimulants: Used to overcome fatigue or to counteract the effect of respiratory depressants; amphetamines are very liable to addictive misuse and can produce a devastating reaction on withdrawal.

amphetamine   (*Benzedrine*) dexamphetamine
bemegride   (*Megemide*)

Anti-convulsants: Used in the treatment of epilepsy. Side effects can include gastro-intestinal upset, headache and dizziness, disturbance of speech and vision etc. The best known is *Epanutin*.

Other classes of drugs which could affect driving (*Clarke* 1982) and which might possibly be encountered in this context are:

anorectics (appetite suppressants used for slimming);
anti-hypertensives (for the treatment of high-blood-pressure);
broncho-dilators (for asthma and bronchitis);
drugs for cardiac rhythm control;
drugs dilating the pupils and therefore possibly affecting the
   focusing of the eyes.

Some other terms that may be encountered in this context are:

analeptic: stimulant counteracting the effect of
                           respiratory depressants.
anti-psychotic: a general name for major tranquillisers.
ataractic: more or less synonymous with anti-
                           psychotic.
beta-adrenergic   used in treatment of certain heart
   blocking: conditions.
neuroleptics: tranquillisers and related drugs.
psychotomimetic: hallucinatory drugs such as LSD.
psychotropic: affecting the mind.

Illicit drugs:

Probably, the best known and most widely used of these is Cannabis, which is defined as "the dried flowering or fruiting tops of the plant Cannabis sativa" or the resin extracted from it. It is generally known in North America as marihuana, and has about 250 names in all, including "Indian hemp," "bhang," 'hashish," "pot," "grass" and many others. (*Multilingual List of Narcotic Drugs under International Control*: United Nations 1963). Its active principle is generally accepted as being the compound $\triangle$-9-tetrahydrocannabinol (THC). It has been reported that in 1976 more American high-school pupils smoked Cannabis than drank alcohol. (*Cooper, Schwär and Smith* p. 345).

The use of other illicit drugs such as lysergide (LSD), mescaline, "STP," the active principle of hallucinogenic mushrooms, Morning Glory seeds, "angel dust" and various others, tends to depend on fashion—at any given time certain drugs tend to be "in."

The current menace of "glue-sniffing" should also be mentioned. This utilises the intoxicating effect of the solvent vapour from certain adhesives or (though less commonly) dry-cleaning liquids, hair lacquers, etc., (*Watson* 1978). Rather improbable though it may seem, a man was convicted in December 1981 in Glasgow of driving under the influence of sniffed butane (petrol-lighter fuel), for which he had acquired a taste, having started with petrol (*Guardian*, December 12, 1981).

TESTING AND EFFECTS

As was mentioned earlier in this chapter, it would be a prodigious task to collect for each possibly impairing drug the quantity of information about its effects which we now have for alcohol (Chap. 4). Nevertheless, during the last 10–15 years a considerable body of published work on this subject has accumulated. This has come from many countries; Australia, Finland and the United States have all been particularly active. It would be impossible within the limits of this book to deal in detail with either the various ways in which the tests have been planned or the results obtained. (A representative collection of papers on the subject will be found on pp. 415–468 of *Alcohol, Drugs and Traffic Safety*—the report published in 1975 by the Addiction Research Foundation of Ontario on the conference on the subject held in Toronto in 1974.)

The two most extensively tested drugs have probably been the tranquilliser diazepam (*Valium*) and Cannabis. There has been, which is perhaps unfortunate, no universally agreed experimental design, so that the results are rarely directly comparable. *Betts et al.* (1972) considered that low-speed and vehicle-handling tests afforded the best compromise with practical considerations. In some cases simple tests such as the effect on bodily posture or eye-hand coordination were considered sufficiently diagnostic (*Sep-*

pälä et al. 1976–2; *Linnoila* 1976). The specific effect of dizepam on willingness to take risks was investigated by *Wetherell* (1979); this may be compared with the investigations of the effect of alcohol in this respect (see pp. 55–57). In general, however, the tests were more elaborate and sophisticated than those used in the earlier trials of the effects of alcohol; in particular, researchers have been at pains to discriminate among the various faculties which might be affected—perception, reaction time, judgment, risk-taking, motor performance and others (*cf.* pp. 71–73). To this end more or less elaborate combinations of visual and auditory response meters, tracking simulators and actual driving have been used. A particularly well-designed series of experiments on the combined effect of alcohol and Cannabis on ocular tracking was reported in 1976 by *Flom et al.* Some workers (for example, *Forney* 1973) used a variety of verbal and arithmetical mental tests; that group also in one series of tests maximised the element of motivation by arranging a sports-car "gymkhana" on a disused airfield. A particularly sophisticated test was to examine the effects of a drug, with or without the simultaneous consumption of alcohol, during exposure to delayed auditory feedback of the sound of the subject's own voice, a procedure which induces a stressful state of divided attention. (See, for example, *Forney, loc. cit.*) *Seppälä et al.* (*loc. cit.*) thought that the maximum effect of a drug coincided with its peak concentration in the body; it has however been suggested (see, for example, *Linnoila and Mattila* 1973–3; *Clarke* 1982) that, as with alcohol (*cf.* pp. 48 and 55) the effect is greatest while the concentration is still rising. The reports of the trials have usually compared the dose of drug administered with the normal therapeutic dose and have almost invariably compared, using a placebo in the experimental design, the effects of the drug itself with its interaction, if any, with alcohol.

In some cases only the dose of drug administered is recorded, but in others its subsequent concentration in body fluids has been determined; for this, advantage has been taken of some of the most sensitive modern analytical methods; it has, for example, only quite recently become possible to determine the active constituent(s) of Cannabis in body-fluids. (See, for example, *P. L. Williams et al.* 1978; *Harvey et al.* 1980; *Harvey* 1982.) The choice of fluid depends upon the distribution of drugs in the body, and this is not as straightforward as in the case of alcohol (*Osselton et al.* 1980). Blood, urine or saliva can all be used, but the last two have the advantage over blood that a larger specimen is easily collected, which, in spite of the sensitivity of modern analytical techniques, makes the analyst's task easier. Another difficulty here is however that the drugs encountered most commonly in this context, such as diazepam, are among the most difficult to detect and assay in body fluids, largely because they are rapidly metabolised in the body to other compounds (*Finkle* 1980).

No clear unambiguous picture emerges from the results of all these trials. Some workers found that some tranquillisers and antidepressants could by themselves in sufficient dosage produce some significant impairment, others that they did not, but most agreed that they interacted with, and increased the effects of, alcohol. It is however probably significant that the more recent the research the more clearly does an association of tranquillisers and similar drugs with impairment appear, and that a combination of most of these drugs with alcohol is always dangerous. Different drugs of these general classes did not however always produce similar effects. It seems to have been established that, of the two commonest tranquillisers diazepam (*Valium*) and chlordiazepoxide (*Librium*), the former interacts more dangerously with alcohol than the latter. (*Burford et al.* Toronto 1974, p. 423; *Smiley et al.* Toronto 1974, p. 433; *Moskowitz* Stockholm 1980, p. 881). The similarity of the effects of barbiturates to, and their additive effect on, those of alcohol, which had long been known (see, for example, *Joyce et al.* 1959; *A. I. Miller et al.* 1963), though not necessarily in connection with driving, was re-emphasised. Subjectively, drivers to whom a barbiturate had been given seemed unaware on subsequent testing how much they were affected by the drug; moreover, the effect even if subjectively unperceived could sometimes be objectively demonstrated on the following day. *Legg et al.* (1973) found that the actual effects of tranquillisers and hypnotics depended upon the psychological type of the subject. (*cf.* the effect of alcohol in this respect—pp. 50 and 60). *Hauck and Spann* (1974) considered that stimulants were liable to produce a dangerously false subjective assessment of driving skill.

Probably no reader needs to be reminded that at the present time the use of Cannabis is a most contentious topic. Practically all workers agree that it and similar drugs are apt to produce not only a change of mood but also a distorted perception of time and space. The former can lead to irresponsible behaviour, such as disregarding red lights or weaving about the road just for fun; the latter to wrong estimates of distance and speed as well as increased braking time. It has been stated (*Davis* 1972) that even hallucinatory inversion of the roadway can occur. *Forney* (1973), *Hansteen and Jones* (1976) and *Franks et al.* (Toronto 1974, p. 461) are satisfied that the effects of Cannabis and alcohol are additive. On the other hand, there is a respectable body of opinion that the euphoria which these drugs induce makes the users less inclined to drive at all, and less aggressive when they do. (See, for example, *Moskowitz* 1976.) It has also been found that regular users seem less impaired than occasional. *Linnoila* (1974–1) thought that young drivers and Cannabis were a less dangerous combination than middle-aged ones and alcohol.

As already mentioned (p. 136), it has not very long been possible, thanks to the great sensitivity of modern analytical techniques, to detect the active principle of Cannabis in the body fluids of users of it. One interesting fact which this possibility has elucidated is that, whereas the blood alcohol of the liquor drinker takes probably half-an-hour to three-quarters of an hour to "peak" (*cf.* p. 13), the tetrahydrocannabinol peak of the Cannabis smoker occurs within 5–10 minutes.

Some conclusions have also been recorded about other drugs than the hallucinatory ones. *Kreuzer* (1974) states that a series of probing interviews with young heroin addicts led him to believe that they frequently drove with faculties impaired but undetected by the police. On the other hand, *Gordon* (1976) believed that neither heroin addicts nor methadone users had driving records significantly worse than those of the general population, and *dal Monte et al.* (Stockholm 1980, p. 160) found that in northern Italy the number of accidents in which addicts were involved was lower than statistically predicted.

The following sources were also consulted in the compilation of the preceding paragraphs:
Casswell (Melbourne 1977, p. 238): Cannabis and alcohol in closed-circuit driving. *Clayton et al.* (Melbourne 1977, p. 230): anti-depressants and driving performance. *Crancer et al.* (1969): comparison Cannabis and alcohol in simulated driving. *Deutsche medizinische Wochenschrift* (1971), p. 1027: editorial on drugs and driving.; *Goldman et al.* (1969): beta-adrenergic blocking agents in simulated driving. *Hansteen and Jones* (1976): effects Cannabis and alcohol. *Hauck and Spann* (1974): effects of various drugs. *Helmer et al.* (1972): interaction alcohol and carbromal. *Huffmann et al.* (1963): tranquillisers and driving. *Kielholz et al.* (1973): Cannabis and driving. *Kolenda* (1975): interaction alcohol and drugs. *Landauer and Milner* (1971): tranquillisers, anti-histamines, etc.,

and their interaction with alcohol. *Legg et al.* (1973): effect of psychological type of driver. *Linnoila et al.* (1973–1, 1973–2, 1973–4, 1974–2, 1974–3): effects of various drugs, chiefly tranquillisers and related compounds. *Malpas* (1970): slow elimination of barbiturates and other sedatives. *Manno et al.* (1971): effects of Cannabis. *Manton* (Melbourne 1977, p. 247): effects of sedatives on human performance. *J. G. Miller* (1962): effects tranquillisers, anti-depressants, amphetamine on simulated driving. *Milner and Landauer* (1971, 1973): effects of tranquillisers and anti-depressants. *Missen et al* (1982): drugs and driving in New Zealand. *Moskowitz et al.* (Melbourne 1977, p. 184): the Mellanby effect. *Nouvelle presse medicale* (editorial 1972): effects of prescribed drugs. *im Obersteg and Bäumler* (1967): early experiments on interaction alcohol and tranquillisers. *Patman et al.* (1969): alcohol and amitriptyline. *Rafaelson et al.* (1973–2): effect Cannabis plus alcohol on simulated driving. *Saario and Linnoila* (1975, 1976): effect alcohol, drugs and sleep deprivation. *Seppälä et al.* (1975, 1976–1, 1976–2): effects of hangover and various drugs. *Sharma* (1976): correlation drug intake and accident rate. *Staak et al.* (1976): effect diazepam plus alcohol on traffic behaviour.

Miscellaneous

There are a few other points which should be mentioned before we leave the subject of drugs:

(1) The circumstances in which a laboratory analysis of a body-fluid specimen for drugs may be requested have already been mentioned (p. 131). If a significant level of any possibly impairing drug was detected, and no alcohol was present, then a medical witness might well be asked whether he thought the impaired driving could be due to the effects of the drug. On the other hand, it is probably safe to say that, if any alcohol was present along with the drug, no doctor would be prepared to offer an opinion as to how far the observed effects were due to the alcohol and how far to the drug.

(2) The withdrawal of a drug on which a degree of dependence has been acquired (*e.g.* a barbiturate) may produce marked and unpleasant effects which would be incompatible with safe driving, yet any impairment of driving so produced could not lead to a charge of driving whilst under the influence of drugs, since there might be no trace of the withdrawn drug in the driver's body.

(3) It was pointed out on p. 127 that the full implementation of

the Transport Act 1981 may result in a greatly increased laboratory work-load of drug analyses. This will require totally different
analytical techniques from those used for alcohol: the analysis of
body-fluid specimens for drugs forms part of the methodology of
toxicological analysis, and is too large and complex a subject to be
dealt with here. In general, the analysis may require preliminary
screening tests for the presence of drugs and provisional clues as to
their identity, followed by confirmatory identification and
determination using all the available modern analytical techniques. Several procedures for routine testing have recently been
published (for example, *Smith* Stockholm 1980 p. 469; *Taylor*
Stockholm 1980, p. 478), and several writers (*e.g. Smith loc. cit.*;
Arnold and Brinkman Stockholm 1980, p. 506) also describe the
use in this context of one of the most sophisticated and ultra-
sensitive modern methods of analysis—namely radio-immuno
assay. The detection of volatile compounds in blood specimens,
necessary when dealing with "glue-sniffers" (see p. 135), can be
accomplished with the aid of the extreme sensitivity possible with
gas chromatography.

Carbon monoxide

This notoriously poisonous gas is not of course a drug, but it is
convenient to mention it here. It may form up to 5–10 per cent. of
car exhaust gases; it may therefore constitute a hazard in a closed
car, coming either from a leaky exhaust system of the car itself, or
(more probably) by being sucked in by a heater fan from the
exhaust of the car in front in a stationary line of traffic, and this
reason is sometimes advanced as a cause of apparent intoxication
in a driver. This danger is naturally greater in winter, when windows will be tightly closed and the engine is kept running for
warmth even when the car is stationary. Experiments by *Naess-
Schmidt* (1971) and by *Russell et al.* (1973) suggest that smoking in
a confined space (such as a closed car) could produce saturations
of as much as 5–15 per cent. in the smokers and of perhaps around
2 per cent. in non-smokers confined with them.

A healthy person can stand 5–10 per cent. saturation of his
blood with carbon monoxide without noticeable effects, whilst the
fatal dose varies from about 30 per cent. saturation for the aged
and sufferers from heart disease to about 75 per cent. for a healthy
young adult. One may therefore perhaps guess (no figures are
available) that the saturation level in an otherwise healthy person

whose driving is impaired for this reason might be of the order of 20 per cent. Some rather tenuous support for this estimate is given by figures for American accident victims published by *Sunshine et al.* in 1968, and for 577 Puerto Rican victims by *Kaye* (Toronto 1974, p. 85).

Clinically, carbon monoxide poisoning can closely resemble alcoholic intoxication, except that it does not produce nystagmus. Nothing is known of the combined effect of carbon monoxide and alcohol, but *Sunshine et al.* suggest that an additive effect may usually be presumed. This conclusion is tentatively supported by *Fazekas and Rengei* (1969) from their investigation of human fatal cases and from their animal experiments. The results of investigations into the effects of carbon monoxide poisoning on the course of the blood-alcohol curve are inconclusive, but the most trustworthy seem to show that there is no effect (*Elber and Schleyer* p. 103).

Carbon monoxide can easily be determined in quite small blood specimens provided that they are taken within a fairly short time of the exposure to the gas and that they are tightly sealed. However, no laboratory would make this examination unless specifically requested, as the method of analysis is totally different from those used for alcohol or drugs.

The preceding discussion is in fact somewhat academic, chiefly because carbon monoxide disappears fairly rapidly from the blood when exposure to it has ended and pure air is being breathed; recovery therefore is rapid and a blood sample unless taken within an hour or two would not show its presence in significant amount. Even if we assume therefore that carbon monoxide poisoning may be retrospectively suspected if

(1) the breath test for alcohol is negative, *and*

(2a) the driver claims that he was affected by exhaust fumes, *or*

(2b) the medical examination suggests this possibility, alcohol being absent and the driver showing a rapid recovery
it is unlikely that this suspicion would have become firm enough in time for the taking of an adequate blood specimen to be useful.

If, however, in these circumstances the driving was sufficiently impaired for the police to consider charging the driver with some traffic offence not concerned with drink or drugs, and if he alleged that a faulty exhaust in his own car was responsible for his impairment, then the air inside the car should be tested for carbon monoxide with the engine running and the windows shut. Any forensic science laboratory would probably be willing to do this, but it would of course mean depriving the driver of his car for at least a day.

FURTHER READING

As is mentioned on p. 126, and as will be obvious from the number of references mentioned in the text, much has been published in recent years on the topic of this chapter. Although making any selection can be invidious, it is probably safe to recommend the following. When only a name, title and date are given, the full reference to the source will be found in the list of scientific references beginning on p. 253.

Drugs in General:

The Drugs Handbook, Paul Turner and Glyn Volans (Macmillan Reference Books, 2nd revised ed. 1980). Lists, with their properties, most of the drugs commonly prescribed and used in the U.K.

Martindale's Extra Pharmacopoeia (Pub. The Pharmaceutical Society; frequent new and updated editions). *The* complete and authoritative list of drugs and their uses and properties. Should be found in any good reference library.

Harvey, D.H. (1982): *Report to the Advisory Council on the Misuse of Drugs* (H.M.S.O. 1982).

Drugs and Driving:

Kibrick, E. and Smart, R.G., *Psychotropic Drug Use and Driving Risk*: *A Review and Analysis* (1970).

Conference on Drugs and Driving, Basel (1972): Reported in *Pharmakopsychiatrie/Neuro-Psychopharmakologie*, (1973), Vol. **6**, part 2.

Milner, Gerald, *Drugs and Driving* (1972), (Pub. S. Karger, Basel).

Silverstone, J.T., *Drugs and Driving* (1974), (Editorial article with bibliography).

Accident Analysis and Prevention (1976): Vol. **8**, part 1. Issue of this journal devoted to drugs and driving.

Cooper, W.E., Schwär, T.G. and Smith, L.S. *Drugs and Driving* (1979) (Chap. 28, p. 340).

Lundberg, G.D., White, J.M. and Hoffmann, K.I., *Drugs* (other than or in addition to Ethyl Alcohol) *and Driving Behaviour* (1979).

Manton, J.C., *The Effect of Sedative Drugs upon Human Performance* (1979).

Seppälä, T., Linnoila, M. and Mattila, M.T., *Drugs and Driving* (1979) A review of over 150 papers and articles on the subject published in 1969–78.

Moskowitz, H., *Alcohol and Drug Interactions* (1980).

Terhune, K.W. and Fell, J.C., *The Role of Alcohol, Marihuana and other Drugs in the Accidents of Injured Drivers* (1981).

Cannabis:

Encyclopaedia Britannica (15th ed.) Article "Cannabis."

Klein, A.W., Davis, J.H. and Blackbourne, B.D. *Journal of Drug Issues* (1971) vol. 1, p. 18. Marihuana and automobile crashes.

Canadian Medical Association Journal (1972): Vol. 107, p. 269—editorial on "Cannabis and Driving Skills."

Kielholz, P. *et al. An Experimental Investigation about the Effect of Cannabis on Car Driving Behaviour* (1973) A thorough and detailed investigation of the subject.

Klonoff, H., *Marihuana and Driving in Real-Life Situations* (1974).

Casswell, Sally *Cannabis and Alcohol: Effects on Closed-Course Driving Behaviour* (1977).

Testing and Analysis:

Alcohol, Drugs and Traffic Safety: Proceedings of the 6th Annual Conference, **Toronto**, 1974; Analytical Section, pp. 469–636.

Osselton, M.D., Hammond, M.D. and Moffat, A.C., *Distribution of Drugs and Toxic Chemicals in Blood* (1980).

CHAPTER 9

EFFECTS OF ALCOHOL ON THE DRIVER: ATTEMPTS AT STATUTORY DEFINITION

"DRUNK IN CHARGE"

The law has long taken cognisance of excessive drinking. The offence of being "drunk and incapable" was recognised in statute law and in many local private Acts in the eighteenth and nineteenth centuries. Though drunkenness itself was not directly penalised, the anti-social results of persistent and public drunkenness and of drunkenness of those in charge of dangerous machinery, animals and the like were proscribed. The Locomotives Act 1865 limited road speed to four miles per hour in the country and two miles per hour in town and required a flagman to precede the vehicle. Statutory recognition was given by section 12 of the Licensing Act 1872[1] to the offence of being drunk in charge of any carriage, horse, cattle or steam engine. The 1872 Act provision as to drunk and disorderly behaviour was replaced in England by section 91 of the Criminal Justice Act 1967 which gave power to arrest without warrant. Legislation subsequent to 1872 imposed penalties for drunkenness in those having positions of special responsibility such as engine drivers, ships' masters, pilots, taxi-drivers and service personnel. Following the Motor Car Act of 1903 and the Royal Commission on the Motor Car of 1906 the age of the motor car could be said to have begun.

The Criminal Justice Act 1925, by section 40, penalised a person drunk while in charge on any highway or other public place of any mechanically propelled vehicle, and this enactment may be regarded as the foundation of the modern attempts in Britain to control the drinking driver. Because of the terms used it is likely that only a fairly gross degree of drinking could be brought within the scope of the offence, and when in *R.* v. *Presdee*[2] it was confirmed that "drunk" in the 1925 Act meant drunk as it is com-

[1] And the Licensing (Scotland) Act 1903, s.70.
[2] (1927) 20 Cr.App.R. 95.

144

monly understood[3] it became clear that the time was ripe for a more precise definition of the driving offence. For similar reasons it is clear that the expression "drunk" ought no longer to be used in describing the modern offence: *R.* v. *Carr.*[4] The opportunity for re-definition might, following Continental law, have led to an emphasis on the element of public danger resulting in injury or death, but instead the wider concept of impairment of general driving control was chosen: (Lasok).

"UNDER THE INFLUENCE OF DRINK OR DRUGS"

In the event, the increasing flow of motor traffic following the First World War and the urgent need for closer control produced the Road Traffic Act 1930 which, recognising that it was not necessary to be drunk to be a danger to road-users, re-defined the offence in the following terms in section 15(1):

"Any person who, when driving or attempting to drive or when in charge of a motor vehicle on a road or other public place is under the influence of drink or a drug to such an extent as to be incapable of having proper control of the vehicle . . . [shall be guilty of an offence]."

This statute thus established a single offence applicable throughout Scotland, England and Wales, triable both summarily and on indictment. (For the law affecting Northern Ireland see *Hagan* and *Osborough*). In such circumstances the desirability of uniform construction of the law is obvious: *cf. Cording* v. *Halse.*[5] Despite this the differences in legal systems north and south of the Border produced practical results which brought about a more critical situation in England and Wales than that which obtained in Scotland. According to English practice, since the maximum possible sentence exceeded three months' imprisonment the accused over 14 years of age if proceeded against summarily could claim trial by jury,[6] an option which was sometimes exercised despite the possibility of heavier sentence on conviction. The reason seemed to be that juries, mainly composed of motorists, tended to sympathise with the driver and, as events proved, were rather unwilling to convict even in serious cases. Moreover the use of the word

---

[3] See also *R.* v. *Burdon* (1927) 20 Cr.App.R. 80.
[4] (1934) 24 Cr.App.R. 199.
[5] [1955] 1 Q.B. 63.
[6] But the Magistrates' Courts Act 1952, s.25 was repealed by s.15 of the Criminal Law Act 1977.

"incapable" provided an unfortunate reminder of the old offence of "drunk and incapable" and some juries looked for a standard of gross drunkenness which the law certainly did not intend. The proportion of convictions by judges turned out to be significantly higher than that of juries in similar cases. In Scotland where cases of driving under the influence of drink or drugs were brought almost exclusively in the summary courts there was no option for jury trial and convictions were more readily obtained.[7] There was moreover growing concern throughout the country that the figures returned by the police for accidents caused by the effects of drink did not reflect the true proportions of the problem, partly because of the diffidence of English juries, and partly because the police could attribute to drink only those cases where there was conclusive evidence of drink and nothing else. In 1951, for example, the figure for accidents caused through drink was a mere 1,300. Figures of this kind seriously understated the problem and ceased to be relied upon.[8]

The definition of the offence of driving, attempting to drive or being in charge while under the influence of drink or drugs nevertheless served for over 25 years. In time, however, the enormously increased number of vehicles using the congested roads of these islands, together with the difficulties of proving by observer evidence and clinical examination that a particular driver was "under the influence," combined to lead the British Medical Association (B.M.A.) in 1951 to revive an earlier Committee for the purpose of reviewing the tests for drunkenness, and the relation of alcohol to road accidents.

In 1954 this Committee produced a report "The Recognition of Intoxication" in which they recorded their belief that many accidents were caused by persons whose degree of intoxication was insufficient to attract the attention of the police, and yet whose skills were sufficiently impaired to constitute a danger on the road. The report also included a model outline clinical examination, the main purpose of which, was to exclude any possibility of the accused's condition being due to illness. The clinical examination included tests for lack of co-ordination and alertness as well as for the more obvious manifestations of excessive drinking. The 1954 report went on to consider the better techniques then becoming available for analysis of the alcohol concentration of body fluids,

---

[7] See "Chemical Tests, etc." (Murphy, 1964).
[8] Cf. p. 61.

and the experience of this work gained in particular by the Scandinavians. Conversion tables were provided which were thought to enable some estimate to be made of the minimum intake of alcohol required to yield particular urine or blood-alcohol figures.

In 1956 the Road Traffic Act of that year separated, by section 9, the offence of driving while under the influence of drink or drugs from that of being in charge of (but not driving) a vehicle while under the influence. It gave the expression "unfit to drive" as meaning "under the influence of drink or a drug to such an extent as to be incapable of having proper control of a motor vehicle" and brought pedal cyclists not under the new law but under the offence as it had been defined in the 1930 Act.[9] A revised edition of the B.M.A. report on "Recognition of Intoxication" issued in 1958 repeated its suggested scheme of medical examination, emphasising that it offered no more than a guide to clinical examination, and devoted some attention to the re-defined offence of driving "under the influence."

In 1960 the B.M.A. Committee produced a further report "Relation of Alcohol to Road Accidents" in which the accumulating evidence as to the effect of small quantities of alcohol on driving performance and related skills and also the statistical evidence linking accidents to alcohol intake[10] were examined, see page 60. This report contained an interesting table giving in brief the situation in other countries and showing that Finland, West Germany, Iceland, Norway, Sweden, Switzerland and some states of the United States of America had adopted mandatory blood testing to provide evidence of impairment based upon blood-alcohol concentration. Of these countries some prescribed no limit while others adopted fixed levels beyond which driving impairment was presumed. The report advocated reform of the United Kingdom law: by fixing an arbitrary level above which an offence would be committed.

In recommending a prescribed alcohol level offence the Committee were endeavouring to reach out towards an objective standard which had previously been lacking in the law, for as well as being tautologous and confusing in its use of the expression "drink or a drug," as though alcohol were not a drug, the 1930 definition, even when amended in 1956, still associated in the lay mind the idea of being under the influence with the idea of gross drunken-

---

[9] Later the Road Traffic Act 1960, s.11.
[10] *Cf.* pp. 60–71. For foreign limits see Chap. 16.

ness which the law had used in its first attempt to designate the offence.

Unfit Through Drink or Drugs

There followed a further amendment whereby the offences were by section 6 of the Road Traffic Act 1960, re-stated (with a statutory defence to the "in-charge" offence) as follows:

(1) A person who when driving or attempting to drive a motor vehicle on a road or other public place, is unfit to drive through drink or drugs shall be liable . . . [to certain penalties].

(2) A person who when in charge of a motor vehicle which is on a road or other public place (but not driving the vehicle) is unfit to drive through drink or drugs shall be liable . . . [to certain penalties].

A person shall be deemed for the purposes of this sub-section not to have been in charge of a motor vehicle if he proves—

(i) that at the material time the circumstances were such that there was no likelihood of his driving the vehicle so long as he remained unfit to drive through drink or drugs; and

(ii) that between his becoming unfit to drive as aforesaid and the material time he had not driven the vehicle on a road or other public place.

Impairment

A further amendment of the offence of unfitness which had been established by section 6 of the 1960 Act was effected by section 1 of the Road Traffic Act 1962 whose most important provision in this connection stated:

"For the purposes of section 6 of the principal Act (which imposes penalties for driving, attempting to drive, or being in charge of a motor vehicle while unfit through drink or drugs) a person shall be taken to be unfit to drive if his ability to drive properly is for the time being impaired."

Attention was thus switched from unfitness to drive the vehicle to impairment of driving ability, and the offence apparently penalised any diminution whatever in proper driving ability. Together with the provisions of section 2 of the Road Traffic Act 1962, which required the court to have regard to the proportion of alcohol or drug in a driver's body as evidenced by blood and urine tests, and permitted refusal of such tests to be treated as supporting the prosecution case, those amendments brought the offence into its modern and still subsisting form. No guidance whatever was given as to the degree of impairment to be imputed to different alcohol levels and it is possible to criticise the chemical testing law as leaving too many variables to the individual expert (Murphy). At all events this left only the B.M.A.'s recommendation for fixed-level legislation to set up an offence which could be easily and undeniably proved still to receive attention.

THE PRESCRIBED LEVEL

Despite its introduction of powers to require courts to have regard to analytical evidence of blood and urine-alcohol levels, the 1962 Act failed to bring about widespread reliance upon these methods of proof, and observation of the driver's conduct coupled with clinical examination remained the standard method of proving the offence of unfitness and impairment of ability to drive. Analytical evidence was restricted mainly to urine specimens, and where blood was used the specimens had to be large enough to permit macro-analysis. The fact that courts were inexperienced in interpreting (and indeed without expert guidance could not interpret) evidence that blood alcohol had reached a particular figure and the difficulties of translating urine-alcohol to blood-alcohol concentrations combined to restrict the use made of scientific evidence. Efforts were made in some cases to calculate back from the levels demonstrated to show that a given quantity of alcohol had been taken, but the tables which had been supplied since 1954 in the B.M.A. reports gave, particularly in conditions of social drinking, a most unrealistic picture.[11] Accordingly the giving in evidence of quantities of liquor so calculated came to be recognised as misleading and unreliable.[12]

An answer to these difficulties was eventually provided on the lines recommended by the B.M.A. by the introduction of a fixed-level offence. The White Paper on Road Safety Legislation 1965–66 clearly set out the Government's intentions, and after a false start when the first Road Safety Bill of January 1966 lapsed on the dissolution of the Government, a second Bill was introduced later in the year and passed into law with only a modification of the original random testing proposed by the White Paper.

[11] B.M.A. Report: The Drinking Driver, 1965.
[12] But see Chap. 7.

The newly defined offence was one of driving or attempting to drive a motor vehicle on a road or other public place, alcohol having been consumed in such a quantity that the proportion thereof in the blood as ascertained from a laboratory test exceeds the prescribed limit at the time of sampling, which was set at 80mg of alcohol per 100ml of blood.[13] This offence did not supersede the offence of driving with ability impaired through drink or drugs but was supplementary to it. There was no provision to prevent conviction of both offences and both are sometimes charged, particularly where post-driving drinking is likely to be alleged: *R*. v. *Stanley Richards*.[14] Conviction of both offences must however be extremely rare. In a Canadian case an accused pleaded guilty to the prescribed-level offence and was sentenced and two months later was charged and convicted of the impairment offence in relation to the same incident.[15] It was held on appeal that this was multiple conviction for the same offence and his conviction was quashed.

The law accordingly seems to distinguish the two offences. In 1972, as part of a consolidation of road traffic law, the prescribed-level offence provisions of the Road Safety Act were re-enacted in the Road Traffic Act and a very considerable body of case law had accumulated on all aspects of the drink driving offences. The Blennerhassett Committee set up in 1974 to examine the operation of the law of drinking and driving and to make recommendations recognised that the initial impact of the prescribed level offence (reckoned in its first year to have saved over 1,000 lives) had worn off and that proof of the offence (which had been defined in a complicated way) had become inextricably bound up with proof that the procedures had been rigidly followed, while loopholes and limitations in the law had been discovered and exploited. The Transport Act 1981 made various changes. It re-defined the prescribed-level offence[16] radically amended the definition of the impairment offence, and introduced in Schedule 8 a new code of drink-driving law. This code now forms the re-enacted sections 6 to 12 of the Road Traffic Act 1972 which describe amongst other things the offence of driving or being in charge of a vehicle with

---

[13] Road Safety Act 1967, s.7 re-enacted in the Road Traffic Act 1972, s.6.
[14] [1974] R.T.R. 520.
[15] *R*. v. *Lachance* [1974] R.h. 125 (Que.).
[16] The change became operative from May 1983.

alcohol concentration above the prescribed limit, measured in the ordinary case by instrumental analysis of breath alcohol. A further amendment in section 59 of the Transport Act 1982 completed the code. These newly defined offences will be discussed in the next chapter.

CHAPTER 10

THE APPROACH TO THE PRESENT OFFENCES

ESSENTIAL ELEMENTS

Motor vehicle

The Road Traffic Acts and the related legislation deal with driving or being in charge of motor vehicles upon the roads or other public places, and some account must be given of how these terms have come to be defined.

The offences of driving a motor vehicle while unfit through drink or drugs on a road or other public place[1] and driving a motor vehicle on a road or other public place after consuming so much alcohol that the proportion of it in the driver's breath, blood or urine exceeds the prescribed limit[2] imply certain essential elements. The most important of these are the terms "motor vehicle," "driving" and "road or other public place."

In the ordinary way the least uncertainty is likely to apply to the term "motor vehicle" defined by section 190(1) of the Road Traffic Act 1972 as "a mechanically propelled vehicle intended or adapted for use on roads." The vast majority of drink and driving offences involve either private cars or commercial vehicles. It should be noted however that mechanical dumpers have been held excluded from the definition since they are not generally adapted for use on the public roads: cf. *MacDonald* v. *Carmichael*[3]; *Daley* v. *Hargreaves*[4]; *MacLean* v. *McCabe*,[5] as have Go-Karts: *Burns* v. *Currell*[6]; *Chalgray Ltd. & Anor.* v. *Aspley*[7] and a mini car rebuilt for Autocross racing: *Nichol* v. *Leach*.[8] However, where these unsuitable contraptions do venture on the highway, especially in

[1] Road Traffic Act 1972, s.5(1), (the impairment offence).
[2] *Ibid.* s.6(1), (the prescribed level offence).
[3] 1941 J.C. 27.
[4] [1961] 1 All E.R. 552.
[5] 1964 S.L.T. (Sh. Ct.) 39.
[6] [1963] 2 Q.B. 422.
[7] [1965] Crim. L.R. 440.
[8] [1972] R.T.R. 476.

unsteady hands, they are probably a greater danger than regular vehicles. But an earth scraper seems to fall within the definition of a motor vehicle: *Childs* v. *Coghlan*[9] as does a road roller: *Waters* v. *Eddison Steam Rolling Co.*[10] One is tempted to wonder why case law throws no light on the powered lawn mower until one realises that this is specifically excluded from the definition by section 193 of the Road Traffic Act 1972. A defective vehicle may be repaired so that it remains a "motor vehicle": *Elliott* v. *Grey*,[11] even when the engine is removed: *Newberry* v. *Simmonds*,[12] but a stage may be reached at which a cannibalised hulk is no longer repairable and ceases to fall within the definition: *Smart* v. *Allan*[13]; *MacLean* v. *Hall.*[14] An auto cycle from which the cylinder and piston had been removed was held to be a pedal cycle rather than a motor vehicle: *Lawrence* v. *Howlett.*[15] Whatever the driver may think, a car with a flat battery remains a motor vehicle: *R.* v. *Paul.*[16]

Driving

"Driving" implies having some control either of steering or of propulsion: *R.* v. *Roberts (No. 2)*[17]; *Burgoyne* v. *Phillips.*[18] Sitting astride a motor cycle with a blood alcohol concentration of 141mg/100ml is not driving: *Trevor Pearson.*[19] Where these acts are shared as in driving instruction each participant is regarded as a driver[20]: *Langman* v. *Valentine*[21]; *R.* v. *Wilkins*[22]; *Evans* v. *Walkden*[23] or as aiding and abetting the driver: *Carter* v. *Richardson*[24]; *Valentine* v. *Mackie.*[25] But a supervisor may be able to satisfy the Court that there was no likelihood of his driving: *Sheldon* v. *Jones.*[26] A person who released the handbrake of a lorry and

[9] (1968) 112 S.J. 175.
[10] [1914] 3 K.B. 818.
[11] [1960] 1 Q.B. 367.
[12] [1961] 2 Q.B. 345.
[13] [1963] 1 Q.B. 291.
[14] 1962 S.L.T. (Sh. Ct.) 30.
[15] [1952] 2 All E.R. 74.
[16] [1952] N.I. 61.
[17] [1965] 1 Q.B. 85.
[18] [1983] R.T.R. 49.
[19] Bodmin Crown Court: *Sunday Express* May 21, 1978.
[20] *Cf.* 1960 Road Traffic Act, s.257.
[21] [1952] 2 All E.R. 803.
[22] (1951) 115 J.P. 443.
[23] [1956] 3 All E.R. 64.
[24] [1974] R.T.R. 314.
[25] 1980 S.L.T. (Sh. Ct.) 122.
[26] [1970] R.T.R. 38.

coasted it down a hill was driving: *Saycell* v. *Bool*,[27] and even a
passenger who set a vehicle in motion by switching on the ignition
and starting the engine while the gears were engaged: *R.* v.
Levy.[28] In general the person who steers a towed vehicle is driving
if they have some measure of control, *McQuaid* v. *Anderton*[29];
Carse v. *Wright*[30] and a front seat passenger leaning across and
steering a car (the "driver" operating only the foot pedals) was
held in *Tyler* v. *Whatmore*[31] to be driving. But a passenger who
momentarily seized the wheel and put the car into a field, was
unaccountably held not to be driving in *Jones* v. *Pratt*.[32] Where a
vehicle pushed from behind was steered conflicting decisions have
been rendered as to whether the steersman was driving: *R.* v. *Spin-
dley*[33]; *R.* v. *Arnold*.[34] In *Ames* v. *MacLeod*[35] the person pushing
and steering a vehicle through the open window backwards down a
slope was held to be driving but not so in the rather similar case of
R. v. *MacDonagh*.[36] The act of driving requires volition. Accidental contact with the controls is not enough: *Blayney* v. *Knight*.[37]
The English courts have had to consider whether the onset of disease might produce a state of automatism, proof of which by the
party alleging it would relieve of criminal liability: *Hill* v. *Baxter*[38]
and in that case the judges figured such a situation as where the
hapless driver was attacked by a swarm of bees. It would seem that
such a state could hardly be sustained over any substantial distance
without amounting to driving: *Watmore* v. *Jenkins*[39]; *Moses* v.
Winder[40] cf. the case of hysterical fugue *R.* v. *Isitt*.[41] Self-induced
incapacity will not avail: *R.* v. *Quick*.[42] The Scottish courts have
been at pains to make clear that nothing short of insanity is likely
to negative the responsibility of the driver *H.M. Advocate* v. *Cunn-
ingham*[43] although in practice this decision may be applied in its
full rigour only in the more serious cases cf. *Stirling* v. *Annan*.[44] In
Farrell v. *Stirling*,[45] a case of alleged hypoglycaemia, the test was
said to be whether his driving at the material time depended on a
conscious effort of will and whether his movements were volun-

---

[27] [1948] 2 All E.R. 83. But cf. R. v. Roberts [1965] 1 Q.B. 85.
[28] [1956] Crim. L.R. 340.
[29] [1980] R.T.R. 371.
[30] [1981] R.T.R. 49.
[31] [1976] R.T.R. 83.
[32] [1983] R.T.R. 54.
[33] [1961] Crim. L.R. 486.
[34] [1964] Crim. L.R. 664.
[35] 1969 J.C. 1.
[36] [1974] R.T.R. 372.

[37] [1975] R.T.R. 279.
[38] [1958] 1 Q.B. 277.
[39] [1962] 2 Q.B. 572.
[40] [1981] R.T.R. 37.
[41] [1978] R.T.R. 211.
[42] [1973] 1 Q.B. 910.
[43] 1963 S.L.T. 345.
[44] 1983 S.C.C.R. 396.
[45] 1975 S.L.T. (Notes) 71.

tary. The case of the driver suffering a slight stroke at the wheel would probably depend upon whether the driver had any degree of control: see the civil action *Roberts* v. *Ramsbottom*[46] and see Glanville Williams. In *R.* v. *Kitson*[47] however the accused who awoke from a drunken sleep in the passenger seat of a moving vehicle and resourcefully guided it by steering erratically into the verge was held to have driven the vehicle. A passenger who momentarily grabs the steering wheel is probably not to be regarded as driving: *Jones* v. *Pratt*.[48]

The expression "driving" and "a person driving or attempting to drive" have attracted more judicial attention than any other expressions in the Road Safety Act and its successors. The context makes it clear that a more extended interpretation than a purely literal one must have been intended if the Act were not to call for dangerous, not to say acrobatic, feats by the police administering breath tests. A series of cases culminating in *Pinner* v. *Everett*[49] and *Sakhuja* v. *Allen*[50] gave the House of Lords the opportunity to consider the expressions. Although the speeches are not entirely consistent it can be said that "driving" extends beyond the actual control of a vehicle whilst in motion. For the purposes of the Acts a driver is still to be regarded as driving although the vehicle may be at rest and although the driver may have left the vehicle, provided his purpose is still connected with driving. A motorist filling his tank at a self-service garage, or visiting a roadside toilet, or buying a road map, is thus likely to be considered to be still driving, and a person only ceases to drive when he has severed his connection with the vehicle in a way which shows he had ended his journey, or if he interrupts his journey to do something unconnected with driving. Getting out of the car to discuss with a constable whether an offence has been committed may still be driving: *R.* v. *Reid*[51] and stopping at a police check for stolen sheep: *R.* v. *Herd*.[52] But in *R.* v. *Rees*[53] a driver who stopped, removed his ignition keys, parked the car and set off to look for a fish-and-chip shop was no longer driving. Nor was a driver followed by the police because he had taken a roundabout rather fast who drove

[46] [1980] 1 All E.R. 7.
[47] (1955) 39 Cr. App. R. 66 (C.C.A.).
[48] [1983] R.T.R. 54.
[49] [1969] 3 All E.R. 257.
[50] [1972] R.T.R. 315.
[51] [1973] R.T.R. 536.
[52] [1973] R.T.R. 165.
[53] [1977] R.T.R. 181.

home, left and locked his car and was walking towards his house smelling of drink when the police intercepted him. He had been unaware of their presence and had voluntarily concluded his journey: *Sanaghan* v. *Galt*.[54] A driver who surrendered his ignition keys, albeit not to the police, could no longer be regarded as a person driving: *Harman* v. *Wardrop*.[55] But the circumstances in which the keys are handed over have to be taken into consideration: *R.* v. *Cooper*.[56] Where the police stopped the driver, suspected alcohol, reached into the car and took the ignition keys from the dashboard before requiring a breath test, the accused was still to be regarded as "a person driving": *R.* v. *Maidment*.[57] In a Scottish case[58] a driver who pulled off the road to spend 20 minutes kissing his girl friend was held no longer to be a person driving. See also *R.* v. *Price*[59] and *Campbell* v. *Tormey*.[60] In an impairment case the driver who crashed his car into a tree and minutes later was arrested by a pursuing policeman was held to be committing the offence and so driving: *R.* v. *Roff*.[61] In *Brooks* v. *Ellis*[62] a motorist who was chased by the police and finally came to rest in his own private driveway was held to be still driving as was the driver seen to be driving without lights called back as he was entering his hotel: *McNaughton* v. *Deenan*.[63] These matters were reviewed in *Edkins* v. *Knowles*.[64] A person who is prevented or persuaded from driving can no longer be considered to be driving. In *Purvis* v. *Hogg*[65] a person found slumped over the wheel by police after a period of 20 minutes was held to be driving; but in *Ritchie* v. *Pirie*[66] a driver with mechanical trouble who stopped for about half an hour to attempt repairs and who bumped his head on the bonnet so that he had to be taken to hospital was not still driving. It is thought that similar principles will be applied to the expressions as they are now to be found in the amended Road Traffic Act 1972. In *R.* v. *Farrance*[67] a driver sitting at the wheel trying to engage gear and revving the engine was attempting to drive even though the clutch was burnt out so that the vehicle would not move. In addition to the foregoing cases there are numerous cases in which the Court has had to decide whether a motorist is a driver

[54] 1981 S.L.T. 9.
[55] [1971] R.T.R. 127.
[56] [1974] R.T.R. 489.
[57] [1976] R.T.R. 294.
[58] *Nield* v. *Douglas:* Justiciary Appeal Court January 22, 1980.
[59] [1968] 3 All E.R. 814.
[60] [1969] 1 All E.R. 961.
[61] [1976] R.T.R. 7.
[62] [1972] R.T.R. 361.
[63] 1981 S.L.T. (Notes) 105.
[64] [1973] R.T.R. 257.
[65] [1969] Crim. L.R. 378.
[66] 1972 J.C. 7.
[67] [1978] R.T.R. 225.

from whom it is proper to require a breath test[68] and when a driver having reached a destination must no longer be regarded as driving.[69] Detailed and dovetailing circumstantial evidence will usually be sufficient: *Topping* v. *Scott*.[70]

It also has to be kept in mind that section 168 of the Road Traffic Act 1972 requires the keeper of a vehicle to give information in certain circumstances as to the identity of the driver. In *Macnaughtan* v. *Buchan*[71] it was held justifiable by this means to elicit that the owner has been driving and because his breath suggested drink to charge him with the prescribed level offence.

Road

It was clearly established in the case of *Harrison* v. *Hill*[72] that the definition of "road" adopted by the Road Traffic Act 1930 and which is repeated in the later Acts included a place to which the public had access by permission or tolerance but not a place where they had to trespass to gain entry: *cf. R.* v. *Waters*.[73] The addition of the words "or other public place" connotes a significant extension and the question is, first: is it a road, and second, is it a place to which there is public access? *Oxford* v. *Austin*.[74] A car park may not be a road as understood by the Acts[75] (where there was a free public car park to which the public had access) but may yet be a "public place" in which it is an offence to drive while proper driving ability is impaired through drink or drugs or while the blood-alcohol concentration exceeds the permitted level. A forecourt serving for goods delivery though not for through passage is not a road: *Henderson* v. *Bernard*[76]; *cf. Thomas* v. *Dando*[77]; *MacNeill* v. *Dunbar*[78]; *Purves* v. *Muir*[79]; *Baxter* v. *M.C.C.*[80] A titled English landowner who drove while in such a state on the estate policies over which the public had access to view his stately home would almost certainly be committing an offence, as would even a recluse Scotsman driving up his private avenue: *Davidson* v. *Adair*[81] whether or not the public were admitted: but see *Hogg* v. *Nicholson*.[82] The latter factor is vital in England. So a field used

[68] See p. 155.
[69] See p. 156.
[70] 1979 S.L.T. (Notes) 21.
[71] 1980 S.L.T. (Notes) 100.
[72] 1932 J.C. 13.
[73] (1963) 107 S.J. 275.
[74] [1981] R.T.R. 416.
[75] *Cf. Griffin* v. *Squires* [1958] 3 All E.R. 468.

[76] 1955 S.L.T. (Sh. Ct.) 27.
[77] [1951] 2 K.B. 620.
[78] 1965 S.L.T. (Notes) 79.
[79] 1948 J.C. 122.
[80] [1956] Crim. L.R. 561.
[81] 1934 J.C. 37.
[82] 1968 S.L.T. 265.

for a point-to-point meeting was a public place: *R.* v. *Collinson*[83]; and one at an agricultural show: *Patterson* v. *Ogilvy*[84]; *MacDonald* v. *McEwan*[85]; and the car park behind an inn: *Elkins* v. *Cartlidge*[86]; but the matter is one requiring evidence of the public's access: *Williams* v. *Boyle*[87]; and the intention is to protect those who resort there, however few: *R.* v. *Warren*[88]; *R.* v. *Waters*.[89] Even a place to which access is forbidden may be held to be a "road" if access by the public is established: *Adams* v. *Commissioner of Police*[90]; *Cheyne* v. *McNeill*.[91]

Attempt

Attempting to drive while unfit through drink or drugs, and attempting to drive while the blood alcohol level exceeds the prescribed limit are both specific offences. In *R.* v. *Cook*[92] a man caught in the driving seat with the dashboard lit and fiddling with the ignition was convicted of attempting to drive whilst impaired. In *Kelly* v. *Hogan*[93] a driver trying to fit the wrong key in the ignition lock was convicted of attempting to drive while impaired.

In Charge

Although the 1930 Road Traffic Act treated the offence of driving while under the influence of drink or a drug on the same basis as that of being in charge of a vehicle while under the influence of drink, its failure to distinguish the quality of culpability gave rise to criticism. Accordingly the Road Traffic Act 1956, by section 9, separated the offence of being in charge from the principal offence and treated it more leniently. This approach was continued by the 1960 Road Traffic Act which, when it came to re-define the driving offence, maintained the separation of the offence of being in charge. In addition that statute provided a specific defence for in-charge cases where, (a) there was no likelihood of the vehicle being driven so long as unfitness persisted, and (b) no driving had in fact taken place since impairment. The second of these qualifications was repealed by section 1(5) of the Road Safety Act 1967, presumably to encourage drivers on feeling the effects of drink to

[83] (1931) 23 Cr. App. R. 49.
[84] 1957 J.C. 42.
[85] 1953 S.L.T. (Sh. Ct.) 26.
[86] [1947] 1 All E.R. 829.
[87] [1963] Crim. L.R. 204.
[88] (1932) 96 J.P.J. 301.
[89] (1963) 107 S.J. 275.
[90] [1980] R.T.R. 289.
[91] 1973 S.L.T. 27.
[92] [1964] Crim. L.R. 56.
[93] [1982] R.T.R. 352.

cease driving and more readily bring themselves within the scope of the in charge offence. The 1972 Road Traffic Act in its original and later its amended form still differentiates the "in charge" from the "driving" offence both as regards the impairment and the pre-scribed-level offences, but there is no difference in sentence other than that the former variant involves discretionary and the latter mandatory disqualification.

Alongside the impairment offence for driving there accordingly stands the different and lesser offence[94] of being in charge whilst impaired. To this charge there is a statutory defence similar to that just mentioned, that at the material time circumstances were such that there was no likelihood of the accused driving so long as he remained unfit to drive through drink or drugs. The onus of estab-lishing such a defence rests upon the accused and would normally require evidence from him sufficient to satisfy the court on a balance of probabilities. The case of *Thaw* v. *Segar*,[95] in which it was said that the standard demanded was proof beyond reasonable doubt, was disapproved in *Neish* v. *Stevenson*[96] when the statutory defence to a charge under section 1(2) of the Road Safety Act 1967[97] was under consideration. In general something more than intention not to drive must be proved: *Morton* v. *Confer*[98]; and delivery of the ignition key to another party is often an element in such cases: *e.g. Farrell* v. *Campbell* [99]; though perhaps not an invariable one: *R.* v. *Harnett*.[1] Merely to immobilise the engine may not be sufficient for there can conceivably be driving: *Saycell* v. *Bool*,[2] and therefore the possibility of being in charge, without the engine having been started. A person simply using a car as a place to sleep off an excess of drink may not be in charge of the vehicle but he is very vulnerable to the suggestion: *Williams* v. *Osborne*.[3] The comparable and lesser offence of being in charge while exceeding the prescribed blood-alcohol limit,[4] was also created alongside the offence of driving while exceeding that limit and a rather similar statutory defence follows: "It is a defence for a

---

[94] *Cf. Jones* v. *English* [1951] 2 All E.R. 853.
[95] 1962 S.L.T. (Sh. Ct.) 63.
[96] 1969 S.L.T. 229.
[97] Now s.6(2) of the Road Safety Act 1972.
[98] [1963] 2 All E.R. 765.
[99] 1959 S.L.T. (Sh. Ct.) 43.
[1] [1955] Crim. L.R. 793.
[2] [1948] 2 All E.R. 83.
[3] [1975] R.T.R. 181.
[4] Road Traffic Act 1972, s.6(2)(*b*).

person charged. . . . to prove that at the time he is alleged to have committed the offence the circumstances were such that there was no likelihood of his driving the vehicle whilst the proportion of alcohol in his breath, blood or urine remained likely to exceed the prescribed limit."

The Court may, in considering either of these defences, disregard the fact that the accused may have been injured or his vehicle damaged, so that it need not prejudice an accused that his being in charge has resulted in a spectacular accident or injury. It is to be noted that the in-charge offence is not an alternative to which the prosecution may automatically resort in the event of their failing to establish that an accused was driving whilst impaired or over the prescribed limit; they are different substantive offences. Alternative charges may of course be preferred.

There is some varied case law on what constitutes being in charge, much of it relating to the original variant of the principal offence. This, although it may be of assistance in considering the modern offences of being in charge, must be applied with care. In *Crichton* v. *Burrell*,[5] for instance Lord Keith said that "the words 'in charge' mean being responsible for the control or driving of the car . . . the person who is for the time being in control of the vehicle." But in that case the car owner was standing by the open car door with a friend with the ignition key in his possession waiting for an employee to come to drive him away: he was not in charge, which is essentially a matter of fact: *R.* v. *Harnett*.[6] Nor was an insensible drunk in the back of an immobilised car: *Dean* v. *Wishart*[7]; nor the owner of a car sitting in the front passenger seat, his wife holding an expired provisional licence, occupying the driving seat with the engine running: *Winter* v. *Morrison*[8]; nor an accused slumped over the driving wheel with no licence or insurance while his companion occupied the front passenger seat with licence, insurance and ignition keys: *Fisher* v. *Kearton*.[9] See also- *MacDonald* v. *Bain*,[10] *MacDonald* v. *MacDonald*,[11] *MacDonald* v. *Kubirdas*,[12] and *Farrell* v. *Campbell*.[13]

[5] 1951 J.C. 107.
[6] [1955] Crim. L.R. 793.
[7] 1952 J.C. 9.
[8] 1954 J.C. 7.
[9] [1964] Crim. L.R. 470 (D.C.).
[10] 1954 S.L.T. (Sh. Ct.) 30.
[11] (1955) 71 (Sh. Ct.) 17.
[12] 1955 S.L.T. (Sh. Ct.) 43.
[13] 1959 S.L.T. (Sh. Ct.) 43.

On the other hand a person in possession of ignition keys looking for his car and arrested before he could enter it was held to be
in charge: *Leach* v. *Evans*,[14] as was the supervisor of a learner
driver: *Clark* v. *Clark*[15]; a taxi-driver awaiting a tow in his broken-
down taxi: *MacDonald* v. *Crawford*,[16] and a motor cyclist whose
companions were arranging that someone else should ride his
cycle: *Haines* v. *Roberts*.[17] It may be a nice question when a person ceased to be in charge. In *Ellis* v. *Smith*[18] a bus driver who
went off duty leaving his bus on the road was held still in charge
until he handed over to another driver: and in *Woodage* v. *Jones*
(No. 2)[19] a driver who left his car on a garage forecourt and
walked a distance of half a mile remained in charge. In *Walker* v.
Rowntree[20] a driver lying half outside his car, his ignition key being
lost, was still held to be in charge. Only abandonment seems to
terminate a person's charge of a vehicle according to *R.* v. *Short*.[21]
There may be circumstances where a driver has abandoned his
vehicle so decisively that he could no longer be held in charge.
What is clear is that mere delivery of the ignition key to a drinking
companion will avail nothing: *Thaw* v. *Segar*.[22]

It appears from *Northfield* v. *Pinder*[23] that evidence in support
of the statutory defence to the in-charge variant of the prescribed-
level offence must go so far as to show on a balance of probabilities
that there is no likelihood of the accused driving so long as his
excess alcohol level persists. This may be difficult to establish since
the presence of excess alcohol can only be revealed by repeated
checks. Section 11 of the Road Traffic Act 1972 provides the police
with power to detain a person from whom breath or laboratory
specimens have been requisitioned until such time as they have
been satisfied that the blood-alcohol level has dropped to the
extent that the person, were he to drive, would be committing no
offence. As the rule is not mandatory, in suitable cases an accused
may be released leaving his vehicle behind. Because there was
considerable delay in obtaining the result of an analysis of blood or

[14] [1952] 2 All E.R. 264.
[15] 1950 S.L.T. (Sh. Ct.) 68.
[16] 1952 S.L.T. (Sh. Ct.) 92.
[17] [1953] 1 All E.R. 344.
[18] [1962] 3 All E.R. 954.
[19] [1975] R.T.R. 119.
[20] [1963] N.I. 23.
[21] *The Times*, December 10, 1955.
[22] 1962 S.L.T. (Sh. Ct.) 63.
[23] [1969] W.L.R. 50.

urine it used to be said that a person arrested for the prescribed-level offence, unlike any other, did not have to be brought immediately before a magistrate but this is no longer the case.

The practical feature of the in-charge offences which distinguishes them from the principal offences is that though disqualification may be ordered it is not a mandatory punishment.

The Impairment Offence

Having established that the accused drove a vehicle on a road or public place the central nature of the impairment offence must be examined—driving or attempting to drive while unfit through drink or drugs. The offence is one, but may be committed by indulgence in drink or in drugs or, of course, in both. It is not therefore bad for duplicity: *Thomson* v. *Knights*.[24]

The offence is committed, it is to be observed, at the moment of driving. But it has to be remembered that driving is given an extended meaning in the Road Traffic Acts.[25] To bring the offence to an end requires, therefore, that the person who has been driving, or in charge of a vehicle, should cease driving and sever his connection with the vehicle. The immediacy of the offence used to introduce a problem since the evidence of impairment had to be related to the material time. However section 10(2) of the Road Traffic Act 1972 provides that in regard to evidence of the proportion of alcohol or any drug in a specimen of breath, blood or urine it shall be assumed that the proportion of alcohol in the accused's breath, blood or urine at the time of the alleged offence was not less than in the specimen and this is so for the prescribed-level and for the impairment offence. Frequently that evidence of impairment takes the form of observation of the driving. Evidence of driving observed three miles away was acceptable in *R.* v. *Burdon*[26] but the fact of unexceptionable driving over as little as 200 yards was not sufficient to rebut medical evidence of unfitness in *Murray* v. *Muir*.[27] It is perhaps more common to find a vehicle driven by one whose ability is impaired by drink to be travelling slowly rather than too fast, *cf. R.* v. *McCall*.[28] Sometimes the observer describes the vehicle as zig-zagging in the road almost as

[24] [1947] K.B. 336.
[25] See *supra* pp. 153 *et seq.*
[26] (1927) 20 Cr. App. R. 80.
[27] 1949 J.C. 127.
[28] [1974] R.T.R. 216.

one might imagine a drunk pedestrian to walk. Failure to relate to traffic conditions, driving too near the kerb, negotiating corners awkwardly, responding slowly or not at all to signs and signals may suggest impairment, but may of course also be attributable to other causes. Linked with other evidence these matters may be of importance in particular because they are suggestive of impairment at the material time. Evidence of breath, blood or urine alcohol level is admissible in relation to the impairment offence[29] cf. *R. v. Stanley Richards,*[30] and may have to be interpreted, but the Court have a discretion and may disregard it: *MacNeill v. Fletcher.*[31] Where a driver collided with a stationary vehicle and had 2·5 times the prescribed blood alcohol level the inference that his driving was impaired was a proper one to make, *R. v. Hunt.*[32] But in the extraordinary case of *P.F. v. Thomas*[33] the accused was acquitted of the impairment offence despite a blood alcohol level of 224mg/100ml. He was said to have an exceptional tolerance to alcohol.

A question is sometimes raised whether incidental evidence of drink is admissible in cases of other driving offences such as causing death by dangerous driving where no drink-driving offence applies. In *R. v. Norrington*[34] evidence of urine-alcohol tests was admitted in such a case, while in *R. v. Sibley*[35] evidence of visits to public houses was allowed to stand, but it had not been suggested that drink was the cause of the accident. No doubt the factors to be regarded would be the relevance and materiality of the evidence, fair notice and absence of prejudice to the accused. It is arguably better practice, however, to avoid evidence of drink in such cases altogether.

The attention of the police may in impairment cases be drawn to a vehicle by an informant, by its involvement in an accident or by the way in which it is driven. Police evidence is generally given of the encounter between the police and the driver, often of their request that he should leave his vehicle, produce his licence, and accompany them under arrest to the police station. The power of arrest without warrant[36] may be exercised if the police reasonably

[29] Road Traffic Act 1972, s.10(2).
[30] [1974] R.T.R. 520.
[31] 1966 J.C. 18.
[32] [1980] R.T.R. 29.
[33] Glasgow Sheriff Court, May 5, 1976.
[34] [1960] Crim. L.R. 432.
[35] [1962] Crim. L.R. 397.
[36] Road Traffic Act 1972, s.5(5).

conclude from his conduct or condition or from other evidence that the driver is unfit to drive, even though this may later prove not to be so: *Wiltshire* v. *Barrett*.[37] Clearly, weight may be attached to the driver's behaviour and appearance, but such facts as that his breath "smells strongly of drink" and that he fumbles in producing his licence from his pocket, though almost invariably given, seem in themselves of limited value. In America sound films of the accused's behaviour have been used as evidence (Sweeny) (Taylor) and as most British police forces have video equipment it is only a matter of time until such evidence is given in Britain. The question of arrest is dealt with more fully in Chapter 11.

At the police station the accused person is normally cautioned and charged with the offence and if arrested in Scotland is always entitled to an interview in private with his solicitor.[38] In England he may be admitted to bail by the station officer.[39] In Scotland this can also be done by the police,[40] though application may be and normally is made at the accused's first appearance in court.[41] Although it is technically possible to make it a condition of bail that the accused shall not drive this can give rise to problems: *R.* v. *Kwame*.[42] When a driver is arrested for the impairment offence the police are at liberty to search his car: *P.F. Kirkcaldy* v. *Chalmers*.[43] He must be brought before the court at the earliest practicable time, and should not be detained overnight uncharged: *R.* v. *Morgan*.[44] Where it is inconvenient to have the accused brought before the court the following day he may instead be released and ordained to appear at a fixed date.

Where he is to be medically examined (and this should follow in most cases to exclude illness or injury and to satisfy the police of his fitness to be detained) the accused must be informed by the police doctor of what is proposed, and his consent sought and obtained. The fact of consent to examination need not be corroborated, even in Scotland: *Farrell* v. *Concannon*.[45] The accused may not be medically examined against his will, or at least without

---

[37] [1966] 1 Q.B. 312.
[38] Criminal Procedure (Scotland) Act 1975, s.305.
[39] Magistrates' Courts Act 1980, s.43.
[40] Bail (Scotland) Act 1980, s.8.
[41] Criminal Procedure (Scotland) Act 1975, s.298.
[42] [1975] R.T.R. 106.
[43] The Scotsman, August 15, 1981.
[44] [1961] Crim. L.R. 538.
[45] 1957 J.C. 12.

his concurrence: *Taylor* v. *Irvine*[46] though where he declines his conduct may and should be circumspectly observed. It is proper for the doctor to inform the accused that, failing consent, his conduct will be observed: *Wishart* v. *Fenwick*.[47] The accused must be permitted to request the attendance of a doctor of his own choosing, though it is unusual for such a request to meet with enthusiastic response from medical men. In Scotland the law requires the police doctor's examination to be carried out privately and without questions directed to elicit information bearing on the accused's guilt: *Reid* v. *Nixon*[48]; *Dumigan* v. *Brown*[49]; *Harris* v. *Adair*[50]; but in England it is more usual for the police to be present though preferably out of earshot[51]: and the propriety of observation of a nonconsenting driver has been questioned[52]: cf. *Wishart* v. *Fenwick*.[53] The results of medical examination carried out before caution and charge are inadmissible in Scotland: *Gallacher* v. *H.M. Advocate*,[54] and have been excluded from evidence in England where the accused was not told of his right to refuse: *R.* v. *Urech*[55] or where he gave consent on the understanding that the examination was purely to eliminate the possibility of illness or injury: *R.* v. *Payne*.[56] Consent obtained through a mistaken belief that the proceedings were regular might well be held to be ineffective should the arrest for example have been made without the necessary circumstances warranting it.

Something has been made of the fact that in England the evidence of the police doctor is to be regarded as "that of a professional man giving independent expert evidence with no other desire than to assist the Court," *R.* v. *Nowell*[57]: "an impartial witness,"[58] while in Scotland he is simply a prosecution witness and so (as was conceded in *Reid* v. *Nixon, supra*) "the hand of the police." The medical evidence in such a case is to be regarded in the

[46] 1958 S.L.T. (Notes) 15.
[47] 1968 S.L.T. 263.
[48] 1948 J.C. 68.
[49] 1948 J.C. 68.
[50] 1947 J.C. 116.
[51] *The Drinking Driver*, B.M.A. 1965.
[52] *The New Police Surgeon*, S.H. Burges (Ed.), Chap. 15.
[53] 1968 S.L.T. 263.
[54] 1963 S.L.T. 217.
[55] [1962] C.L.Y. 587.
[56] [1963] 1 All E.R. 848.
[57] [1948] 1 All E.R. 794.
[58] *The Drinking Driver*, B.M.A. 1965.

same way as that of any other independent witness: *R.* v. *Lan-fear*[59] and doctors involved on whichever side will for professional reasons avoid an unduly partisan approach.

The layman may give evidence as to whether the accused has been drinking, but the question whether he is fit to drive, being the issue before the court, is not a proper one even for an experienced driver: *R.* v. *Davies*[60]; though where in substance the evidence amounts to the observation of an experienced driver it may be permitted as in *R.* v. *Neal.*[61] The police doctor's opinion, though dealing with fitness to drive, is not initially related directly to the material time of driving and is rarely attacked on the ground that it tends to usurp the issue before the court. Should the accused have managed to consume additional drink after the material time it might be impossible for the court to decide what his condition was before having taken the drink, though the circumstances of the additional drinking could themselves be suggestive of guilt. The Road Traffic Act 1972, section 10(2), now contains a statutory provision for this eventuality. This so-called "hip flask defence" is discussed at pp. 121 and 206.

It is often forgotten that drugs too may be consumed after the driving incident with a consequential effect upon the accused's condition. For a case of impairment by glue sniffing see *Bradford* v. *Wilson*[62]; and the Scottish case of impairment through toluene (a container of Evostik was found in the car): *Duffy* v. *Tudhope.*[63] The quantity of drink consumed is frequently proved by the evidence of the accused or by that of his companions, often with wildly optimistic estimates of its lack of effect. The fact of having taken drink or drugs is essential to the impairment offence and it is now competent to produce evidence of the proportion of alcohol in breath, blood or urine in impairment cases. It is of course possible to be affected by drugs which have not been "consumed," and it seems that the expression "through drink or drugs" is deliberately a wide one. A person who had taken drink but whose ability to drive was impaired by illness would not necessarily be guilty of

---

[59] [1968] 2 Q.B. 77, disapproving the statement of law in Archbold (36th Ed.) para. 2849, which could give a false impression of the weight to be attached to the evidence.

[60] [1962] 3 All E.R. 97.

[61] [1962] Crim. L.R. 698.

[62] [1983] Crim. L.R. 482; [1984] R.T.R. 116, D.C.

[63] 1984 S.L.T. 107.

an offence. There have been cases of drivers claiming to be affected by the fumes of distilleries *cf. Brewer* v. *Metropolitan Police Commissioner*[64]; *Collins* v. *Lucking*[65] and unwitting carbon monoxide poisoning from leaking exhaust fumes can simulate the effects of drink, though this can easily be revealed by a blood test (p. 140). In *P.F.* v. *Niven*[66] a youth pleaded guilty to driving under the influence of butane gas. Seventeen containers were found in his car. In *P.F.* v. *Arthur Morgan*,[67] a youth pleaded guilty to driving while impaired through glue sniffing. In the Canadian case of *R.* v. *Marianchuk*[68] a youth was charged with driving while his ability to drive was impaired by sniffing toluene. It was held that not being used for a medical purpose, that substance was not a drug. In this connection "drug" means in England any medicine given to cure, alleviate or assist an ailing body and includes insulin; in *Armstrong* v. *Clark*[69] *cf.* p. 125 Lord Chief Justice Goddard expressed the cautious opinion that the term "drink" means alcoholic drink. In Scotland a drug is any material which has a drugging effect on driving capacity: *Duffy* v. *Tudhope.*[69a] A diabetic who, due to an unforeseen shift of body metabolism, becomes subject to a hypoglycaemic episode may be acquitted of the impairment offence: *Watmore* v. *Jenkins*,[70] though he might be unwise to expect to fare so well on a second occasion. The offence for a driver lies not in taking the drink or drugs nor even in having taken them, but in the impairment of proper driving ability to which this may later lead. As indicated in the earlier chapters of this book there may well be a lapse of time before the offence is committed. That is to say a driver may set out able to drive properly but in the course of his journey the effect of drink or drugs may begin to make itself felt on his driving ability. In such a situation the offence is committed as soon as driving ability begins to be affected. Even a driver whose original impairment arises in a way not punishable within the scope of the law, and who persists in driving after realising its effects, risks prosecution.

---

[64] [1969] 1 All E.R. 513.
[65] [1983] R.T.R. 312; [1983] Crim. L.R. 264.
[66] Unreported, December 24, 1981.
[67] Perth Sheriff Court, August 10, 1982.
[68] [1977] 5 W.W.R. 444.
[69] [1957] 2 Q.B. 391.
[69a] 1983 S.C.C.R. 440.
[70] [1962] 2 Q.B. 572.

THE RE-DEFINED IMPAIRMENT OFFENCE

Following the amendments introduced by the Transport Act 1981 the rules for the impairment offence have been revised.[71] A person suspected of the impairment offence may be given an opportunity of providing a screening breath test[72] but this is optional. Most police forces are likely to follow the screening breath test procedure as a matter of good police/public relations but its omission will not itself vitiate subsequent procedure. Where a specimen of breath for a breath test is validly required, failure to provide it without reasonable excuse will constitute an offence subject to discretionary disqualification and mandatory endorsement. In this respect the previous immunity of the "in charge" motorist from breath testing has been removed, and breath tests may now be required both from the driver and from the person in charge in impairment cases. It is now perfectly acceptable for a compliant motorist to accompany the police either before or after a positive breath test to the police station without the necessity of a formal arrest. However a constable may arrest a person without warrant if he has reasonable cause to suspect that that person is or has been committing the impairment offence, and in England may enter, by force if need be, any place where that person is or where the constable suspects him to be. This provision largely reverses the Court's decision in *Morris* v. *Beardmore*.[73] In Scotland the police already have common law power in these circumstances to enter premises to make such an arrest.

Having reached the stage where a suspect is shown either to have given a positive breath test or to have refused to provide a specimen for such a test, or where, without these enquiries, it is desired to investigate whether a suspect may indeed have committed a drink-driving offence, the police may move on to the requirement of specimens for analysis of breath which is the principal innovation brought about by the Transport Act 1981 reforms.

That procedure is described on page 195.

The provisions of section 10 of the Road Traffic Act 1972 now applied to impairment cases allow the Court to have regard to evidence of the proportion of alcohol or any drug in a specimen of breath, blood or urine both for the impaired driver and the impaired person in charge. The procedures regarding proof by cer-

---

[71] See now road Traffic Act 1972, s.5.
[72] See *infra*, pp. 174 *et seq*.
[73] [1980] 3 W.L.R. 283.

tificate apply. It appears that the previous incentives to urge a driver who felt himself the worse for drink to cease driving and remain only in charge have not been heeded, because the law following the Transport Act 1981 offers no lesser punishment to the person in charge, except that disqualification for that offence is discretionary rather than obligatory.

If any question arises that evidence of this kind is for any reason incompetent or inadmissible it is important that objection should be taken in court at the earliest opportunity. For the consequences of failure to do so in England see Newark and for the peremptory Scottish rule see Criminal Procedure (Scotland) Act 1975, the proviso to section 454(i) and *Reid* v. *Nixon*.[74] So far as evidence of the proportion of alcohol or any drug in breath, blood or urine is concerned section 10(2) of the Road Traffic Act 1972 provides that such evidence shall in all cases be taken into account, and this is apparently intended to render such evidence admissible even though improperly or illegally obtained. It remains to be seen whether the courts will so interpret the provision. This is less likely in Scotland than in England where the case of *R.* v. *Sang*[75] confirmed that the English courts already have power to hear evidence although it may have been illegally obtained. See also *Smith* v. *Ross*.[75a]

THE STANDARD OF UNFITNESS

It is curious that despite much criticism of the terms of the impairment offence there has been no close judicial examination of its meaning either in its original or in its amended form. It is arguable that the amendment made in 1962 brought about no significant improvement in its clarity (Smith J.C.). No doubt impairment means impairment in however small a degree, and ability to drive, though necessarily subjective, is an intelligible matter for enquiry, but ability to drive properly seems to imply reference to an objective standard of proper driving which is still remarkably elusive to define. It is sometimes argued that any observable physical consequence of taking alcohol, such as *nystagmus*, must imply impairment of driving ability, but rarely if ever is evidence given that *nystagmus* is correlated with diminished driving ability, let alone with a diminution which falls below the standard of proper driving.

---

[74] 1948 J.C. 68 at p. 73.
[75] [1979] 2 All E.R. 1222.
[75a] 1983 S.C.C.R. 109.

Since it must be accepted that driving ability varies from person to person, and even perhaps in the same person on different occasions, it seems unlikely that there can be a truly objective and fixed standard of proper driving ability. Does it therefore mean that impairment of a person's ability to drive as well as that person would otherwise have driven is the mischief aimed at by the statutory offence? What, if any, are the tolerances allowed? The absence of answers to these questions necessarily gives scope for the defence in borderline cases, though it may well avail nothing in the grosser cases where control of the vehicle is almost absent. This unsatisfactory situation also led to much criticism of the law and strengthened the demand for the creation in 1967 of the complementary prescribed alcohol-level offence which survives in a much amended form to the present day.

The Prescribed-Level Offence

The prescribed alcohol-level offence was created by section 1 of the Road Safety Act 1967 but radically re-enacted by the amendments of the Transport Act 1981, Schedule 8 of which substituted a set of new sections 6 to 12 in the Road Traffic Act 1972. The 1967 prescribed-level offence provided that if a person drives or attempts to drive a vehicle on a road or other public place having consumed alcohol in such a quantity that the proportion thereof in his blood as ascertained from a laboratory test exceeds the prescribed limit at the time he provides a specimen of blood or urine for the purpose of the test he shall be guilty of an offence. In practice this tortuous definition proved too complicated to be readily applicable and the very complexity of the definition gave rise to many defences in prosecutions for the offence. The main defects were that the definition did not make driving with too much alcohol an offence in itself. The criminal character of the driving only appeared from a subsequent analysis. It could thus be justly argued that many drivers had no idea whether or not they were committing an offence, and it was often not possible to know for certain whether an offence had been committed until the specimen had been analysed.

In its 1967 form the prescribed-level offence could only be established after a preliminary screening breath test which could be applied only in certain defined circumstances. Only those who failed the screening test or refused it without reasonable excuse could be proceeded against. The others were discharged by compliance: *Brennan* v. *Farrell*.[76] The 1967 Act then provided for those who failed or refused the screening test to be required to supply blood or urine specimens for laboratory testing on pain of punishment for refusal if they did not comply. An accused who had failed or refused to supply a breath test, or who had failed or refused to supply either blood or urine in response to a require-ment under the Act was treated in substantially the same way as a person who has been convicted of the prescribed-level offence.

The original prescribed-level offence concerned blood alcohol only and had no relevance to the misuse of drugs despite the rubric of the Road Safety Act which read "An Act to make further pro-vision with respect to persons driving or being in charge of motor vehicles after consuming alcohol or taking drugs. . . . " The inclu-sion of the reference to drugs was necessary because amongst other things the Act amended the previous law of driving while impaired through drink or drugs. Although the language describ-ing the offence seemed to create an offence of strict liability appli-cable to all who showed a blood-alcohol level above that prescribed, the use of the expression "having consumed alcohol" seemed inadequate to cover those to whom it had unknowingly been administered and the voluntary act of the accused in knowingly consuming the alcohol was necessary for conviction. See "laced drinks," at p. 205.

The evidential restriction of the 1967 offence to alcohol level "as ascertained from a laboratory test" seemed to mean that the offence could be proved in one way only, and therefore a convic-tion was vulnerable to any substantial doubt raised in regard to the laboratory tests. The procedures preliminary to demanding screening breath tests were as strictly dependent upon compliance with the statutory provisions as were the breath tests themselves, and it followed that any failure or irregularity might be fatal to conviction. Each step in the procedure was justified only if every preceding step had been properly carried out: *Scott* v. *Baker*.[77] For these reasons the 1967 prescribed-level offence, which set out to be precise and unchallengeable, turned out in practice to be just as open to attack as the looser and vaguer impairment offence ever was.

It is important to keep in mind that the prescribed-level offence has in law nothing to do with actual impairment. It is possible that

---

[76] [1969] Crim. L.R. 494, *per* Lord Walker.
[77] [1969] 1 Q.B. 659.

the most habituated of drinkers could tolerate 80mg of alcohol per 100ml of blood without adverse effect on driving ability, although most suffer at least some impairment at that level. Conversely a driver may be obviously impaired and yet may not have attained the prescribed level.

The 1967 Act and its successors made great demands upon, and required surrender of some of the cherished privileges of the public. It allowed the police wide powers to set enquiries in motion, demanded submission to rather humiliating tests, virtually forced, or at least induced, the accused to supply evidence upon which alone he might be convicted, and permitted the luxury of non-co-operation only in exchange for conviction of an offence virtually identical with that in regard to which co-operation was refused. These inroads upon the liberties of the subject could only be justified if they were acceptable to the public and resulted in a marked diminution in the toll of road accidents as, indeed, they did. Generally the statutory rules operated moderately well, if unevenly, and produced an initial reduction in casualties, though the originally sharp public reaction to screening breath tests soon wore off. The 1967 Act seemed to have proved socially acceptable, a situation which might have been unlikely to continue if the Minister of Transport had exercised his power to lower the prescribed limit. There are however some who consider the present limit too high; and the view has been expressed that no limit is better than one which is too high (Havard 1963).

THE RE-DEFINED PRESCRIBED-LEVEL OFFENCE

In its re-defined form following the Transport Act 1981 amendments, the prescribed-level offence[78] provides that if a person drives or attempts to drive a motor vehicle on a road or other public place or is in charge after consuming so much alcohol that the proportion of it in his breath, blood or urine exceeds the prescribed limit he shall be guilty of an offence.

This new definition simplifies the offence; it restores the *actus reus* of the offence to driving with excess alcohol; no longer is the criminality of the offence dependent upon the result of a future analysis. The point at which to consider the motorist's alcohol level is at the time of sampling rather than the time of driving so that the intervening period of delay cannot be argued to have

---

[78] Road Traffic Act 1972, s.6.

raised the blood-alcohol from an acceptable to a criminal level. This is because section 10(2) of the 1972 Act provides that in regard to evidence of the proportion of alcohol or any drug in a specimen of breath, blood or urine it shall be assumed (unless post-driving alcohol has been consumed to a certain level) that the proportion of alcohol in breath, blood or urine at the time of the alleged offence was not less than in the specimen. For the situation where post-driving alcohol has been consumed see p. 206. No longer will it be essential to show that the person to whom the tests were applied is a driver; the definition contemplates also a person who has been driving; but a new difficulty will be to determine how long after a person has ceased to drive the enquiry can be made. There is also a statutory defence if the accused alleged to be in charge can establish that there was no likelihood of his driving while the proportion of alcohol in his breath, blood or urine remained likely to exceed the prescribed-level. Since the offence applies now to persons who "have been driving" the statutory defence will be of material importance. The standard of proof will be balance of probability: *Morton* v. *Confer*[79]: *Neish* v. *Stevenson*[80] but the standard of proof required will be high. In *P.F.* v. *McRitchie*[81] a driver who ran out of petrol and was stranded at the roadside failed in such a defence. Section 12(2) of the 1972 Act now defines the offence by reference to breath, blood or urine.

CROSSING OVER

The Road Safety Act 1967 at first sight introduced a statutory pathway for procedure in the prescribed-level offence which was stricter and more detailed than that for the impairment offence. It soon became clear, however, that crossing over from one to the other was possible, even when this seemed to relieve the Crown of the necessity of fulfilling all the safeguards for the accused enacted in the stricter of the procedures. In *Campbell* v. *Tormey*[82] the possibility of a driver arrested for the impairment offence being convicted of the prescribed-level offence arose. Lord Dilhorne referred *obiter* to the same thing in *D.P.P.* v. *Carey*.[83] This happened in *R.* v. *Jones R.W.*[84] In *R.* v. *Sadler*[85] it was confirmed that

---

[79] [1963] 2 All E.R. 765.   [80] 1969 S.L.T. 229.
[81] Unreported Perth Sheriff Court, March 17, 1977.
[82] [1969] 1 All E.R. 961.
[83] [1969] 3 All E.R. 1662.
[84] [1969] 3 All E.R. 1559.
[85] [1970] R.T.R. 127.

an analysis of blood taken for the prescribed-level offence was admissible in support of the impairment offence. In the Scottish case of *Cairns* v. *MacNab*[86] the appeal court expressed a view similar to that of Lord Dilhorne. In *Norman* v. *MacGill*[87] a youth initially charged with being in charge while sitting in the driver's seat, his girl friend passenger having the ignition keys, was eventually convicted of the prescribed-level offence. So also in *Woodage* v. *Jones* (*No. 2*)[88] a person arrested for being in charge was then required to provide a laboratory specimen leading to conviction of the prescribed-level offence. A suggestion that, having been arrested for the impairment offence, blood tests then obtained could not be used for the prescribed-level offence, was negatived in *R.* v. *Dixon*.[89] The police may charge a person alternatively, or even cumulatively, for the impairment and prescribed-level offences: *Sharpe* v. *Perry*[90] although this is uncommon in practice.

SCREENING BREATH TEST

The original prescribed-level offence had to be preceded by a request for a screening breath test but no set form of words was required: *R.* v. *Clarke*.[91] The constable who made the request had to be in uniform; the court having to determine what was uniform: *Wood* v. *Brown*.[92] It mattered not that when he first suspected alcohol he was wearing an overcoat: *Taylor* v. *Baldwin*.[93] And the test had to be carried out "there or nearby," another term to be construed by the court: *Donegani* v. *Ward*[94]; *Arnold* v. *Kingston-upon-Hull Chief Constable*.[95] In Scotland the test could be administered at a police station if the accused was voluntarily present there: *Mackenzie* v. *Smith*.[96] These requirements have now been varied or modified. The screening test is now optional to the police. Where a constable in uniform has reasonable cause to suspect that a driver or person in charge has alcohol in his body or has committed a traffic offence whilst the vehicle was in motion: or that a person has been driving or attempting to drive or in charge with alcohol in his body and that he still has alcohol in his body, or

---

[86] 1971 S.L.T. (Notes) 56.
[87] [1972] R.T.R. 81.
[88] [1975] R.T.R. 119.
[89] [1980] R.T.R. 17.
[90] [1979] R.T.R. 235.
[91] [1969] 1 W.L.R. 1109.
[92] 1969 S.L.T. (Notea) 75.
[93] [1976] R.T.R. 265.
[94] [1969] 1 W.L.R. 1502.
[95] [1969] 1 W.L.R. 1499.
[96] 1971 S.L.T. (Notes) 81.

that a person has been driving or attempting to drive or in charge and has committed a traffic offence while the vehicle was in motion the constable may, provided the person is not a hospital patient, require a specimen of breath for a breath test. In *Baker* v. *Oxford*[97] the police had reasonable cause to believe that a particular person had been driving where other police information claimed it to be so and the person admitted it. There is a distinction between "reasonable cause to believe" and "reasonable cause to suspect:" *Johnston* v. *Whitehouse*.[98] Where the constable has two reasons for requiring a breath test and discloses the faulty one to the driver, the latter is not prejudiced if the other reason is sound. If a vehicle accident occurs the person suspected of having been driving or attempting to drive may be required to provide a specimen of breath for a breath test. If the requirement is made by the police the driver must provide the specimen at or near the place where the requirement is made or, in the case of an accident, if the police think fit, at a police station. Failure without reasonable excuse to provide such a specimen of breath constitutes an offence. Under the previous legislation it was not an offence for a person in charge to refuse a breath test. Under the earlier rules it had been necessary for the test to be required as soon as reasonably possible after commission of the offence, *cf. R.* v. *Coleman*[99]; and *Ely* v. *Marle*[1] where a motorist who would wait only 10 minutes for the arrival of the Alcotest device and then tried to walk away had to be restrained: he was refusing. Similarly in *R.* v. *Mackey*[2] a driver who when asked to provide a breath test began eating Tic-Tac mints and would not desist was refusing. That requirement (for the breath test to be given as soon as possible) has not been re-enacted. It seems also that a constable requesting a breath test after an accident need not now be in uniform.

The purpose of the re-defined offence seems to be to rely in the majority of cases upon the analysis of breath specimens by instrumental methods.

What amounts to reasonable cause to suspect that a person has alcohol in the body must be a matter of particular circumstances, a few examples of which were given by Seago.[3] Bad driving in itself

[97] [1980] R.T.R. 315.
[98] [1984] R.T.R. 38.
[99] [1974] R.T.R. 359.
[1] [1977] R.T.R. 412.
[2] [1977] R.T.R. 146.
[3] [1969] Crim. L.R. 293.

may well be insufficient to found such a suspicion: *Williams* v. *Jones*[4]; but where a jury came to such a conclusion it was not disturbed: *R.* v. *Fardy*.[5] So in *Sinclair* v. *Heywood*[6] an ostentatiously fast 3-point turning drew attention to a driver who was justifiably breath-tested. The suspicion need not be aroused during the period of actual driving if the requirement of breath is made from a person driving; *Pinner* v. *Everett*,[7] although it would have to be closely related to it. It is sufficient that the driver's breath smells of drink in circumstances which point to an offence. Smell of drink by itself was not sufficient to support suspicion of impairment (justly so, since alcohol has no smell): *R.* v. *Way*.[8] But in *Mulcaster* v. *Wheatstone*[9] where a driver was stopped because of the manner of his driving (which did not support the inference of drinking) and wound down his window, smelt of drink and admitted he had taken two pints there was then material to found reasonable suspicion. And a police driver in *Regan* v. *Anderton*[10] who drove to the police garage in response to a radio call and while sitting in his vehicle spoke to his Inspector, who smelt drink, provided material for reasonable suspicion whilst still driving. In *Such* v. *Ball*[11] the police followed and stopped a driver, smelling drink and requiring a breath specimen. Although there had been no moving traffic offence and no reasonable grounds for believing an offence to have been committed, there was no positive finding of malpractice or random testing and the driver was rightly convicted. It may be a reasonable inference in regard to any person leaving licensed premises, particularly at closing time, or driving with a bottle of liquor on display in the vehicle. It does not matter what the objective truth happened to be, unknown to the police constable at the time: what matters is whether the constable had reasonable cause to suspect the presence of alcohol: *McNicol* v. *Peters*.[12] Where two constables are acting jointly, one may suspect drink and require a breath test, while the other makes the arrest: *Knight* v. *Taylor*.[13] Since a constable in uniform has power under section 159 of the Road Traffic Act 1972 to stop the driver of any vehicle on a road, it

[4] [1972] R.T.R. 4.
[5] [1973] R.T.R. 268.
[6] 1981 S.L.T. (Notes) 98.
[7] [1969] 1 W.L.R. 1266.
[8] 1970 R.T.R. 348.
[9] [1980] R.T.R. 190.
[10] [1980] R.T.R. 126.
[11] [1982] R.T.R. 140.
[12] 1969 S.L.T. 261.
[13] [1979] R.T.R. 304.

is clear that there is not in practice much difference between the original random testing proposed in the White Paper of 1965 and the limited power to call for a screening breath test as it has turned out in section 7(1) of the Road Traffic Act 1972. Parliament, however, though frequently debating the use of random tests, has never yet sanctioned them, presumably because their use would be likely to impair police/public relations. In *Winter* v. *Barlow*[14] where the police stopped a vehicle, smelt drink and obtained a laboratory specimen, analysed at 180mg/100ml, it was argued that the tests had been random; but the English court saw no reason to exclude the evidence.

The interpretation of requiring a breath test from "a person driving or attempting to drive or in charge of a vehicle" must obviously be given some latitude and the interpretation of these words has been discussed *supra* at pp. 153 *et seq*. In Scotland the fact of driving will require corroboration. See also *McLeod* v. *Nicol*[15] and *Douglas* v. *Pirie*.[16] There may be circumstances where it is by no means clear that the accused person is shown to have been the driver at the material time. In the Scottish case of *Breen* v. *Pirie*[17] the police, having a report of an accident, went to the locus where at one point they found the accused the worse for drink behind a dyke, and a mile away a Land Rover in a field with the engine warm and the ignition keys in place. This was insufficient to justify the inference of driving.

The term "accident" is undefined by the Act but it describes an unintended occurrence such as bumpers interlocking: *R.* v. *Morris*[18] or a deliberate driving through a closed gate *Chief Constable of Staffordshire* v. *Lees*,[19] or a vehicle crashing: *R.* v. *Harling*[20]; *Chief Constable of West Midlands Police* v. *Billingham*.[21] In a Scottish case the term "accident" was held to include a car coming round a corner at such speed that two pedestrians had to jump out of the way: *Pryde* v. *Brown*.[22] If the driver is at hospital as a patient the breath test can only be given if (a) the intention to require it is notified to the doctor in immediate charge of the

[14] [1980] R.T.R. 209.
[15] 1970 S.L.T. 304.
[16] 1975 S.L.T. 206.
[17] 1976 S.L.T. 136.
[18] [1972] R.T.R. 201.
[19] [1981] R.T.R. 506.
[20] [1970] R.T.R. 441.
[21] [1979] R.T.R. 446.
[22] 1982 S.L.T. 314.

patient and (b) the doctor does not raise the objection that the demand for the breath test or laboratory specimen or the taking of blood or urine or the associated warning, would be prejudicial to the proper care and treatment of the patient. Whether a doctor's surgery, a nursing home, a private clinic or a health centre would qualify as a "hospital" remains to be seen. The doctor's concurrence in the breath test being administered at the hospital may be proved at second hand: *R.* v. *Chapman.*[23]

A breath test is defined in section 12(2) of the Road Traffic Act 1972[23a] as a preliminary test for the purpose of obtaining an indication whether the proportion of alcohol in a person's breath or blood carried out by means of a device of a type approved by the Secretary of State is likely to exceed the prescribed limit. The definition of a breath test together with the former evidential restriction upon the method of proof of the prescribed-level offence had the effect of rendering evidence of the Alcotest result incompetent in support of the original prescribed-level offence itself but the present provisions of the Road Traffic Act 1972 do not seem to prevent the giving in evidence of the result of a breath test performed either with the Alcotest R 80 or with one of the hand-held instruments approved by the Secretary of State. Inferences can and have been drawn from the fact that a screening breath test was positive: for example: *Lomas* v. *Bowler.*[24] Failure to provide a breath specimen includes refusal to do so, but probably excludes circumstances which are beyond the driver's control such as defective equipment or absence of equipment: *Hoyle* v. *Walsh.*[25] Where the driver has taken no exception at the time to reasonable police instructions, the procedure in Scotland is acceptable: *McLeod* v. *Milligan*[26]: *Farrell* v. *Coakley.*[27]

Only a constable in uniform may require a person to provide a specimen of breath for a breath test except where an accident has happened, in which case it appears that the requirement may be made by a constable whether or not in uniform. There is no set formula: *R.* v. *O'Boyle.*[28] A constable, of course, would include a constable of any rank[29] and one constable can make the require-

[23] [1969] 2 W.L.R. 1004.
[23a] Amended by s.59 of the Transport Act 1982.
[24] [1984] Crim. L.R. 178.
[25] [1969] 1 All E.R. 39.
[26] (1969) 14 J.L.S. 253.
[27] (1969) 14 J.L.S. 253.
[28] [1973] R.T.R. 445.
[29] Police Act 1964, s.19.

ment on information supplied by another constable: *Erskine* v. *Hollin*[30]; *Copeland* v. *McPherson*[31] in which case it is necessary to have some record of what that information was: *Moss* v. *Jenkins*.[32] The breath test is the successor to what the 1965–6 White Paper called the "screening breath test" and is to be distinguished from the requirement to provide two specimens of breath for analysis by instrumental means which will be described in a following section. The procedures of breath testing and breath analysis have already been briefly described at pages 174 and 168 respectively. From 1967 the pre-requisites for requiring a breath test were that the constable had reasonable cause to suspect a person driving or attempting to drive on a road or other public place of having alcohol in his body or of having committed a traffic offence while the vehicle was in motion whether he had committed it or not: *R.* v. *Downey*.[33] In the latter case the requirement had to be made as soon as reasonably practicable after commission of the traffic offence, say within 5 minutes: *Rickwood* v. *Cochrane*.[34]

In either case the test was to be carried out there or nearby. Where, following an accident, the police stopped the wrong car and smelt drink, they were unable to secure a conviction for failure to provide a breath specimen because they could not substantiate their reason for stopping the particular driver: *Clements* v. *Dams*.[35] The provisions of the re-enacted section 7 of the Road Traffic Act 1972 now widen the power to require a breath test. Where a constable in uniform has reasonable cause to suspect that such a person has alcohol in his body or has committed a traffic offence while the vehicle was in motion, or that such a person has in the past had alcohol in his body and still has it, or where such a person has been driving or attempting to drive and has committed such an offence, the constable may require him to provide a specimen of breath for a breath test to be carried out either at or near the place where the requirement was made or (following an accident) at a police station. What is meant by "at or near" will be a matter for the Court but under the previous law in *Arnold* v. *Hull Chief Constable*[36] one and a half miles did not fall within the simi-

---

[30] [1971] R.T.R. 199.
[31] 1970 S.L.T. 87.
[32] [1975] R.T.R. 25.
[33] [1970] R.T.R. 257.
[34] [1978] R.T.R. 218.
[35] [1978] R.T.R. 206.
[36] [1969] 3 All E.R. 646.

lar phrase "there or nearby," while in *Donegani* v. *Ward*[37] the Divisional Court would not disturb a finding that 160 yards was likewise not within the latter phrase. The re-enacted section 7 catches not only the driver, the person who *has* been driving, and indeed the person believed to have been driving or in charge, but also permits the requirement even following some delay after the traffic offence, and allows the requirement and the test to take place wherever the police direct. The definition of traffic offence has been widened to include offences under Part 1 of the Transport Act 1980. There has been considerable case law as to whether the suspicion has to arise while the vehicle is being driven. It appeared that it might arise before: *R.* v. *Furness*[38] or during the driving and while the driver retained some connection with his vehicle and could still be regarded as within the extended description of "a person driving," but (until the recent amendments) not when the person was no longer driving in that extended sense: as for example when the driver had surrendered his ignition keys to someone else: *Cruickshank* v. *Devlin*[39]; *Harman* v. *Wardrop*[40]; or was prevented from driving: *R.* v. *Bates*.[41] The Scottish courts have tried to obviate the examination of when the motorist is "a person driving" by interpreting the Act as applying to the category of persons from whom a test can be required: *Farrell* v. *Brown*[42]; *Taylor* v. *Houston*[43]; *Swan* v. *Houston*.[44] It is a question of fact and degree in each case whether a person is in the category from whom such a request can be made: *Smith* v. *Fyfe*.[45] So an injured driver whose car was driven away from the locus by a third party was not in the category: *Carbis* v. *Hamilton*,[46] nor was a keyholder of premises called out by the police after 10 minutes spent examining the premises: *Hogg* v. *Martin*,[47] nor a motorist who had returned home after a crash and who was then roused by police who had no knowledge of the events other than information received from those involved: *Seaton* v. *Allan*.[48] The new provisions are less stringent. A motorist stopped by the police, relieved of his ignition keys and engaged in conversation for 15 minutes until the breath test equipment arrived was still driving:

[37] [1969] 3 All E.R. 636.
[38] [1973] Crim. L.R. 759.
[39] 1973 S.L.T. (Sh. Ct.) 81.
[40] [1971] R.T.R. 127.
[41] [1973] R.T.R. 264.
[42] 1971 S.L.T. 40.
[43] 1971 S.L.T. 39.
[44] 1971 S.L.T. 39.
[45] 1971 S.L.T. 89.
[46] 1971 S.L.T. (Notes) 58.
[47] 1971 S.L.T. (Sh. Ct.) 14.
[48] 1974 S.L.T. 234.

Swankie v. *Milne*.[49] However a driver observed and followed by other road-users, who suspected drink, removed his ignition keys and kept him in conversation for eight minutes till police arrived was no longer driving, the nexus having been broken by the confiscation of the keys: *Cruickshank* v. *Devlin*.[50] There are no specific terms laid down in which the requirement for a breath test must be made: *R.* v. *O'Boyle*[51]; *R.* v. *Clarke*,[52] and, if made in good faith by a constable who believes it is being heard by the driver, it is valid even if it is neither heard nor understood: *R.* v. *Nicholls*.[53]

There may of course be reasonable suspicion of alcohol although in truth no alcohol has been consumed: *McNicol* v. *Peters*,[54] and it may be that where the reasonableness of the constable's suspicion is impugned the requirement of the breath test may still be upheld in view of the new provision that evidence of the proportion of alcohol in a specimen shall *in all cases* be taken into account[55]; and absence of alcohol would probably not constitute reasonable excuse for failing to provide a breath specimen. In addition a valid arrest and a positive breath test are no longer essential pre-requisites for requiring a specimen for analysis. The constable's suspicion may arise in all sorts of circumstances: when a vehicle has been stopped for a reason or for no particular reason: *Harris* v. *Croson*,[56] or for alternative reasons: *Atkinson* v. *Walker*[57]; *McNaughton* v. *Deenam*,[58] and a questionable reason is often confirmed by the smell of the driver's breath: *Hay* v. *Shepherd*[59]; *Shersby* v. *Klippel*[60] but (under the old rules) not after the driving is finished: *Solkins* v. *Knowles*.[61] The basis for the reasonable suspicion may be information from another police officer: *R.* v. *Moore*[62]; *Erskine* v. *Hollin*,[63] or plain clothes officer: *Copeland* v. *McPherson*[64]; *R.* v. *Evans*,[65] or from a layman: *Monaghan* v. *Corbett*.[66] The police do not have to explain to the driver how their suspicion is founded: *Atkinson* v. *Walker*[67]; *Clements* v. *Dams*,[68] but any reason given should be correct and justified: *Williams* v.

[49] 1973 S.L.T. (Notes) 28.
[50] 1973 S.L.T. (Sh. Ct.) 81.
[51] [1973] R.T.R. 445.
[52] [1969] 2 All E.R. 1008.
[53] [1972] R.T.R. 308.
[54] 1969 S.L.T. 261.
[55] Road Traffic Act 1972, s.10(2).
[56] [1973] R.T.R. 57.
[57] [1976] R.T.R. 117.
[58] 1981 S.C.C.R. 97.

[59] [1974] R.T.R. 64.
[60] [1979] R.T.R. 116.
[61] [1973] R.T.R. 257.
[62] [1970] R.T.R. 486.
[63] [1971] R.T.R. 199.
[64] 1970 S.L.T. 87.
[65] [1974] R.T.R. 232.
[66] *The Times*, June 23, 1983.
[67] [1976] R.T.R. 117.
[68] [1978] R.T.R. 206.

Jones.[69] There is no valid provision of a specimen for a breath test unless the specimen is sufficient for the test or analysis[70] and provided in such a way as to enable the objective of the test or analysis to be satisfactorily achieved. The test must of course be carried out on an approved device. The Alcotest R 80 became so familiar to Courts that evidence of approval was not always required: *R.* v. *Jones*[71] and *Bentley* v. *Northumbria Police*.[71a] In Scotland in the absence of contrary evidence a copy letter from a Government department was enough evidence of approval: *Hunter* v. *Herron*,[72] in England evidence of a breath test was assumed to be evidence of the Alcotest R 80: *Cooper* v. *Rowlands*.[73] In *Lee* v. *Smith*[74] where the matter was not challenged the Court accepted the evidence of the police who used the Alcolyser, that the device was approved by the Secretary of State: *cf. R.* v. *Jones*.[75] The other hand-held devices have also been approved by the Secretary of State and their approval may for a time have to be demonstrated.

Manufacturer's Instructions

In England failure to observe the manufacturer's instructions in using the Alcotest R 80 would only vitiate the procedure if the police did not act in good faith. The manufacturer's instructions form no part of the device as approved by the Secretary of State and meticulous compliance is not required. It is for the accused to draw attention to drinking or smoking within 20 minutes of the test (and to lay a foundation in cross examination if the point is to be tested in Court), and no obligation rests on the police to enquire: *D.P.P.* v. *Carey*,[76] *Halbert* v. *Stewart*.[77] As to the effect of smoking see *Watkinson* v. *Barley*[78]: *Darnell* v. *Portal*,[79] *Attorney General's Reference (No. 2 of 1974)*.[80] As to storage conditions (under 30° Centigrade) see *Sayer* v. *Johnston*[81]: *Gill* v. *Forster*.[82] As to recent drinking (within 15 minutes) see *R.* v. *Aspden*[83]: *Wright* v. *Brobyn*.[84] Likewise non-compliance with the manufacturer's instructions for the Alcotest R 80 need not be fatal unless shown to have invalidated the result: *Attorney General's Reference (No. 1 of*

[69] [1972] R.T.R. 4.
[70] Road Traffic Act 1972, s.12(3).
[71] [1969] 3 All E.R. 1559.
[71a] [1984] R.T.R. 276.
[72] 1969 S.L.T. (Notes) 54.
[73] [1971] R.T.R. 291.
[74] 1982 S.L.T. 200.
[75] [1969] 3 All E.R. 1559.
[76] [1970] R.T.R. 14.
[77] 1971 S.L.T. 43.
[78] [1975] R.T.R. 136.
[79] [1972] R.T.R. 483.
[80] [1975] R.T.R. 142.
[81] [1970] R.T.R. 286.
[82] [1970] R.T.R. 372.
[83] [1975] R.T.R. 456.
[84] [1971] R.T.R. 204.

1978).[85] In *Butcher* v. *Catterall*[86] where the breath test was commenced 15 seconds after the last inhalation of smoke the case was remitted back to enquire what effect this had on the colour of the granules. In *Attorney General's Reference* (*No. 2 of 1974*),[87] the view was expressed that where a constable ignored a smoking driver and proceeded at once with a breath test the results would be invalid. Ignoring the fact that a driver smoked right up to the time of the test was one of the reasons for quashing a conviction in *R.* v. *Callum.*[88] The mischief would only be where there was a heavy concentration of smoke in the lungs: *Watkinson* v. *Barley.*[89] But in *R.* v. *George Moore*[90] where the driver said his last drink was "a short while ago" the procedure at once to require laboratory tests was not faulted. In *Blake* v. *Bickmore*[91] a prescribed-level case, the breath testing was by the Lion Alcolmeter SL2. The first test failed to illuminate both lights A and B. The driver tried again and a reading was obtained. The blood-alcohol level was eventually found to be 201mg/100ml. An attempt to criticise the use of the Alcolmeter failed because the manufacturer's instructions were not in evidence. Disregard of manufacturer's instructions may now be of less importance than it was in view of the provisions of section 10(2) of the Road Traffic Act 1972 that evidence shall in all cases be taken into account. An incorrectly assembled Alcotest R 80 is not an approved device (the green end of the tube must be inserted in the bag): *R.* v. *Coates*[92] nor is a device with a hole in the plastic bag: *Rayner* v. *Hampshire Chief Constable.*[93] In *Mackay* v. *MacLeod*[94] the driver did not fill the bag at his first attempt and was given a second which he inflated giving a positive reading. At the police station the confirmatory test (now discontinued) was given with a defective bag, and the accused refused to proceed. This was held not to be a confirmatory test under the Statute (a breath test with a defective device is not a test as called for by statute) and the refusal of another test entitled the police to require a laboratory specimen. Although the driver is entitled to only one breath test the police sometimes accept the

[85] [1978] R.T.R. 377.
[86] [1975] R.T.R. 436.
[87] [1975] R.T.R. 142.
[88] [1975] R.T.R. 415.
[89] [1975] R.T.R. 136.
[90] [1979] R.T.R. 98.
[91] [1982] R.T.R. 167.
[92] [1971] R.T.R. 74.
[93] [1971] R.T.R. 15.
[94] 1970 S.L.T. 29.

first test as a non-starter and allow a second. In *R.* v. *Broomhead*[95] it was questioned whether the first (negative) breath test was properly done and conviction follow from the second (positive) breath test. In *Gwyn-Jones* v. *Sutherland*[96] the police required breath from a lady driver who collapsed and fell hitting her head. She was taken to hospital and on discharge was again required to give breath and failed. On trial for her later failure to provide a specimen she was acquitted. She should have been charged with her first failure to provide. In *R.* v. *Kaplan*[97] the bag burst, but as the granules had already shown a positive result the driver was rightly convicted. In *Price* v. *Davies*[98] it was noticed that the Alcotest device was wrongly assembled. The constable took it from the driver's mouth and adjusted it before giving it back to the driver who was unable to inflate it. It was held that the procedure should have been re-started with a new unsullied tube. In *Brennan* v. *Farrell*[99] a driver who inflated the bag in two breaths and refused to try again was acquitted of refusing a breath specimen because there was no statutory power to require a second specimen if the first was sufficient in quantity. The accused was discharged by compliance. There was however no reference to the detail of the manufacturer's instructions in that case. Where a bag is inflated in an irregular manner but in such a way as to give a positive recording the test is satisfactory and the driver should not be said to have failed to supply a specimen: *R.* v. *Holah.*[1] Disregard of the instructions to inflate the bag in one breath of not less than 10 nor more than 20 seconds does not matter if the result is positive: *Attorney General's Reference (No. 1 of 1978)*[2]: *Rendall* v. *Hooper*[3]: *Walker* v. *Lovell*[4]: *Sheridan* v. *Webster.*[5] In Scotland it was held to be not unreasonable for the police to require the breath test in one continuous breath of not less than 10 nor more than 20 seconds though there is no specific statutory warrant: *MacLeod* v. *Milligan*,[6] *Farrell* v. *Oakley.*[7] In all cases the device should be examined. The arrest of a driver who had inflated the bag "hardly at all" was held to be unlawful because the police had not thought it worth while examining the granules: *Spicer* v. *Holt*[8]: *Seniveratne* v. *Bishop.*[9] In

[95] [1975] R.T.R. 558.
[96] [1982] R.T.R. 102.
[97] [1978] R.T.R. 119.
[98] [1979] R.T.R. 204.
[99] 1969 J.C. 45.
[1] [1973] R.T.R. 74.
[2] [1978] R.T.R. 377.
[3] [1970] R.T.R. 252.
[4] [1975] R.T.R. 377.
[5] [1980] R.T.R. 349.
[6] 1970 S.L.T. 2.
[7] 1970 S.L.T. 2.
[8] [1976] R.T.R. 389.
[9] [1978] R.T.R. 92.

Stoddart v. *Balls*[10] where the driver failed twice to inflate the bag it was unnecessary for the constable to check the granules. Likewise in *Shepherd* v. *Kavulok*[11] where a driver, following an accident, gave several puffs but failed to inflate the bag and was allowed to try again and was unable to inflate the bag and was taken to the police station and afforded a third opportunity to give breath, it did not matter that on neither occasion were the granules examined, because, if positive, he would have been arrested and required to provide laboratory specimens, and if negative he would have been arrested for failure to provide breath with a similar outcome. In *R.* v. *Littell*[12] a driver gave a breath specimen in 10 puffs. He was allowed three further attempts but could not improve on that. The Court, canvassing the English and Scottish cases, agreed that such a response must be regarded as failure to provide a specimen of breath. In *Wilson* v. *Cummings*[13] a driver appealing against conviction for refusing a breath test was shown to have put the device to his lips blowing one or two short breaths which did not inflate the bag. Despite the police not examining the granules he had clearly failed to provide a specimen. In *Corp* v. *Dalton*[14] a driver blew into the bag for 10 seconds, stopped and continued till the bag was full, for 40 seconds in all. The granules did not change colour. He was arrested for failing to provide a breath specimen. His blood was analysed at 149mg/100ml. and it was argued that he had complied with the requirements of the breath test despite his disregard of the manufacturer's instructions. It was observed that disregard of these instructions will not produce a false positive but may produce a false negative. Where the manufacturer's instructions are not observed and the result is negative it is a question of fact and degree whether there has been failure to provide a breath specimen. In this particular case the dismissal of the charges against the driver could not be faulted. The Court in this case do not seem to have had in mind the disregard of manufacturer's instructions regarding recent drinking which *could* provide a false positive. However in the Scottish case of *Jeffrey* v. *McNeill*[15] where the police had reasonable cause to believe that the accused had been drinking in the past 20 minutes it was held

[10] [1977] R.T.R. 113.
[11] [1978] R.T.R. 85.
[12] [1981] R.T.R. 449.
[13] [1983] R.T.R. 347.
[14] [1983] R.T.R. 160.
[15] 1976 S.L.T. 134.

that this knowledge rendered it improper for them to exercise an immediate power of arrest. But where an accused in police custody claimed he had been drinking in the past two minutes the police were entitled to disregard this statement and go ahead: *Sloan* v. *Smith*.[16] In *R.* v. *Parsons*[17] a device showing what was described as corrosion of the wire gauze causing green discoloration was held to be acceptable because the police acted in good faith. Previously the police in England could not require a breath test from a driver in his own property when the police were trespassers: *Clowser* v. *Chaplin*[18]: *Morris* v. *Beardmore*[19] but by section 7(6) of the Road Traffic Act 1972 the police in a case where they have reasonable cause to suspect that an accident has involved injury or where they wish to arrest a person who has given a positive breath test or failed to give a specimen of breath for a breath test, may enter, if need be by force, the place where such person is or where they reasonably suspect him to be. This power somewhat modifies the *Beardmore* decision and is declared not to apply in Scotland where the police have this power at common law. Where an arrest has taken place the police may of course enter a house if need be to recapture the accused: *Hart* v. *Chief Constable of Kent*.[20] In circumstances not involving injury the police will no doubt approach those they wish to breath test under the implied licence which normally exists and try to make the requirement before that licence is withdrawn. Vulgar abuse will be insufficient to signify withdrawal: *Snook* v. *Mannion*[21]: *Gilham* v. *Breidenbach*.[22]

Accident

If an accident occurs owing to the presence of a vehicle on a road, see *Welch* v. *Phipps*,[23] or other public place, see *R.* v. *Vardy*,[24] a constable by virtue of section 7(2) of the 1972 Act may require any person who he has reasonable cause to believe (not suspect) was driving or attempting to drive or in charge of the vehicle at the time to provide a specimen of breath for a breath test. For the definition of an accident see p. 177. In such circum-

[16] 1977 S.L.T. (Notes) 27.
[17] [1972] R.T.R. 425.
[18] [1981] R.T.R. 317.
[19] [1980] R.T.R. 321.
[20] [1983] Crim. L.R. 117.
[21] [1982] R.T.R. 289.
[22] [1981] R.T.R. 481.
[23] [1955] 2 All E.R. 302.
[24] [1978] R.T.R. 202.

stances no suspicion of alcohol need be involved. Where the officer requiring the specimen was not shown to have the necessary belief that the accused had been driving, a prosecution failed: *Moss* v. *Jenkins*.[25] Where an accident occurred on the Scottish side of the Border it was competent in a Scottish prosecution for the police to follow the accused into England and to require a breath specimen there: *Binnie* v. *Donnelly*.[26] In a curious Scottish case where police found a driver alone in his car with the engine warm, fresh injuries to his head and damage to the car, it was held there was no evidence from which they could conclude than an accident had happened owing to the presence of a vehicle on the road.[26a]

Failure to provide breath specimen

A person who, without reasonable excuse, fails to provide a specimen of breath when required to do so in pursuance of section 7 of the 1972 Act shall be guilty of an offence. This is so despite the fact that the breath test procedure is optional to the police. If they choose to follow it and make a requirement, it must be complied with. A constable may (but need not) arrest a person without warrant who is shown from a breath test probably to have breath or blood alcohol above the prescribed level, or a person who has failed to provide a specimen of breath for a breath test, provided the constable has reasonable cause to suspect that he still has alcohol in his body.[26b] The previous case law dealing with faulty arrest will no longer necessarily be relevant. As under previous legislation "fail" includes "refuse." The driver who refused to wait for the Alcotest had refused the breath test: *R.* v. *Wagner*[27]: *R.* v. *Clarke*[28]: *Ely* v. *Marle*.[29] To agree to supply breath when a solicitor attends is to refuse: *Pettigrew* v. *Northumbria Police Authority*[30]: *Payne* v. *Diccox*.[31] Reasonable excuse would have to amount to physical or mental inability to provide a specimen. What is reasonable excuse will be for the courts to decide, and would seem to be a question of fact: *Leck* v. *Epsom Rural D.C.*[32]

[25] [1975] R.T.R. 25.
[26] 1981 S.L.T. 294.
[26a] *Merry* v. *Doherty* 1977 S.L.T. 117.
[26b] S.7(5) of the 1972 Act.
[27] [1970] R.T.R. 422.
[28] [1969] Crim. L.R. 441.
[29] [1977] R.T.R. 412.
[30] [1976] R.T.R. 177.
[31] [1980] R.T.R. 82.
[32] [1922] 1 K.B. 383.

Perhaps the fact that the accused suffered from a critical lung complaint, from an uncorrected hernia, or from chronic asthma, would serve, though the view has been expressed (*Havard* 1967) that asthmatics are used to breathing out against resistance and should be exceptionally proficient at inflating the bag. Certainly the disability would have to be backed up by medical evidence: *cf. R.* v. *Kelly*[33] (permanent tracheotomy) and *Hirst* v. *Wilson*[34] (a bronchitic condition which prevented sufficient exhalation). These conditions supplied "reasonable excuse" for not providing a specimen. The burden is on the prosecution to disprove reasonable excuse: *R.* v. *Clarke.*[35] Being too drunk to inflate the bag is obviously no excuse: *R.* v. *Chapman.*[36] Professional glass blowers may find the Act not unduly burdensome. A person may be acquitted of failing to provide a breath specimen and convicted of failing to give a laboratory specimen: *R.* v. *Haslam.*[37]

One of the more oppressive features of the drink-driving legislation was that while it is no offence to refuse to supply a breath specimen where reasonable excuse exists, the accused who wished to vindicate himself might have to submit to arrest and the indignity of police procedure followed by a court hearing before he could do so. This remains true except that arrest may not now be necessary in every case. In *R.* v. *Miles*[38] the police required a driver to provide breath.[38a] His wife interfered, sat on his knee, and made a nuisance of herself so that he failed to give a specimen and was rightly proceeded against. The police, in arresting a person failing to provide a breath specimen, have no concern with reasonable excuse. This is a matter entirely for the court. In Scotland the fact of refusal will have to be corroborated: *Farrell* v. *Concannon,*[39] but in general the requirement of corroboration need not be exceptionally burdensome. Apart from the essential elements in the offence any other facts being procedural in character may be proved by the evidence of a single witness: *McLeod* v. *Nicol*[40]: *Torrance* v. *Thaw.*[41] There is no requirement to warn a

[33] [1972] R.T.R. 447.
[34] [1970] R.T.R. 67.
[35] [1969] 1 W.L.R. 1109.
[36] [1969] 2 W.L.R. 1004.
[37] [1972] R.T.R. 297.
[38] [1979] R.T.R. 509.
[38a] *Bunyard* v. *Hayes*, *The Times*, November 3, 1984.
[39] 1957 J.C. 12.
[40] 1970 S.L.T. 304.
[41] 1970 S.L.T. 304.

driver of the consequences of failing to provide a breath specimen. In one case where a warning was given the driver claimed to have been "pressured" but he was held to have been validly convicted. For a driver on being required to provide a breath specimen to run to his house in order to obtain drink is to attempt to defeat the course of justice: *R. v. Britton*,[42] as well as to refuse the test.

As under previous legislation the conduct of the breath test is in the hands of the police constable. Where in the constable's judgment the Alcotest indicates that the proportion of alcohol exceeds the prescribed limit (*i.e.* where the granules turn green beyond the yellow line) the constable may arrest the accused without warrant and proceed to the next stage. Where the breath test is properly carried out and the granules do not turn green beyond the line, the accused under previous legislation could not be further proceeded against and had to be released or dealt with as for the impairment offence. For a case where it was questioned whether the granules *had* turned green beyond the line see *R. v. Sittingbourne Justices ex parte Parsley*.[43] Whether a driver who survives a breath test is immune from further proceedings, is uncertain since the breath test procedure is in any event optional to the police, but having cleared that hurdle it would seem unfair if the police were then to require submission to instrumental breath analysis. The interpretation of the Alcotest in borderline cases is not easy and could perhaps be variously assessed. Since the matter is for the police constable the accused is not entitled to examine the Alcotest device: *R. v. Grant*,[44] though in most cases he is in practice allowed to do so. In some courts the device is produced as an exhibit at the trial, though the reading on the tube may long since have deteriorated, and for this reason, among others, many police forces routinely destroy the tubes, a procedure approved in *Miller v. Howe*.[45] Although the device is of little assistance after an interval for determining whether or not it registered a positive reading, the accused may have an interest to show whether it was obstructed or defective, and there is much to be said for retaining the device until the hearing of the case. In one case, *R. v. Parsons*,[46] the Police gave the tubes to the accused. English law no longer insists on production of the best evidence where physical

[42] [1973] R.T.R. 502.
[43] [1978] R.T.R. 153.
[44] [1980] R.T.R. 280.
[45] [1969] 3 All E.R. 451.
[46] [1972] R.T.R. 425.

objects are concerned.[47] In *R.* v. *Orrell*[48] it was held that absence of the bottle and urine specimen was not fatal to conviction. Scottish courts still require that such an object should be produced where it is practicable and convenient to do so: *Walker* v. *Walker*.[49]

At hospital as a patient

The foregoing provisions for requiring a breath test and the power to arrest a person failing to provide a specimen or showing a positive result do not apply when the person in question is at a hospital as a patient. In that event section 9 of the Road Traffic Act 1972 provides that he shall not be required to provide a specimen of breath for a breath test or to provide a specimen for laboratory test unless the medical practitioner in immediate charge of his case has been notified. It is not wrong to obtain consent from the doctor in charge to both breath and laboratory specimens at the same time: *Ratledge* v. *Oliver*.[50] If such a requirement for breath is made it must be for provision of a specimen at the hospital and if the medical practitioner objects on the ground that the requirement or the provision of the specimen, or in the case of a blood or urine specimen, the warning which accompanies it, would be prejudicial to the proper care and treatment of the patient, the requirement shall not be made. Arrest is not appropriate where the person is in hospital: *Goodley* v. *Kelly*.[51] The warning should be proved, not just assumed to have been given; *Foulkes* v. *Baker*.[52] Hospital is defined as an institution which provides medical or surgical treatment for in-patients or out-patients, but does not include an ambulance on its way to hospital: *Hollingsworth* v. *Howard*[53]; *Manz* v. *Miln*.[54] However taking a breath test in an ambulance at hospital while awaiting the doctor was improper: *R.* v. *Crowley*.[55] Where a driver was taken to hospital after being required to provide a laboratory specimen because of a head

---

[47] Cross, *Evidence* (3rd ed.) p. 11.
[48] [1972] R.T.R. 14.
[49] *Law of Evidence*, p. 445.
[50] [1974] R.T.R. 394.
[51] [1973] R.T.R. 125.
[52] [1975] R.T.R. 50.
[53] [1974] R.T.R. 58.
[54] 1977 J.C. 78.
[55] [1977] R.T.R. 153.

injury he became an out-patient and it was wrong to go ahead to take that specimen without observing the correct hospital procedure: *MacNeill* v. *England*.[56] On the other hand a patient released from hospital for a day clear of treatment could be considered a free agent: *Attorney General's Reference (No. 1 of 1976)*.[57] Where a prescribed-level driver discharged himself from hospital after validly giving the first of two laboratory specimens of urine it was held that the second could be given notwithstanding that he was no longer a patient, and he was convicted: *Edwards* v. *Davies*.[58] The police are generally able to identify the doctor in immediate charge: *Jones* v. *Brazil*[59] and may give evidence that the doctor did not object: *Burn* v. *Kernohan*.[60] The request to the doctor for permission to take laboratory tests may be made in the patient's hearing: *Oxford* v. *Lowton*.[61] Since instrumental breath analysis is only undertaken at police stations an analysis of breath cannot be carried out on a patient at hospital. It is a question of fact and circumstance when a person ceases to be a patient, see *Bosley* v. *Long*,[62] *Bourlet* v. *Porter*[63] and *Watt* v. *MacNeill*.[64] In Scotland the constable need not explain to the hospital doctor that a warning as to consequences of failure to supply a specimen will be involved: *McGuinness* v. *Thaw*[65] disapproving *R.* v. *Knightley*.[66] In *Cunliffe* v. *Bleasdale*[67] a patient agreed to provide a laboratory specimen but absconded before doing so. Under the former rules he could not be convicted, but would probably be convicted of failing to provide a specimen under the present rules. Provision, partly at hospital and partly after discharge, as a private individual was competent in *Edwards* v. *Davies*.[68] Under the provisions which obtained from 1967 the description of the prescribed-level offence precluded the advancing of any evidence except the result of a laboratory test in proof of the accused's blood-alcohol level. Now that the prescribed-level offence has been simplified and that restriction removed it would seem to be possible for evidence of a positive breath test to be given as an indication whether the proportion of alcohol in the driver's breath or blood is likely to exceed

[56] 1971 S.L.T. 103.
[57] [1977] R.T.R. 284.
[58] [1982] R.T.R. 279.
[59] [1970] R.T.R. 449.
[60] [1973] R.T.R. 82.
[61] [1978] R.T.R. 237.
[62] [1970] R.T.R. 432.

[63] [1973] R.T.R. 293.
[64] 1980 S.L.T. 178.
[65] 1974 S.L.T. 237.
[66] [1971] R.T.R. 409.
[67] [1973] R.T.R. 90.
[68] [1982] R.T.R. 279.

the prescribed level. For an example see *Lomas* v. *Bowler*.[69] It
may be an oversight that this is not specifically forbidden.

LABORATORY TESTS

Under the law prior to 1983 a person arrested for providing a
positive breath test or for failure to provide a breath specimen
could be required to provide blood or urine samples for laboratory
testing. Such a person would first have had an opportunity to provide a confirmatory breath test at the police station (a safeguard
now dispensed with) and the whole procedure had to be completed
at the same police station: *Pascoe* v. *Nicholson*,[70] not at a doctor's
house: *Cruickshank* v. *Moncur*.[71] But in Scotland an averment
that after arrest the accused was taken to a police station may not
be required, it is plainly inferred: *McIlhargey* v. *Herron*.[72] Where
no doctor was available at the first police station it was acceptable
in a Scottish case to proceed to the second police station: *Milne* v.
McDonald.[73] It was necessary to warn such a person initially that
failure to comply with a request for laboratory specimens could
render him liable to fine and disqualification: *R.* v. *Brush*[74]; *R.* v.
Chippendale.[75] As to the effect of a defective warning see *Bryant*
v. *Morris*[76] and *O'Sharkey* v. *Smith*.[77] The time of giving a blood
or urine specimen was the time of giving the specimen, not the
time of giving consent. A person who expressed willingness but
from whom the doctor failed to obtain a specimen would nevertheless be treated as refusing to provide a specimen. Blood would
have to be taken by a doctor but if the accused helped by guiding
the needle this is still taken by the doctor: *R.* v. *Burdekin*.[78]
Absence of consent in England would be likely, and in Scotland
would be certain, to vitiate the procedure: *R.* v. *Palfrey*,[79] *R.* v.
Sadler.[80] No guidance was given as to the size of the specimen.
The original directions called for the specimen being divided, a
part given to the driver, and the remainder retained for analysis.
Under the old procedure the driver had to ask for his part of the
sample: *R.* v. *Byers*.[81] Sometimes a part was kept in case a repli-

[69] [1984] Crim. L.R. 178.
[70] [1981] R.T.R. 421.
[71] 1971 S.L.T. (Sh. Ct.) 14.
[72] 1972 S.L.T. 185.
[73] 1971 S.L.T. 291.
[74] [1968] 3 All E.R. 467.
[75] [1973] R.T.R. 236.
[76] [1972] R.T.R. 214.
[77] 1982 S.L.T. 91.
[78] [1976] R.T.R. 27.
[79] [1970] 2 All E.R. 12.
[80] [1970] 2 All E.R. 12.
[81] [1971] R.T.R. 383.

cate analysis was called for. Where there was dispute as to whether the blood specimen produced was taken from the accused, blood grouping tests have been used: See the case of *Hughie Green*.[82]

Although a 1956 Government leaflet ("The New Law of Drinking and Driving") described a method of giving capillary blood, the universal practice quickly became for specimens to be taken by venepuncture. In *Rushton* v. *Higgins*[83] the offer of capillary blood was held to be a refusal to provide blood. And following some silly suggestions by drivers the site from which blood could be taken was held to be for the doctor to decide: *Solesbury* v. *Pugh*.[84] It is not wrong for the police to ask the driver to sign a form of consent to blood tests before summoning a doctor, but refusal to sign is not necessarily refusal to provide a specimen: *Hier* v. *Read*.[85] On being required to provide blood where both the police doctor and the driver's doctor were present and willing to take a blood specimen, it was held not to be refusal for the driver to require that his own doctor took the specimen. He was imposing a condition capable of being instantly satisfied: *Bayliss* v. *Thames Valley Police*.[86] If blood is refused or cannot be provided or if the doctor's will not turn out: *R.* v. *Paduch*,[87] the driver is to be asked to provide two specimens of urine within an hour, the first of which would be disregarded *i.e.* thrown away: *R.* v. *Welsby*[88] and should urine not be provided, the accused will again be asked for a blood specimen. If the accused makes it clear that he is not going to supply urine there is no need to wait for an hour: *Jones* v. *Roberts*.[89] A second urine specimen provided just after expiry of the hour was acceptable in *Roney* v. *Matthews*[90]; *Tudhope* v. *Stevenson*.[91] An hour is the period the police must wait, in the absence of surrender, before declaring failure. Should there be a failure to supply both blood and urine the correct order and timing of these requests is essential for conviction. And the requirements of the law cannot be extended: a third specimen of urine is not admissible in a prescribed-level case: *Gabrielson* v. *Richards*.[92] But where the second urine specimen is lost because of the accused's action in an impairment case it is permissible to use a third specimen for analy-

---

[82] November 29, 1977, Richmond Magistrates Court: *Sunday Express* November 30, 1977. See also *Hall* v. *Allan* 1984 S.L.T. 199 (consenting to provide a specimen).

[83] [1972] R.T.R. 456.
[84] [1969] 2 All E.R. 1171.
[85] [1978] R.T.R. 114.
[86] [1978] R.T.R. 328.
[87] [1973] R.T.R. 493.

[88] [1972] R.T.R. 301.
[89] [1973] R.T.R. 26.
[90] [1975] R.T.R. 273.
[91] 1980 S.L.T. 94.
[92] [1976] R.T.R. 223.

sis: *R.* v. *John Moore*.[93] Where a person stole a urine specimen the procedure was vitiated: *R.* v. *Rothery*.[94] If the urine specimen is accidentally lost before delivery to the police it has not been validly provided: *Ross* v. *Hodges*.[95] And where a blood specimen was accidentally lost when the doctor was dividing it the driver had discharged his obligation: *Beck* v. *Watson*.[96] Similarly where the police by misjudgment threw away a second urine specimen as insufficient, the accused had discharged his obligation: *Poole* v. *Lockwood*[97]; *R.* v. *Hyams*.[98] Even though the accused has not emptied his bladder on giving the first urine sample, an analysis of the second (which is unlikely to be an accurate representation of his body-fluid alcohol, *cf.* p. 80) is acceptable in law: *R.* v. *Radcliffe*.[99] Where the police directed the motorist to urinate, stop and then two minutes later continue in what was essentially a single transaction, it was held that the analysis was not admissible: *Prosser* v. *Dickeson*.[1]

The accused must be given part of the specimen of blood or urine if he requests it, and what is given should be sufficient for analysis. Even a partly clotted blood specimen may be acceptable: *Nicholson* v. *Watts*,[2] but it must be capable of analysis with ordinary skill and equipment: *Nugent* v. *Hobday*.[3] Should he be in custody the sample may be provided by being put amongst the accused's belongings: *R.* v. *Colin James*.[4]

Although the intention of the recent changes in the law is to make instrumental breath analysis the principal means of ascertaining the driver's body-fluid alcohol level, laboratory tests will still be relied upon when the device is not available, not in good working order, or without its trained operator. This can happen where the police believe that for medical reasons a specimen of breath should not be required or cannot be provided, or in an impairment case, where the police have been advised by a doctor that drugs may be involved, or on February 29, each leap year (when the Intoximeter at least will be out of commission since its calendar makes no provision for leap years). In these circumstances and at the option of the accused in the case provided for by

[93] [1978] R.T.R. 384.
[94] [1976] R.T.R. 550.
[95] [1975] R.T.R. 55.
[96] [1980] R.T.R. 90.
[97] [1981] R.T.R. 285.
[98] [1973] R.T.R. 68.
[99] [1977] R.T.R. 99.
[1] [1982] R.T.R. 96.
[2] [1973] R.T.R. 208.
[3] [1973] R.T.R. 41.
[4] [1974] R.T.R. 117.

section 8(6) where the lower of two breath specimens contains no more than 50 microgrammes of alcohol per 100ml the procedure by way of laboratory tests may be followed through and the breath analysis shall not be used. It is to be noted however that in their re-enacted form these rules for laboratory tests are more closely fenced. The accused need not be under arrest; a warning is to be given in connection with every request for breath, blood or urine: the driver has the option to claim laboratory tests if his breath alcohol falls within the specified limits, but it is the police who decide whether blood or urine shall be given, subject to any medical opinion that blood cannot or should not be taken. The test is to be administered at or near the place where the requirement was made and covers both drivers and persons said to be or to have been in charge. Subject to these changes it seems that the previous case law will still apply. The rules however about post-driving drinking have been given statutory form and these are described at p. 206.

INSTRUMENTAL BREATH ANALYSIS

The principal innovation brought about by the Transport Act 1981 was the introduction of instrumental breath analysis which is obviously intended to replace analysis of blood and urine in the great majority of cases. Perhaps the most significant change compared with the previous procedure is that the instrument will give an immediate print-out, thus obviating the delays which hitherto were involved before the analytical results of blood or urine specimens could be obtained. The detailed arrangements are set out alongside the re-enacted provisions for breath tests which have been described above, and form a code of procedure which the police may follow in sequence having established either a positive breath test or a failure to supply a specimen for a breath test (if they decide to allow a screening breath test at all) and whether the suspect has been arrested or not. There is no longer any requirement for a confirmatory screening breath test at the police station. Section 8 of the Road Traffic Act 1972 now permits a constable in the course of an investigation whether a person has committed the impairment or the prescribed level offence to require that person to provide two specimens of breath for analysis or to provide a specimen of blood or urine for a laboratory test. The requirement for the breath specimens can be made only at a police station. The

requirement for blood or urine can be made only at a police station
or at a hospital, and the former only if, (1) the constable has cause
to believe that for medical reasons breath cannot or should not be
provided, or (2) the approved breath testing instrument is not
available or it is impracticable to use it, or (3) in the case of a suspected impairment offence where medical advice indicates to the
police that drugs may be involved. In the latter case the requirement may be made or made again notwithstanding that the person
may already have provided or been required to provide two specimens of breath. At a hospital, subject to the protection for hospital patients already described, a constable may require the
provision of a specimen of blood or urine. Elsewhere if the police
in pursuance of section 8 require blood or urine, the decision
whether the specimen is to be one or other is reserved to the constable making the requirement, not as in the past to the suspect.
However where a medical practitioner considers that for medical
reasons a specimen of blood cannot or should not be taken, the
specimen shall be of urine. This establishes the order of preference
of the legislators as breath followed by blood followed by urine. A
simplified version of the previous rather complicated provisions in
recognition of the difference between taking a specimen of con-
stantly circulating blood and of intermittently accumulating urine
(*cf.* p. 80) remains, in that a specimen of urine is to be provided
within one hour of the requirement and (as the statute quaintly
puts it) after the provision of a previous specimen of urine which
presumably is to be disregarded. The suspect must of course consent to the taking of breath, blood or urine. Blood can only be
taken by a medical practitioner.

One of the differences between analysis of body fluids and
instrumental analysis of breath lies in the inability of the machine
to replicate the strict mathematical precautions adopted by analysts in the laboratory to guard against too high a figure being
reported. As a matter of police practice prosecutions will therefore
probably not be undertaken unless the breath analysis figure
reaches 40 microgrammes/100ml. Furthermore to accommodate
the possibility of some variation of blood/breath ratio (no two consecutive breath samples will be absolutely identical in composition, having come from marginally different levels in the lungs,
see p. 32) it is declared by section 8(6) that of the two specimens of
breath provided for instrumental analysis, the lower shall be used
and the other disregarded; but if the specimen with the lower proportion of alcohol contains no more than 50 microgrammes of

alcohol per 100ml of breath the suspect may claim that it should be replaced by a laboratory specimen.[4a]

If such a specimen is then provided neither specimen of breath shall be used. In practice of course this means that a suspect whose lower analysis falls between 35 and 50 microgrammes may opt for a blood specimen to be taken instead. A constable requiring a person to provide a specimen of breath, blood or urine in pursuance of this section of the Act is obliged to warn him that failure to provide the specimen may render him liable to prosecution.[4b] No particular form of warning is prescribed. Under the previous laboratory test provisions the court had a discretion, in the event of failure to deliver the warning, to acquit or dismiss the charge, but no such power is given by section 8(8). It remains to be seen what effect if any this would have upon a prosecution. Curiously, there is no specific requirement that the police should inform the suspect of his right to exercise this option, but it is certain that they will do so. Where blood or urine specimens are provided the specimen is to be divided into two parts at the time of provision, if the suspect then requires it, and one part is to be supplied to the suspect and the other retained for analysis. The implication is that the part delivered will be sufficiently large for analysis. If part is not delivered when requested, evidence of the proportion of alcohol or drugs in the specimen shall not be admissible. If the suspect does not request a part of the specimen at the time it will be too late to ask later, and the evidence of analysis will be admissible. There is of course no question of supplying the accused with a breath specimen. A person who, without reasonable excuse, fails to provide a specimen of breath, blood or urine for analysis in pursuance of section 8 shall be guilty of an offence.

Where such a requirement has been made a person required to provide such a specimen may thereafter be detained at a police station until it appears to the constable that were that person then driving or attempting to drive a motor vehicle on a road he would not be committing either the impairment or the prescribed-level

---

[4a] As a result of adverse newspaper publicity concerning the Intoximeter the Home Office decided that, in England and Wales only, for a period of six months from April 16, 1984 anyone who gives a breath analysis specimen over the 50 milligramme range shall administratively be allowed the option to give a blood/urine specimen as well. During that period further investigations are to be carried out to demonstrate the reliability of the Intoximeter. See Statement by Mr. Hurd in the House of Commons on March 26, 1984.

[4b] The choice need not relate to the individual but may be made by the constable for policy reasons: *Pine* v. *Collacott: The Times*, July 30, 1984.

offence. However, such a person shall not be detained if it seems there is no likelihood of his driving or attempting to drive whilst his ability to do so is impaired or whilst he exceeds the prescribed blood-alcohol level. In dealing with a person who has taken drugs the police are required to take and act upon medical advice as to the likelihood of such a person's continuing impairment. Reasonable excuse for failure to provide a laboratory specimen would have to amount to something like physical or mental inability to provide the specimen to be an effective defence *R.* v. *Lennard.*[5] The police may agree to allow an accused person to contact his solicitor: *Brown* v. *Ridge.*[6] Conditional acceptance, or agreement to provide a specimen only when a solicitor is present, amounts to refusal: *Law* v. *Stephens*[7]; *R.* v. *Seaman*[8]; *Payne* v. *Dixon.*[9] Provision of a late specimen of urine may not render the specimen inadmissible: *Roney* v. *Matthews*[10]; *Tudhope* v. *Stevenson*[11] but if it is insufficient in quantity it may not be regarded as provision of a specimen: *R.* v. *Coward.*[12] A driver who responded "please yourself" to a request for a specimen of blood or urine was refusing: *MacPhail* v. *Forbes.*[13] In *Hogg* v. *Lockhart*[14] an accused could not supply a second urine specimen and was required to give blood which he refused to do by reason of a powerful aversion to blood and a fear of needles. He was held to have reasonable excuse, having proved his aversion to the satisfaction of the court. See also *Alcock* v. *Reid.*[15] It is refusal if the accused agrees to provide a specimen but only in some particular fashion: *Rushton* v. *Higgins.*[16] But see *Bayliss* v. *Thames Valley Police Chief Constable.*[17] Religious scruples: *R.* v. *Najram*,[18] or other sincere beliefs cannot amount to reasonable excuse for failing to provide a laboratory specimen *R.* v. *Jones.*[19] Nor can the accused's belief that he has committed no offence: *Williams* v. *Osborne.*[20]

A special problem arises in connection with failure to supply a specimen of breath for analysis to the Intoximeter or Camic machine. As already explained (p. 96) the machines are so arranged that some effort is needed to blow the required volume into them to ensure that the specimens of breath provided are

[5] [1973] 1 W.L.R. 483.
[6] [1979] R.T.R. 136.
[7] (1971) 115 S.J. 369.
[8] [1971] R.T.R. 456.
[9] [1979] Crim. L.R. 670.
[10] [1975] R.T.R. 273.
[11] 1980 S.L.T. (Notes) 94.
[12] [1976] R.T.R. 425.
[13] 1975 S.L.T. (Sh. Ct.) 48.
[14] 1973 S.L.T. (Sh. Ct.) 40.
[15] [1979] Crim L.R. 534.
[16] [1972] R.T.R. 456.
[17] [1978] R.T.R. 328.
[18] [1973] R.T.R. 451.
[19] [1974] R.T.R. 332.
[20] [1975] Crim. L.R. 166.

likely to come from the lower part of the lungs. As in previous legislation the definition of failing to provide a specimen includes refusing to provide a specimen. Where a motorist fails to provide a specimen of breath therefore the possible explanations include (a) that he is deliberately refusing to provide it, (b) that the machine's pressure switch is defective, (c) that he is too drunk to be able to provide it, (d) that for some other reason he is unable to provide it. Section 8(7) makes it an offence if the motorist without reasonable excuse fails to provide a specimen (whether of breath, blood or urine) when required to do so in pursuance of that section. The matter of reasonable excuse is dealt with at pages 209 *et seq*. In the remaining cases therefore the question is likely to be whether the failure to provide the breath specimen is due to fault in the man or in the machine. Evidence will be given by the police of how it appeared to them that the motorist was trying to provide the specimen, and no doubt as to how the machine functioned both before and after the motorist made his attempt. It is however unfortunate that in a sizeable proportion of cases the evidence will not be of a sophisticated scientific nature, but rather of the "Yes I did" "No you didn't" variety.

The requirement of providing a specimen of breath for a breath test or for analysis was extended in scope when its definition was by section 59 of the Transport Act 1982 augmented to the effect not only that the specimen should be sufficient to enable the test or analysis to be carried out, but also that it should be provided in such a way as to enable the objective of the test or analysis to be satisfactorily achieved. Where the test or analysis is inconclusive it appears that there has been no proper provision of the specimen.

Where consecutive breath analyses produced markedly different readings the question will be raised whether the explanation lies with man or machine. At present it can only be said that the greater the discrepancy the more likely is this to be due to machine failure. Where, however, the Camic machine is apparently performing as it should, the Scottish Courts have held that there is no need for positive independent evidence from the Crown that the machine is functioning properly.[21]

[21] *Tudhope* v. *McAllister* 1984 S.L.T. 395.

CHAPTER 11

ARREST

Under the previous law a constable in uniform had power to arrest, without warrant, a person committing the impairment offence or in charge while impaired. In regard to the prescribed-level offence a constable in uniform had similar power to arrest a driver or person in charge who had either failed to provide a screening breath test when lawfully required to do so, or when such a person had provided a positive breath test. The procedure of requiring laboratory tests could however only be commenced against a pursuer who had been arrested, and it was one of the criticisms of these provisions that they exacerbated the public's confrontation with the police, and failed to provide for the motorist who was perfectly willing to go quietly through the procedures as requested.

Doubtless in response to this criticism by the Blennerhasset Committee the amended provisions of sections 5(5) and 7(5) of the Road Traffic Act 1972 now allow the police discretion to arrest, without warrant, a driver or a person who has been a driver, or a person in charge, or person whom a constable has reasonable cause to suspect of having committed the impairment offence, or to arrest such a person who has given a positive breath test, or who has failed to provide a specimen of breath for a breath test when required to do so under section 7 of the 1972 Act, provided the constable has reasonable cause to suspect that that person continues to have alcohol in his body, and the person is not at hospital as a patient. The relaxation provided by these amendments means that the police need only arrest those who appear unwilling to co-operate, and it will no longer be possible to fault a prosecution because the police failed to make clear that they were arresting the motorist, or because they arrested on the wrong basis, as in *Smith* v. *Ross*.[1]

---

[1] 1983 S.L.T. 491.

Where a driver is arrested he should be told the reason for his arrest: *Christie* v. *Leachinsky*[2]; *Reid* v. *Nixon*[3]; *Harris* v. *Adair*[4]; *R.* v. *Holah*,[5] if it is possible to get through to him: *R.* v. *Gordon*.[6] If the police act in good faith the arrest is not invalidated because it turns out that the accused is deaf and did not understand: *Wheatley* v. *Lodge*.[7] Nor is an arrest rendered unlawful merely because the accused is subsequently released and not further proceeded against: *Wiltshire* v. *Barrett*.[8] Scottish procedure in impairment cases requires that the accused should be cautioned and charged, his consent to clinical examination must be obtained, he should be informed of his right to independent medical assistance, the clinical examination should be conducted in private, there should be no interrogation on the merits by the police and nothing inadvertently elicited by the police doctor must be communicated to the police. Failure to caution and charge the accused before clinical examination will normally render the medical evidence inadmissible: *Gallacher* v. *H.M. Adv.*[9] In *Siddiqui* v. *Swain*[10] the police interviewed and subsequently arrested a person they believed to have been the driver of a car which had crashed earlier the same day without explanation of their belief that he had been drinking. On appeal the conviction was set aside because of their failure to explain. In *Grant* v. *Gorman*[11] a tractor driver driving too fast in a public-house car park was stopped by the police and asked for breath. He refused and attacked the constable, but reinforcements were called in and he was arrested for failing to provide a laboratory specimen. He was then taken to hospital, treated and discharged and eventually gave blood at the police station. It was held that the police failure to explain his arrest was not material under these circumstances: he must have known the reason. See also *R.* v. *Mayer*.[12] In *R.* v. *Birtwhistle*[13] a driver who had an accident and went to report it to the police smelling of drink was invited to remain while they checked his story, but he ran away. Subsequently he argued that he had been illegally arrested and that this vitiated the procedures, but this was held not to be so. In *Lambert* v. *Roberts*[14] a motorist was pursued by the police on to

[2] [1947] A.C. 573.
[3] 1948 J.C. 68.
[4] 1947 J.C. 116.
[5] [1973] R.T.R. 74.
[6] [1970] R.T.R. 125.
[7] [1971] R.T.R. 22.
[8] [1966] 1 Q.B. 312.
[9] 1963 S.L.T. 217.
[10] [1979] R.T.R. 454.
[11] [1980] R.T.R. 119.
[12] [1975] R.T.R. 411.
[13] [1980] R.T.R. 342.
[14] [1981] R.T.R. 113.

private property and required to give breath. It was held that the requirement of breath and the arrest which followed were unlawful and he must be acquitted. On the contrary in *Pamplin* v. *Fraser*[15] a driver showing a reversing light while driving forwards was followed into what turned out to be private property where the police smelt drink and required breath and laboratory specimens. The police had a licence to be there, and it was held that the procedures and the arrest were lawful. In *R.* v. *Allen*[16] after an accident the police came to the accused's private property asking for a breath test as they had reasonable grounds for suspecting that he had been the driver. He immediately ordered them off his property. From then their licence was withdrawn and all that followed was unlawful. In *Clowser* v. *Chaplin*[17] following an accident police went to the accused's house and were told to stay at the door. The accused appeared in his dressing gown and agreed he had been the driver but refused breath, and on being arrested a fight began. It was held that an arrest by a trespassing constable was not lawful in England, and this was confirmed in the House of Lords where Lord Diplock observed "the many loopholes in the law that the ingenuity of defence lawyers has brought to light are in my view doing more to bring the criminal law of this country into disrepute than any other legislation." In *Snook* v. *Mannion*[18] the police followed a drinking driver into his private gateway where he left his car, threw his keys into a flower bed, and abused the police when they asked for breath, and on his failure to provide it he was arrested. It was held that the abuse had not amounted to withdrawal of their licence to be on his land, and they were justified in their procedures. Consent may be inferred from conduct: *Faulkner* v. *Willetts*.[19] In *Gilham* v. *Breidenbach*[20] the police followed a driver without lights to his house. As he walked up the garden path the police asked for breath. He replied in terms of coarse abuse which however did not withdraw their licence, and the arrest which followed was valid. In *Revel* v. *Jordan*[21]—a prescribed-level case—the accused drove erratically until stopped by the police for a positive breath test and arrested. At the police station he was

[15] [1981] R.T.R. 494.
[16] [1981] R.T.R. 410.
[17] [1981] R.T.R. 317.
[18] [1982] R.T.R. 321.
[19] [1982] R.T.R. 159.
[20] [1982] R.T.R. 328.
[21] [1983] R.T.R. 497.

given the confirmatory breath test and was allowed an extra breath test, but the arrest was valid. It was held to be open to the police to allow this latitude. In *Hart* v. *Chief Constable of Kent*[22] a driver who hit a lamp standard was traced to his home where the police asked for breath and the test being positive, arrested him. He pulled back into his private porch and ordered the police to leave. It was held that the arrest being lawful, the police were entitled to follow it through. But at a time when there was no power to arrest a person suspected of the in-charge variant of the prescribed-level offence it was held that a purported arrest was invalid: *Waters* v. *Bigmore*.[23] Until recently it was said in Scotland that a person was either arrested or not arrested and there was no in-between state: cf. *Dunne* v. *Clinton*[24] and *Spicer* v. *Holt*.[25] However not only has section 2 of Criminal Justice (Scotland) Act 1980 produced a statutory type of detention for questioning, but section 11 of the Road Traffic Act 1972 permits the police to detain a person at a police station following a requirement to provide breath, blood or urine until it appears to the police that, were that person then driving or attempting to drive a motor vehicle, he would not be committing a drink-driving offence. Since there is now no necessity to arrest a person to require breath, blood or urine this type of detention can constitute something short of arrest in the usual sense. It is also provided that if there is no likelihood of the accused driving or attempting to drive while impaired or over the prescribed level he may be released, and that if a question of drugs is involved the police shall consult and be guided by a medical practitioner on any question which arises in this context.

The decision of *Morris* v. *Beardmore*[26] that an Englishman's home is his castle has been partially reversed by the provisions of sections 5(5) and 7(6) of the Road Traffic Act 1972 which allow a constable to require entry to a driver's home to arrest him in impairment cases (driving or in-charge) and in prescribed-level cases where an accident has happened and the constable reasonably suspects that injury was caused to some other person. These provisions apply to England only because in Scotland the police have common law powers of arrest in such circumstances. The Scot's home never was his castle.[27]

[22] [1983] R.T.R. 484.
[23] [1981] R.T.R. 356.
[24] (1930) I.R. 366.
[25] [1976] R.T.R. 389.
[26] [1980] R.T.R. 321.
[27] *Keane* 1983 S.C.C.R. 277.

For hospital procedure where arrest is prescribed see p. 190.

There may be situations where it is acceptable for a motorist to be arrested under separate statutory provisions at the same time: *R.* v. *Hatton*.[28] The principle of *Scott* v. *Baker*[29] having been undermined by the amendment of the statutory procedures, it is now established that there can be drink-driving convictions even where the arrest has been unlawful, or indeed where a suspect has refused a breath test not having been driving at all.[30]

[28] [1978] Crim. L.R. 95.
[29] [1969] 1 Q.B. 659.
[30] *Bunyard* v. *Hayes*, *The Times*, November 3, 1984.

CHAPTER 12

ALCOHOL CONSUMED

The impairment offence relates to a person unfit to drive through drink or drugs and would seem to cover a person driving or attempting to drive in that state whether by deliberate or accidental intoxication, and to be an offence of strict liability. The prescribed-level offence on the other hand is limited to a person driving or attempting to drive after consuming alcohol in excess of a prescribed limit. Although it has been described—in *Att.-Gen.'s Ref. (No. 1 of 1975)*[1]:—as an absolute offence the prescribed-level offence does require consumption of alcohol which can be deliberate or sometimes unknowing. In the latter case where a person is unknowingly affected by alcohol he may still be guilty of the prescribed-level offence, at least until the state at which his predicament becomes obvious. Such a situation might come about where for reasons of misguided high spirits a driver's drink is "laced" without the driver's knowledge, particularly where the additive is tasteless colourless vodka—see p. 213. So far such cases have been decided in England only on the basis of special reasons for not disqualifying the driver (see Chapter 13) but it may be that in some circumstances a driver may wish to attempt a complete defence on the merits. In a Scottish case *P.F.* v. *Richmond*[2] a driver was acquitted of the prescribed-level offence where a teetotaller had been given a "lime" which truly contained alcohol. The appeal court observed that "knowing consumption of drink was essential." In *R.* v. *Mersom*[3] a driver, inexperienced in spirits, asked for a small whisky topped up with ginger ale and was served "a treble brandy." This provided special reasons for not disqualifying. His blood alcohol was surprisingly high at 132mg/100ml. In *R.* v. *Krebs*[4] a careful driver who ordered a Harp lager (followed by four

---

[1] [1975] R.T.R. 473. See *Tudhope* v. *Grubb* 1983 S.C.C.R. 350 (defence of necessity).
[2] Campbeltown Sheriff Court: Justiciary Appeal Court: *Scotsman*, November 21, 1980.
[3] [1973] R.T.R. 140.
[4] [1977] R.T.R. 406.

more) for which he was served four Lowenbrau (of almost double alcoholic strength) had shown special reasons for not having his licence endorsed. Compare the examples cited at p. 214. Finally in *Pugsley* v. *Hunter*[5] it was said that the onus was on the accused: he must show that the extra drink caused the offence. In clear cases this might be done without expert evidence, but in the more doubtful cases the Court would value the guidance of the expert. There must of course be *evidence* that the drink was laced: *Flewitt* v. *Horvath*.[6]

ALCOHOL CONSUMED AFTER DRIVING

The prescribed-level offence seeks to penalise a driver who by consuming alcohol raises his blood-alcohol level above the prescribed limit. Where a driver is shown to have taken drink after the completion of driving and before the sampling of his body fluids it follows that his condition, while driving, must have been due to what he consumed before, but not after driving, and the analysis figure would then reflect the aggregate of the pre-driving and the post-driving figures. In the Scottish case of *Wood* v. *Brown*[7] confirmed by *H.M. Adv.* v. *Lawrie*[8] it was held to be wrong for the Court to disregard the drink consumed after ceasing to drive, and in pre-scribed-level cases it then became possible to offer a defence which attempted to prove that the additional drink taken accounted for the excess alcohol above the prescribed limit so that the level at the time of driving was shown to have been below that limit. Practical examples of such a defence are set out at p. 122. The onus of introducing the defence rests on the accused, and the standard of proof is balance of probability: *Ritchie* v. *Pirie*.[9] Where some new element has emerged since the driving the Court will have regard to its effect on what is contained in the certificate of analysis. In *Sutherland* v. *Aitchison*[10] it was said that the requirements were to establish that an ascertained and definite amount of alcohol had been taken after driving, and that that amount was such as to reduce the quantity regarded as taken before driving to below the

[5] [1973] R.T.R. 140.
[6] [1972] R.T.R. 121.
[7] 1969 S.L.T. 297.
[8] 1971 S.L.T. (Notes) 29.
[9] 1972 S.L.T. 2.
[10] 1979 S.L.T. (Notes) 37.

prescribed level: see also *Ferns* v. *Tudhope*.[11] The defence evidence had to be sufficiently definite and conclusive to throw doubt on the evidential value and presumptive effect of the certificate of analysis. The onus of proof is accordingly on the accused, subject to this, that once there has been proof of post-driving drinking, if the defender fails in proving the extent of the drinking, the prosecution must still satisfy the Court beyond reasonable doubt that it is safe to rely upon the certificate of analysis. A substantial doubt may save the accused. In England, however, the Court took the robust view that post-driving drinking following an accident vitiated the certificate of analysis and precluded conviction: *Rowlands* v. *Hamilton*.[12] The so-called "hip-flask defence" in a gross form thus attained some notoriety. Drink taken by a person still deemed to be in the category of "a person driving" would of course be rightly accounted against the driver. It is an offence of perverting the course of justice to take additional drink in order to frustrate a prosecution. Where a motorist established subsequent drinking an onus would be thrown on the prosecution to show that this had not materially affected the reliability of the analysis: *R.* v. *Alyson*.[13] If the motorist were to drive again after the additional drinking he could be convicted on the basis of the first analysis: *R.* v. *Richard Wilson*.[14] However English Courts have now come round to allow evidence of post-driving drinking rather than simply acquitting the accused.

The original prescribed-level offence was so defined as to deem the blood-alcohol level at the time of taking the specimen for analysis to be the level at the time of the offence. All problems of back-calculation were thus avoided. In the amended version of the prescribed-level offence the statutory assumption that the breath, blood or urine alcohol level at the time of the offence was not less than in the specimen applied, but if the proceedings are for the prescribed-level offence or for the impairment offence in a case where the accused is alleged to have been unfit through drink, the assumption shall not be made if the accused proves:

    (a) that he consumed alcohol after he had ceased to drive or be in charge and before he provided the specimen; and

    (b) that had he not done so the proportion of alcohol in his

---

[11] 1979 S.L.T. (Notes) 23.
[12] [1971] 1 All E.R. 1089.
[13] [1976] R.T.R. 15.
[14] [1975] R.T.R. 485.

breath, blood or urine would not have exceeded the prescribed limit or would not have been such as to impair his
ability to drive properly.

This statutory formalising of the hip-flask defence in section
10(2) of the Road Traffic Act 1972, extending to both the impairment and the prescribed-level offences, requires that evidence of
the proportion of alcohol or any drug in a specimen of breath,
blood or urine shall in all cases be taken into account, and that it
shall be assumed that the proportion of alcohol in the accused's
breath, blood or urine at the time of the alleged offence was not
less than in the specimen, save where the aforementioned excep-
tions apply.

The statutory presumption that the blood-alcohol level at the
time of the offence is not less than at the time of sampling, may
now be rebutted. To avail himself of this defence the accused must
shoulder the burden of proving that he consumed alcohol after he
ceased to drive or be in charge and before provision of the specimen, and that if he had not done so the alcohol in his breath, blood
or urine would not have exceeded the limit, or in an impairment
case would not have impaired his ability to drive properly. (See
Chapter 7). There will obviously be a number of cases in which this
extended statutory defence will be attempted, but it would seem
particularly difficult to establish in defence of an impairment case;
and for an "in charge" case (since the individual continues to be
"in charge") it would seem impossible to apply: *R.* v. *Lawrence.*[15]
Whereas in the past evidence of the effect of the passage of time
between the offences and the sampling was inadmissible, it now
seems to be acceptable to offer evidence to prove that the blood-
alcohol level at the time of driving was greater than at the time of
taking the sample, though probably this would rarely be attempted
by the prosecution. What is clear is that there is now scope for
examination of the time lapse and the effect this may have upon
the result of the analysis, and evidence about the blood-alcohol
level is no longer restricted, as it was, to what is "ascertained from
a laboratory test."

The newly defined hip-flask defence will undoubtedly provide
scope for expert evidence where the facts allow such a defence to
be developed, and an increase in cases of this kind is to be
expected.

---

[15] [1973] R.T.R. 64.

CHAPTER 13

REASONABLE EXCUSE

What is reasonable excuse for failing to provide a specimen of breath for a breath test[1] and what is reasonable excuse for failing to provide a specimen of breath, blood or urine for analysis[2] is a matter not for the police, but for the Court. This must be so because under section 7(5) a constable may arrest *every* person who fails to give a specimen provided the constable has reasonable cause to suspect that he has alcohol in his body. The phrase "reasonable excuse" is not defined in the Act but assistance can be gained from case law.

It is not for the motorist to prove reasonable excuse but rather for the prosecution to negative it once it is raised: *R.* v. *Christopher Clarke*[3]; *R.* v. *O'Boyle*[4]; *Earnshaw* v. *H.M. Adv.*[5] There is no need for proof that the subject was driving or in charge: *Commissioner of Police* v. *Curran*[6]; *Roberts* v. *Griffiths*.[7]

In *Hockin* v. *Weston*[8] the driver, after a serious accident, was required to give both breath for a screening breath test and laboratory tests. He equivocated and refused to provide these, and pleaded guilty to failing to provide them. The justices fined him and for special reasons (which they had confused with reasonable excuse) refrained from disqualifying. On appeal it was held that an error had been made and the case was remitted back to the justices to disqualify. In *Mallows* v. *Harris*[9] a driver failed fully to inflate the Alcotest and was arrested for failure to supply breath and asked for blood. The Court found there was reasonable excuse for his failure to provide breath. The accused however had claimed that he *had* inflated the bag, and it was held on appeal wrong for the Court to have found a reasonable excuse established which the accused himself had not claimed. In *Hogg* v. *Lockhart*[10] a driver

---

[1] Road Traffic Act 1972, s.7(4).
[2] *Ibid.* s.8(7).
[3] [1969] 1 W.L.R. 1109.
[4] [1973] R.T.R. 445.
[5] 1982 S.L.T. 179.
[6] [1976] R.T.R. 61.
[7] [1978] R.T.R. 362.
[8] [1972] R.T.R. 139.
[9] [1979] R.T.R. 404.
[10] 1973 S.L.T. (Sh.Ct.) 40.

was required to give a laboratory specimen. He tried to give urine and failed to provide a second specimen. When required to give blood he claimed a natural and powerful aversion to giving blood and a fear of hypodermic needles. It was held, following evidence, that there was reasonable excuse for failing to give blood, and he was acquitted of the prescribed-level offence and convicted of failure to give urine specimens. A similar Pyrrhic victory was achieved in *Milne* v. *Elliot*[11] where there was reasonable excuse for not providing blood but the Court had not given attention to the failure to provide urine: and so the case was remitted back to convict on that score. In *MacDonald* v. *MacKenzie*[12] a driver charged with the impairment offence failed to provide a specimen for a laboratory test. He had agreed to give blood, but the doctor could not locate a vein and proposed to use his thumb which the driver declined; and he was unable to give urine. Later another doctor examined him and reported he was not unfit to drive. The impairment charge was dropped, but it was held that the accused was rightly convicted of refusal to provide laboratory specimens. In *Rowland* v. *Thorpe*[13] it was held that the embarrassment of a woman having to give a urine specimen to male police officers could amount to reasonable excuse for failure to provide. In *Anderton* v. *Goodfellow*[14] a driver refused blood and failed to provide urine because of the embarrassment of having to provide a specimen in a jug in presence of the police, since he did not want them to watch him urinating. The Court found this reasonable excuse but on appeal it was held there had been no evidence to substantiate the claim and he should have been convicted. Concussion of a driver could also amount to reasonable excuse: *R.* v. *Knightley*.[15] The accused's desire to have his solicitor present is not reasonable excuse: *Law* v. *Stephens*[16]; *Payne* v. *Diccox*,[17] nor for an Australian to await his High Commissioner's advice: *R.* v. *Seaman*.[18] The fact of post-driving drinking was in England at least capable of forming reasonable excuse: *Glendinning* v. *Bell*,[19] but in *R.* v. *Lennard*[20] in the Court of Appeal that case was disapproved and it was held that a reasonable excuse must arise out of a physical or mental inability to provide a specimen or a substantial risk to health in its provision:

[11] 1974 S.L.T. (Notes) 71.
[12] 1975 S.L.T. 190.
[13] [1970] R.T.R. 406.
[14] 1980 R.T.R. 302.
[15] [1971] R.T.R. 409.
[16] [1971] R.T.R. 358.
[17] [1979] Crim. L.R. 670.
[18] [1971] R.T.R. 456.
[19] [1973] R.T.R. 52.
[20] [1973] R.T.R. 252.

Glickman v. *MacKinnon*.[21] In *Park* v. *Smith*[22] it was not enough that a driver might have had a bang on the head and not under-stood the request. There had to be evidence to found such a claim to reasonable excuse. In *Alcock* v. *Reid*[23] a driver was charged with refusing a specimen for laboratory tests. He failed to give two urine samples and agreed to give blood, although he then claimed to have a terror of having blood taken and to be mentally incap-able. He produced parole evidence from his Army service of his terror, and failure to provide blood. It was held on appeal that there was evidence of his condition and reasonable excuse was proved. In *R.* v. *John*[24] the driver's sincerely held belief that as a follower of Mesmer with faith-healing powers derived from divine gift he should not give blood was not reasonable excuse for refus-ing laboratory tests. Nor was the existence of a heart murmur reasonable excuse to refuse a blood test in *R.* v. *Philip Coates*.[25] In *Palmer* v. *Killion*[26] the accused rejected giving blood as he claimed to be haemophiliac, but failed three times to give urine. When asked for a fourth time he refused for embarrassment: reasonable excuse was not established. In *Sykes* v. *White*[27] on being required to provide blood a driver became light-headed and had to sit down. However there was no supporting evidence of disability and reasonable excuse was not established. In *Beck* v. *Sager*[28] the accused, a Libyan student pilot with little English, was warned of the consequence of failing to give a laboratory specimen. He did not provide a specimen but was successful in establishing his inability to understand as reasonable excuse for failing to provide a specimen. In future cases it is likely that the absence of a warning will not prevent the Court convicting the accused.

Special Reasons

Section 93 of the Road Traffic Act 1972 deals with disqualification from driving and provides that where a person is convicted of the offences specified in Part II of Schedule 4 of the Act involving obligatory disqualification (including the impairment offence, the

---

[21] 1978 J.C. 81. *Cf. Williams* v. *Critchley* [1979] R.T.R. 46.
[22] [1974] R.T.R. 500.
[23] [1980] R.T.R. 71.
[24] [1974] R.T.R. 332.
[25] [1977] R.T.R. 77.
[26] [1983] R.T.R. 138.
[27] [1983] R.T.R. 419.
[28] [1979] R.T.R. 475.

prescribed-level offence and the offence of failing to provide a specimen for analysis, or for a laboratory test, where required to ascertain ability to drive, or the proportion of alcohol in the blood at the time the offender was driving or attempting to drive) the Court shall order disqualification from holding a driving licence for at least 12 months unless the Court for special reasons thinks fit to disqualify for a lesser period or not to disqualify at all. Although these provisions are not specific to drink/driving offences, and apply to other offences as well, it is convenient to summarise here the attitude of the Courts to the exercise of their discretion in regard to Special Reasons.

Special Reasons are a matter of both fact and law, and the facts require to be proved in evidence: *McLeod* v. *Scoular*[29]; *Jones* v. *English*.[30] The onus is on the accused. The standard of proof is balance of probability: *Pugsley* v. *Hunter*.[31] The reasons must be special to the offence and not to the offender: *Whittall* v. *Kirby*[32]; *Adair* v. *Munn*.[33] If established they confer on the Court a discretion to mitigate the otherwise obligatory penalty: *Taylor* v. *Rajan*.[34] The cases of drivers consuming "laced drinks" can fall within this category: see p. 213. The Scottish courts regard public safety as a primary consideration: *Irvine* v. *Pollock*[35]; *Fairlie* v. *Hill*[36]; *Carnegie* v. *Clark*.[37] The English courts take a rather wider view: *R.* v. *Wickens*.[38] In Scotland the minor degree of blame attaching to the driver could amount to special reasons: *Smith* v. *Henderson*,[39] but this reasoning was disapproved in the English case of *Nicholson* v. *Brown*.[40] Special reasons for the prescribed-level offence are not radically different than for the previous drink-driving offence: *Herron* v. *McDonagh*.[41]

SOME SUCCESSFUL CASES

Since special reasons depend to a great extent upon the facts of each case they are difficult to predict, but it can be said that the following situations qualified as special reasons: in *Farrell* v. *Moir*[42] where the Court believed the driver's evidence that he had been

[29] 1974 J.C. 28.
[30] [1951] 2 All E.R. 853.
[31] [1973] R.T.R. 284.
[32] [1946] 2 All E.R. 552.
[33] 1940 J.C. 69.
[34] [1974] 2 W.L.R. 385.
[35] 1952 J.C. 51.
[36] 1944 J.C. 53.
[37] 1947 J.C. 74.
[38] (1958) 42 Cr. App. R. 236.
[39] 1950 J.C. 48.
[40] [1974] R.T.R. 177.
[41] 1969 S.L.T. 2.
[42] 1974 S.L.T. (Sh.Ct.) 89.

told by the police to drive; in *Skinner* v. *Ayton*[43] the accused, who was careful about drinking while driving, agreed to take a single Bacardi rum with coca cola: unknown to him his friend laced it with four single whiskies; in the case of *Roger Gravelling*[44] the accused was called out by the police as a keyholder of premises and had a blood-alcohol level of 120mg/100ml; in *James* v. *Hall*[45] the fact that the accused drove only a few yards; in *Alexander* v. *Latter*[46] where diabetic lager was supplied without warning that it was double strength; in *R.* v. *McIntyre*[47] where a driver moved his car on police instructions: and in the laced-drink cases of *Williams* v. *Neale*[48] and *R.* v. *Shippam*.[49] In *R.* v. *Anderson*[50] the accused's blood alcohol was 81mg/100ml and having been told he would not be prosecuted, he destroyed his defence specimen and was then charged with the offence. The circumstances of this unique case amounted to special reasons for not disqualifying.

SOME UNSUCCESSFUL CASES

The following situations did not qualify as special reasons: in *Copeland* v. *Sweeney*[51] the accused's daughter, who suffered from an unusual medical condition, was stung by a wasp and her father drove 30 miles unexpectedly to be with her; in *Peaston*[52] the fact that the driver's condition came to light through a random police check; in *P.F.* v. *Brian Kidd*[53] the fact that the accused was the son of a high-ranking officer of the Royal Ulster Constabulary and a prime I.R.A. target; in *Coombs* v. *Kehoe*[54] the fact that the accused drove only 200 yards; in *Adams* v. *Bradley*[55] where the driver drank strong lager without realising its strength; in *Goldsmith* v. *Laver*[56] where the accused suffered from diabetes; in *R.* v. *Scott*[57] where the lady driver after an accident was taking both

[43] 1977 S.L.T. (Sh.Ct.) 48.
[44] Cambridge Magistrates' Court: *Daily Telegraph*, September 15, 1983.
[45] [1972] R.T.R. 228.
[46] [1972] R.T.R. 441.
[47] [1976] R.T.R. 330.
[48] [1971] R.T.R. 149.
[49] [1971] R.T.R. 209.
[50] [1972] R.T.R. 113.
[51] 1977 S.L.T. (Sh.Ct.) 28.
[52] High Court of Justiciary, September 17, 1977 (unreported).
[53] Inverness Sheriff Court, June 9, 1975 (unreported).
[54] [1972] R.T.R. 224.
[55] [1975] R.T.R. 233.
[56] [1970] R.T.R. 162.
[57] [1970] R.T.R. 173.

drink and sleeping tablets; in *Scoble* v. *Graham*[58] where a legless driver following an accident in his invalid carriage was in pain and discomfort; in *Mullarkey* v. *Prescott*[59] where another legless driver was more than twice the limit; in *R.* v. *Jackson*[60]: *R.* v. *Hart*[61] where a liver condition caused retention of alcohol for longer than normal; in *Knight* v. *Baxter*[62] where a small hungry driver argued that alcohol affected him more rapidly than it would a large fed driver; in *Harding* v. *Oliver*[63] the fact that the driver lost his defence blood specimen at the laboratory where it was sent for analysis; in *Holroyd* v. *Berry*[64] the need for National Servicemen to be able to drive in Northern Ireland; in *R.* v. *Baines*[65]; *Jacobs* v. *Reed*[66]; *Taylor* v. *Rajan*[67] and *Evans* v. *Bray*[68] where emergencies arose requiring the accused to drive but alternative methods of travel had not been excluded; in *Newham* v. *Trigg*[69] where the driver had been given whisky and ginger of unknown amount as treatment for a cold; in *R.* v. *David Newton*[70] where a driver's glass, when he put it down, was laced with vodka, but he had lacked care for his condition; in *R.* v. *Shaw*[71] the fact that accused drove only a short distance on a private lane to which the public had access; in *Kerr* v. *Armstrong*[72] that the accused telephoned the police reporting an accident; in *Bullen* v. *Keay*[73] where the accused drove in a drugged state having taken barbiturates in an attempt to end his life; in *R.* v. *Harding*[74] where a fear of needles fell short of a phobia; in *Anderton* v. *Anderton*[75] where the accused was driving to hospital for urgent treatment but the offences were not for driving but for refusing to supply specimens; in *Park* v. *Hicks*[76] where the nature of the medical emergency alleged had not been clearly proved; in *Powell* v. *Gliha*[77] the fact that a wife drove her paraplegic husband home from a party because he needed to use his special lavatory; in *Doyle* v. *Leroux*[78] where the accused threw away his defence blood specimen on hearing mistakenly from the police that there would be no prosecution, but he had not made

---

[58] [1970] R.T.R. 358.
[59] [1970] R.T.R. 296.
[60] [1970] R.T.R. 165.
[61] [1970] R.T.R. 165.
[62] [1971] R.T.R. 270.
[63] [1973] R.T.R. 497.
[64] [1973] R.T.R. 145.
[65] [1970] R.T.R. 455.
[66] [1974] R.T.R. 81.
[67] [1974] R.T.R. 304.
[68] [1977] R.T.R. 24.

[69] [1970] R.T.R. 107.
[70] [1974] R.T.R. 451.
[71] [1974] R.T.R. 225.
[72] [1974] R.T.R. 139.
[73] [1974] R.T.R. 557.
[74] [1974] R.T.R. 325.
[75] [1977] R.T.R. 385.
[76] [1979] R.T.R. 259.
[77] [1979] R.T.R. 126.
[78] [1981] R.T.R. 438.

any attempt to have it analysed in the previous six weeks; in *De Munthe* v. *Stewart*[79] where the accused re-parked his car at the request of the police but had also driven before that; in *Haime* v. *Walkett*[80] where the accused had reversed his car preparatory to driving 200 yards to park for the night; in *Hosein* v. *Edmunds*[81] where the accused refused to supply specimens for laboratory test until he had consulted his own solicitor; and in *R.* v. *Seaman*[82] where a driver refused laboratory tests until he had the advice of the Australian consulate. In none of these cases were special reasons established.

For guidance on the Courts' reaction to cases of sudden emergency see *Jacobs* v. *Reed*[83] and *Copeland* v. *Sweeney*.[84]

[79] [1982] R.T.R. 27.
[80] [1983] R.T.R. 512.
[81] [1970] R.T.R. 51.
[82] [1971] R.T.R. 456.
[83] [1974] R.T.R. 81.
[84] 1977 S.L.T. (Sh.Ct.) 28.

CHAPTER 14

ANALYSIS—EVIDENCE—EXPERT EVIDENCE

Much of the evidence necessary to prove road traffic offences can be given by lay witnesses, including evidence as to the observed effects of drink. Experienced police officers can in such cases often form a reliable opinion. The question of fitness to drive, save in the grosser cases, is not a proper question for another driver to answer: *R.* v. *Davies* (*No.* 2).[1] The evidence of the police surgeon would normally not go beyond a description of the clinical examination, its interpretation, and a provisional opinion whether the accused was fit to be detained, and whether he could properly be proceeded against for impairment. Now that the analysis of blood and urine specimens is widely used the result of the analysis of these body substances may be available and may be referred to as confirming or throwing doubt on the doctor's opinion, provided the doctor had experience of interpreting such evidence. It is probably not right for courts to interpret these analytical figures for themselves in impairment cases unless the figures disclose such gross quantities of blood alcohol that the figures must imply impairment: *R.* v. *Reginald Hunt.*[2] It is well known that the prescribed level of 35 μg/100 ml in breath, 80 mg/100 ml in blood and 107 mg/100 ml in urine do not exactly correspond to a level at which every driver's ability to drive must be impaired. (p. 48). These figures supply not only a correspondence in the different substances, but also a conversion formula: *Gibson* v. *Skeen.*[3]

However section 10(2) of the 1972 Road Traffic Act lays it down that "evidence of the proportion of alcohol or any drug in a specimen of breath, blood or urine provided by the accused shall, in all cases, be taken into account." The Court must therefore make what it can of such evidence where it is offered.

It seems that the result of a screening breath test showing less than a positive reading or a breath analysis showing a reading

[1] [1962] 1 W.L.R. IIII.
[2] [1980] R.T.R. 29.
[3] 1975 S.L.T. (Notes) 52.

below the legal limit would be admissible and competent (for what they are worth) in support of a defence to the impairment offence. However, just as evidence that the prescribed level has been reached does not automatically mean that a driver is guilty of the section 5 offence, so evidence that the prescribed level has not been reached does not automatically eliminate that possibility.

In some courts doctors have been asked to express their views upon the interpretation of particular blood-alcohol or urine-alcohol figures in terms of impairment. It is doubtful if many doctors are qualified by training or experience to do so, and still more doubtful whether they are equipped to give evidence in borderline cases as to the relation of physical impairment to the deterioration of driving skills. Illogically, in England doctors have been allowed to refer to conversion tables relating blood-alcohol to urine-alcohol levels although they may have no personal knowledge of these matters: *R. v. Somers*.[4] The statutory relation of these levels to one another in section 7(4)of the Road Safety Act 1967 and now section 12(2) of the Road Traffic Act 1972 provides some expression of the ratio between them (see pp. 36, 114). In the last mentioned case, minimum destruction-rate tables for elimination of alcohol, a matter closer to the doctor's experience, were allowed to be consulted: *R. v. Somers, supra.*

EVIDENCE OF BREATH, BLOOD OR URINE TESTS UNDER THE ROAD TRAFFIC ACT 1972

Section 10 of the Road Traffic Act 1972 requires the court both in impairment cases and in prescribed-level cases to take account of any evidence submitted regarding the proportion of alcohol or of any drug contained in the body as ascertained by analysis of a specimen of breath or blood taken with consent of, or of urine provided by, the accused.

The analytical evidence necessary to describe the laboratory examination of blood and urine specimens can of course be given in certificate form only by qualified scientific witnesses. Such witnesses must for the purposes of both the impairment offence and the prescribed-level offence be authorised analysts, *i.e.* they must hold a diploma or fellowship of the Royal Institute of Chemistry of Great Britain and Ireland and a certificate granted by that Institute

---

[4] [1963] 3 All E.R. 808.

after examination conducted in the chemistry including the micros-
copy of food, drugs and water, or have held appointment as a public analysist before May 27, 1957: (The Public Analysts
Regulations 1957; the Public Analysts (Scotland) Regulations
1956) or be specially authorised by the Secretary of State for the
purpose. (See also p. 108). Some courts however are not happy
with evidence from public analysts in interpretation of blood-
alcohol levels because the analyst's skill lies in carrying through
the analytical procedures but not necessarily in relating these
levels to driving performance, and evidence given at large on these
technical questions may be given by any suitably qualified and
experienced expert.

CERTIFICATE EVIDENCE

Section 10 of the Road Traffic Act 1972 also provides that the evidence of blood and urine-alcohol levels in both classes of case may
be given by certificate. A certificate purporting to be signed by an
authorised analyst as to the proportion of alcohol or of any drug
found in a specimen identified by the certificate, being a specimen
of blood or urine, is to be evidence of the facts so certified, and of
the qualification of the analyst. Where no part of the specimen was
given to the accused the certificate was not valid: *R.* v. *Roberts*.[5] A
certificate which failed to specify the blood-alcohol proportion,
though it specified the urine-alcohol proportion was not competent
evidence: *MacLeod* v.*Nicol*.[6] But in England the provision of the
Act was regarded as permissive: *R.* v. *Vaughan*.[7] Only a blood
specimen taken from the accused by a medical practitioner with
the accused's consent can be considered. The 1972 Act is doubly
emphatic on this point: a non-consensual specimen is to be disregarded.[8] Where there is error in the identification of the specimen
to the analyst this may be fatal if the court is not satisfied that the
correct specimen was analysed: *Douglas* v. *Wilkinson*[9]; but where
they are so satisfied it need not render the certificate incompetent:
Lawrie v. *Stevenson*[10]; *Alexander* v. *Clatworthy*[11]; *Dickson* v.

[5] (1964) Cr. App. R. 300.
[6] 1964 J.C. 4.
[7] [1976] R.T.R. 184.
[8] ss.10(4) and 12(4).
[9] 1964 S.L.T. (Sh. Ct.) 68.
[10] 1968 S.L.T. 342.
[11] (1969) 113 S.J. 387.

Atkins[12]; *Tudhope* v. *Corrigall*.[13] The normal requirement is to follow the chain of evidence linking the specimen to the accused and to the certificate of analysis. In *Williamson* v. *Aitchison*[14] the blood sample was not produced in evidence but it was held that "such a concatenation of identical adminicles of evidence warranted the inference beyond all reasonable doubt" that the specimen taken and the specimen analysed were one and the same. For the case of an unstoppable gap in the chain of evidence see *R.* v. *Derek Shaw*.[15] Such a certificate of analysis is to be admissible evidence for the prosecution only where a copy has been handed to the accused at the time when it was produced or served upon the accused at least seven days before the hearing. Proof of service is therefore required. But this can be by production of the recorded delivery receipt, not necessarily by police officer: *Donlon* v. *MacKinnon*.[16] In Scotland service before an adjourned trial diet did not cure the failure to save timeously: *Handley* v. *Pirie*.[17] Although the link between a certificate of analysis and the taking of a particular blood specimen might be proved by fact and circumstances, in a case where the certificate of analysis had not been served that link could not be made: *McLeary* v. *Douglas*.[18] Where special privilege is to be accorded to such a certificate the rules of identification and proof of documentary productions must be scrupulously observed: *MacKinnon* v. *Virhia*.[19] As already pointed out, objection to inadmissible evidence must be taken at once (see p. 169) and failure to challenge evidence based on an unserved certificate of analysis can let it in: *R.* v. *Banks*.[20] In *English* v. *Smith*[21] the time limit was calculated by starting to count seven days before the date of trial. Both the date of service and the date of the trial are excluded to leave seven clear days: *McMillan* v. *H.M. Adv*.[22] Where a diet of trial in a prescribed-level case was deserted *pro loco et tempore* and the certificate of analysis had been properly served for that diet, it was held that the certificate was valid for the proceedings based on a new complaint without further service of the certificate because the Act enfranchised it for *any* proceedings: *Buonaccorsi* v. *Tudhope*.[23] If the accused not later than three days before the hearing has served notice on the

[12] [1972] R.T.R. 209.
[13] 1982 S.C.C.R. 558.
[14] 1982 S.L.T. 399.
[15] [1974] R.T.R. 458.
[16] 1982 S.L.T. 93.
[17] 1977 S.L.T. 30.

[18] 1978 S.L.T. 140.
[19] 1980 S.L.T. 36.
[20] [1972] R.T.R. 179.
[21] 1981 S.L.T. (Notes) 113.
[22] 1983 S.L.T. 24.
[23] 1982 S.L.T. 528.

prosecutor requiring the attendance at the hearing of the expert by whom the certificate was signed, the certificate is deprived of its special evidential value: *Herron* v. *Whitehill*.[24] The Court may however extend the period in special circumstances. In Scotland where the accused has given this notice to the prosecutor it seems that the certificate retains its admissibility as sufficient evidence, as does the evidence of the expert so far as facts contained in the certificate are concerned.[25] So in *McNeill* v. *Pirie*[26] the evidence of an analyst, in a case where the certificate of analysis had not been served, being accepted as truthful and reliable was sufficient in itself for conviction. Where the analyst himself gives evidence it is always a question to what extent he may speak to procedures in his laboratory which he has not personally carried out. In England it was sufficient in *R.* v. *Kershberg*[27] that the procedures were carried out in his laboratory under his control and supervision. This would probably not be acceptable in Scotland, but see *R.* v. *Tate*[28] where it was said that "scientific investigation nowadays is far too complicated for one man by himself to carry out every part of it." It would probably be unwise to rely upon this notice as sufficient to bring the witness, and he should be cited to attend in the usual way. (See also p. 219). Another example of a restriction upon the admissibility of analytical evidence is to be found in section 10(6) of the 1972 Act which provides, as a means of ensuring that the accused receives part of the specimen of blood or urine for his own use, that where at the time of taking the specimen the accused asks to be supplied with such a specimen, evidence of its analysis is not to be admissible on behalf of the prosecution unless the accused has been provided with part of the specimen.

DEFENCE ANALYSIS

In the past it has been regarded as necessary to show that the defence has similar opportunity as the prosecution for analysis of a blood or urine specimen.

The provisions for ensuring that the defence have a specimen have now been simplified, and section 10(6) of the Road Traffic Act 1972 merely states that where at the time of providing a blood

[24] 1969 S.L.T. 238.
[25] ss.10(5),(6) and (7).
[26] 1981 S.L.T. (Notes) 29.
[27] [1976] R.T.R. 526.
[28] [1977] R.T.R. 17.

or urine specimen the accused asks for a specimen, evidence of the proportion of alcohol or drug is not admissible unless he is so provided. In the past, when it was obligatory to supply the defence specimen in a "suitable container" difficulties arose if the defence specimen was clotted. This could be due to poor care of the specimen: *Clarke* v. *Stenlake*[29]; and need not be heeded if the prosecution had no such trouble: *Kierman* v. *Willock*[30]; or if the specimen was only partly clotted *Langridge* v. *Taylor*[31]; but where the defence specimen was incapable of analysis, objection would have to be taken at the time to the prosecution evidence: *Hudson* v. *Hornsby*.[32] It is not clear how the courts will regard such cases in future, but it would seem that having discharged the obligation to supply a defence specimen the prosecution evidence will remain admissible whether or not the defence sample is capable of analysis.

DISCREPANCY IN ANALYSIS

Since the prosecution and the defence should be analysing different parts of the same specimen, substantial discrepancies in analysis would not normally be expected. Where these occur the court must decide which of the analytical results is the more reliable or whether both are unsatisfactory. In such cases expert evidence will be required.

It is generally held that the prosecution has to prove exceeding of the prescribed level, rather than a particular blood-alcohol figure: *R* v. *Coomaraswamy*.[33] A contrary direction in *R.* v. *Boswell*[34] was disapproved. In *Froggatt* v. *Allcock*[35] (where the discrepancy was between 230 mg and 93 mg) the duty of the court was said to be, if in reasonable doubt, to acquit; if not to prefer one expert to the other. In *R.* v. *Dawson*[36] the court had to decide (discrepancy 179 mg and 60 mg); so also in *R.* v. *Tate*[37] (discrepancy 84 mg and 91 mg) and in *R.* v. *Marr*[38] (discrepancy 92 mg and 0 mg). In the former prescribed-level case of *R.* v. *Rutter*[39] the prosecution specimen showed 256 mg but the defence, who had thrown away their specimen, attempted to argue that on consumption of

[29] [1972] R.T.R. 276.
[30] [1972] R.T.R. 270.
[31] [1972] R.T.R. 157.
[32] [1973] R.T.R. 4.
[33] [1976] R.T.R. 21.
[34] [1974] R.T.R. 273.
[35] [1975] R.T.R. 372.
[36] [1976] R.T.R. 533.
[37] [1977] R.T.R. 17.
[38] [1977] R.T.R. 168.
[39] [1977] R.T.R. 105.

only four pints of beer this figure was impossible. It was held to be unacceptable to call expert hypothetical evidence to attack the analysis. So in the case of *Hughie Green*[40] blood was analysed at 200 mg/100 ml and 63 minutes later the accused was allowed home after a clear breath test. Leave to appeal on the ground that such a destruction rate was impossible was refused because all the facts had been before the jury. In *Thomas* v. *Henderson*[41] the prosecution analysis certificate showed 338 mg/100 ml and the accused threw his specimen away. It was held wrong to produce written evidence from a defence expert to challenge that figure without calling the analyst. In *McGarry* v. *Chief Constable of Bedfordshire*[42] the accused in a prescribed-level case gave urine analysed at 108 mg/100 ml. Five analyses were done, the lowest of 115 mg being taken with a six per cent. deduction for inherent error giving 108 mg. The accused argued that the proportion of 80/107 should be taken, equivalent to 80·74 mg and, as a fraction is disregarded, this leaves 80 mg which does not exceed the prescribed level. The offence was defined in terms of blood alcohol, not urine alcohol. It was held that calculations were not required: there was an excess over 107 mg/100 ml and the offence was proved. In *Walker* v. *Hodgins*[43] (discrepancy 96 mg and 83 mg) the magistrates felt unable to decide because no deduction for inherent error had been made from the defence analysis, and on appeal it was confirmed that the case was not proved.

The statement automatically produced by the breath analysis machine is discussed on p. 195 and at p. 225 *infra*. In the prescribed-level offence where no additional drink was taken after driving it was held the certificate of analysis was conclusive and reference to lapse of time was not allowed: *Tudhope* v. *Williamson*[44]; *Ferriby* v. *Sharman*.[45]

Where an analyst's certificate showed a very high alcohol content but the doctor conducting the clinical examination refused to certify the driver as impaired and gave evidence that he did not regard the tests as reliable, the trial judge was entitled to reject the evidence of the certificate: *MacNeil* v. *Fletcher*.[46]

[40] November 28, 1977, Richmond Magistrates' Court: *Sunday Express*, November 30, 1977.
[41] [1983] R.T.R. 293.
[42] [1983] R.T.R. 172.
[43] [1984] R.T.R. 34.
[44] 1977 S.L.T. 18.
[45] [1971] R.T.R. 163.
[46] 1966 J.C. 18.

It may be observed that these provisions do not appear to restrict the use of certificate evidence to the prosecution, and indeed there is no such restriction in section 10 of the 1972 Road Traffic Act. So far as that Act is concerned the defence seems to be equally at liberty to submit specimens to an authorised analyst for examination under the Act.

There has been considerable discussion in foreign countries as to whether a person should be convicted on nothing more than the certificate or even the oral evidence of a single analyst: *Ryan*; *Slough and Wilson*. English law permits this if the evidence is accepted and believed, and convictions based upon nothing but unequivocal scientific evidence are by no means unknown. The general rule of Scots law is that evidence however credible of the crucial facts in any criminal prosecution must be corroborated[47] and therefore the prescribed alcohol-level prosecution in Scotland in which the analyst is called to give evidence may raise difficulties unless the analyst who signed the certificate is present. In that case, and where the certificate alone is relied on, the evidence of the certificate or of the witness himself shall be sufficient evidence of the facts stated in the certificate (Road Traffic Act 1972 s.10(7)). There can hardly be a situation in which the evidence to convict is more crucial than in this type of case. It is arguable therefore that in such a situation there must be corroboration of the accused's alcohol level, and this can only be afforded by a second analyst's evidence that he carried out a second analysis or that he independently checked the first analyst's results as he performed the analysis. This can be double-checked in respect of blood and urine specimens where part of the specimen has been made available to the accused. There is not the same difficulty in connection with the impairment offence where other evidence usually points to the accused's ability to drive properly.

As we have explained (p. 101) it is not possible by modern analytical techniques to provide a precisely known figure for the alcohol in any specimen. The working figure must have certain tolerances set off to allow for error. It is common therefore (though the Act does not seem to contemplate it) to give the analytical result in a form "not less than . . . milligrammes/100 millilitres." (See p. 108.) Where this is done and it is necessary to find corroboration of the excess alcohol, the imprecise nature of the

---

[47] Cf. *Bisset* v. *Anderson* 1949 J.C. 106 and *McKillen* v. *Barclay Curle and Co. Ltd.* 1967 S.L.T. 41.

reported figure may render corroboration more difficult than if the figure were absolute. On the other hand, where there is a discrepancy between the prosecution and the defence analysis it is not easy to criticise this if both results show a figure in excess of the prescribed level. Even though the prescribed limit is a precise one, it is no defence that the excess of blood alcohol above the limit is nominal: *Gilligan* v. *Wright*[48]; and this does not supply special reasons for non-disqualification: see p. 212. The *de minimis* considerations which may apply elsewhere, *cf. Briere* v. *Hailstone*,[49] do not apply to this offence.

There is a further provision in section 10(3) of the Road Traffic Act 1972 that in any prosecution for the impairment offence or for the prescribed alcohol-level offence a certificate purporting to be signed by a medical practitioner that he took a specimen of blood from a person with his consent shall be evidence of the matters so certified and of the qualifications of the medical practitioner. This means of avoiding the attendance of the doctor may be acceptable in the prescribed-level offence, but is unlikely to be acceptable in the impairment case unless the doctor was one who was unconcerned with clinical examination. The provision also rules that a certificate signed by an authorised analyst as to the proportion of alcohol or any drug found in a specimen of blood or urine identified by the certificate shall be evidence.

AUTOMATIC PRINT-OUT

The radical new provision is that a statement automatically produced by the machine by which the proportion of alcohol in a specimen of breath was measured and a certificate signed by the constable (whether in the same document or not) that the statement relates to a specimen provided by the accused at the date and time shown in the statement shall be evidence of the proportion of alcohol or a drug in that specimen. In the case of this automatic analysis no allowance can be made for error (see pp. 109 *et seq.*). If the Crown rely upon the automatic print-out they must accept it in its entirety: where an error of date had crept in, the whole certificate was bad, *Smith* v. *Macdonald*.[50] Where the police altered the print-out after it was issued to correct the time of the offence it was

---

[48] [1968] Crim. L.R. 276.
[49] [1969] Crim. L.R. 36.
[50] 1984 S.C.C.R. 190.

held there was no case to answer.[51] In *Gaimster* v. *Marlow*[52] it was held that the automatic print-out produced by a Lion Intoximeter 3000 machine, so far from being in code and being incomprehensible to the ordinary person, was plainly intelligible if considered as a whole, and if it were not immediately intelligible to some people without explanation that did not prevent it from being a statement. Furthermore if further explanation were required of the signs and symbols used in the print-out there was no reason why the trained police officer accustomed to operating the machine should not give evidence to explain their meaning.[53]

In the case of a breath specimen, analysis will be carried out by the machine, whether in connection with the prescribed-level offence or the impairment offence. Unless for some reason the analysis is aborted, the statement automatically produced by the machine will provide evidence, and the only evidence, of the proportion of alcohol in the specimen. Although the terms of section 10(3) of the Road Traffic Act 1972 allow evidence to be given by whichever is appropriate, either the automatic statement or a certificate by an authorised analyst, there is at present no provision by which a breath specimen may be analysed in the laboratory. For practical purposes only the authomatic print-out will be available in Court. Where blood or urine specimens are concerned, of course, the analyst may provide such a certificate as he will do in all cases involving drugs. It is one of the anxious criticisms of the use of the breath testing machines, that for specimens which fall above the 50 µg/100 ml mark there is no means of analysis other than the instrumental analysis which has to be accepted as correct and cannot be counter-checked. Moreover for the breath specimen which shows a reading marginally above 30 micrograms the accused has to make the difficult decision whether to accept the print-out figure and hope that the prosecutor will exercise an administrative decision not to prosecute (see p. 196) or to request a blood test which might show a rather higher figure which would certainly attract prosecution.

As to the absence of the third zero check from the Scottish print-out, see *Aitchison* v. *Meldrum*.[54] The Scottish courts are aware of developments and take judicial notice of them.[55]

[51] *James Floyde*, November 16, 1983, Bulmer East Magistrates, York: *Daily Telegraph*, November 17, 1983.

[52] [1984] R.T.R. 49.

[53] *Jones* v. *MacPhail* 1984 S.C.C.R. 168, and *Aitchison* v. *Matheson* 1984 S.C.C.R. 83.

[54] 1984 S.C.C.R. 241.   [55] *Annan* v. *Mitchell* 1984 S.C.C.R. 32.

CHAPTER 15

PENALTIES

The most important aspect of sentencing so far as drinking drivers are concerned is the law's requirement for mandatory disqualification in certain cases. For the rest there is a considerable variation in the treatment accorded by different courts, or by the same court on different occasions. Doubtless the considerations to be taken into account include the quantity of drink taken, the degree of impairment, the traffic conditions at the time, the locality of the driving, the type of vehicle involved, the actual or apprehended danger or damage caused as well as the personal circumstances of the driver, and the whole background to the offence. Without the fullest knowledge of the circumstances it is therefore important not to read too much into the following examples of sentencing.

In *Wheater* v. *Campbell*[1] a three year disqualification imposed on a driver pleading guilty to the prescribed-level offence at 175 mg/100 ml was held to be excessive and should have been for one year only. But in the unreported case of *Sydney Wiseman*[2] the accused was fined for driving with excess alcohol of 224 mg/100 ml and disqualified for life. That disqualification was not disturbed on appeal. In *R.* v. *McLaughlin*[3] a driver with a blood alcohol of 319 mg/100 ml with three previous convictions was held on appeal to have been properly imprisioned for 20 years. In *R.* v. *Salters*[4] a driver with an umblemished record fell from grace when he drove with a blood alcohol of 267 mg/100 ml and was sentenced to three months imprisonment and eighteen months disqualification. In *R.* v. *Tupa*[5] a case of 298 mg/100 ml—a custodial sentence of five years was sustained on appeal. Indeed a custodial sentence even for a prescribed-level first offender need not be wrong in principle:

[1] 1974 S.L.T. (Notes) 63.
[2] Arbroath Sheriff Court and Justiciary Appeal Court, November 21, 1980.
[3] [1978] R.T.R. 452.
[4] [1979] R.T.R. 470.
[5] [1974] R.T.R. 153.

R. v. *Nokes.*[6] In *R.* v. *Pashley*[7] a years's imprisonment was sustained. In *R.* v. *Michael Jones*[8] a disqualification imposed upon a skilled carpenter was reduced having regard to the public interest.

Since 1983 many English Courts have been making it plain that prison sentences may be expected for drivers driving with high blood-alcohol levels. The Magistrates Association in England published in January 1982 "Suggestions for Road Traffic Penalties" which include suggestions for drink-driving penalties. Where the circumstances of an offence suggest that inexperience or improper driving habits have contributed to the offence or where there is to be a long period of disqualification the Court may order the taking of a driving test under section 93(7) of the Road Traffic Act 1972. This is not to be regarded as a punishment in itself: *R.* v. *Guilfoyle*[9]; *Sweeney* v. *Cardle.*[10]

In *R.* v. *Yoxall*[11] three years disqualification was appropriate for a driver with a blood alcohol of 236 mg/100 ml: in *R.* v. *Thomas*[12] two years' disqualification was appropriate for a driver with a blood alcohol of 292 mg/100 ml and in *R.* v. *Sherman*[13] a similar period was appropriate for 143 mg/100 ml, while in *R.* v. *Mills*[14] a like period was appropriate for 118 mg/100 ml.

It is possible for a person reasonably suspected of having driven while impaired to be prosecuted, although it is not ultimately established that they were either driving or in charge. In such a case no penalty is possible except obligatory endorsement and discretionary disqualification: *Commissioner of Police of the Metropolis* v. *Curran.*[15] Where a person aids and abets an offence of impairment or a prescribed-level offence disqualification is discretionary: *Ullah* v. *Luckhurst.*[16]

It was however made clear in *Herron* v. *Sharif*[17] that the smallness of the excess over the prescribed level in a case of impairment did not justify a modified sentence: *Cf. Delaroy-Hall* v. *Tadman.*[18]

In *Campbell* v. *McLeod*[19] where a notice of penalties specified the wrong maximum period of disqualification, the accused was held not prejudiced and the conviction was sustained. In *R.* v. *Kashyap*[20] the Court remarked on the anomaly that a person may be

[6] [1978] R.T.R. 101.
[7] [1974] R.T.R. 149.
[8] [1977] R.T.R. 385.
[9] [1973] R.T.R. 272.
[10] 1982 S.C.C.R. 10.
[11] [1973] Crim. L.R. 63.
[12] [1973] R.T.R. 325.
[13] [1974] R.T.R. 213.
[14] [1974] R.T.R. 215.
[15] [1976] R.T.R. 61.
[16] [1977] Crim. L.R. 295.
[17] [1974] S.L.T. (Notes) 63.
[18] [1969] 2 Q.B. 208.
[19] [1975] S.L.T. (Notes) 6.
[20] [1972] R.T.R. 78.

disqualified from driving a car and yet remain able to pilot a jet plane.

All drink-driving cases are now triable only under summary procedure.

The penalties provided by Schedule 9, paragraphs 19 to 21 of the Transport Act 1981 and the penalty points derived from Schedule 7 of that Act as amended by section 58 of the Transport Act 1982 are set out on pages 229 and 230.

It is to be noted that in applying the penalty points provisions, the proviso to section 19(3) of the Transport Act 1981 states that if any of the offences was committed more than three years before another, the penalty points in respect of that offence shall not be added to those in respect of the other. There is also a further provision in section 19(2) of the Transport Act 1981 which allows the court a limited discretion to mitigate the consequences of the imposition of penalty points in excess of 12. If satisfied that there are grounds for doing so the court may disqualify for less than the prescribed minimum period or not at all if satisfied that "mitigating circumstances" exist. These are not to be confused with "special reasons" and are to be much more widely construed. Exceptional hardship to the accused person for example would be acceptable but section 19(6) excludes from consideration any trivialising circumstances relative to the offence, hardship of a lesser character than exceptional hardship, and circumstances which have already been given effect to in this way in the three years immediately preceding the conviction in question.

As to repeated convictions for the drink-driving offences see section 93(3) and (4) of the Road Traffic Act 1972.

HIGH RISK OFFENDERS

The Blennerhasset Report "Drinking and Driving" recommended that problem drinkers (whom they described as "high risk offenders") being persons who are disqualified twice within 10 years for the drink-driving offences or who are convicted of a first drink-driving offence having a blood alcohol figure in excess of 200 mg/100 ml or such level as Parliament might enact, should be subjected not only to the disqualification appropriate to their offence, but to a further requirement that they remain disqualified until the court decides that their driving will no longer present an undue risk. Although these provisions have not been enacted in a direct

The Impairment Offences

s. 5(1)	Driving or attempting to drive when unfit to drive through drink or drugs	6 months or £1,000 or both (level 5)	Disqualification obligatory	Endorsement obligatory 4 penalty points
s. 5(2)	Being in charge when unfit to drive through drink or drugs	3 months or £500 or both (level 4)	Disqualification discretionary	Endorsement obligatory 10 penalty points

The Prescribed-Level Offences

s. 6(1)(a)	Driving or attempting to drive with excess alcohol in blood	6 months or £1,000 or both (level 5)	Disqualification obligatory	Endorsement obligatory 4 penalty points
s. 6(1)(b)	Being in charge with excess alcohol in blood	3 months or £500 or both (level 4)	Disqualification discretionary	Endorsement obligatory 10 penalty points

FAILURE TO PROVIDE SPECIMENS

s. 7(4)	Failing to provide specimen for breath test	£50 (level 3)	Disqualification discretionary	Endorsement obligatory 4 penalty points
s. 8(7)	Failing to provide specimen for analysis for laboratory test	where driving or attempting to drive 6 months or £1,000 or both	Disqualification obligatory	Endorsement obligatory 4 penalty points
		Otherwise, 3 months or £500 or both	Disqualification discretionary	Endorsement discretionary 10 penalty points

FOR CYCLISTS

s. 19	Cycling when unfit through drink or drugs	£50 (level 3)

way in the new code of drink-driving legislation the Government have decided to arrange administratively that in these cases, and in cases where a person has been twice disqualified in 10 years for failing to provide a specimen for analysis and where the police suspect an alcohol problem, that the driving licence will not be automatically restored on the expiry of the second period of disqualification. Such drivers will be notified that consideration will be given to the question whether a medical disability exists which would prevent the restoration of the driving licence and the driver will be invited to seek help to deal with his condition during the period of disqualification. The licence will then not be restored unless the driver is able to satisfy the Secretary of State that he does not suffer from an alcohol problem. There will also be an interview and a medical examination to assist the Secretary of State to decide that question. A subsequent blood sample will then be called for which will be examined at the Isaac Woolfson Research Laboratory at Birmingham. In this way the Secretary of State's powers to revoke or refuse a driving licence under section 87 of the Road Traffic Act 1972 will be used to monitor the return to the road of these high risk offenders. In this administrative procedure the Secretary of State will be ascertaining whether the offender suffers from a disability likely to cause his driving of a motor vehicle to be a danger to the public, and there will be the usual appeal under section 90 of the 1972 Act to the Magistrates' Court in England and to the Sheriff in Scotland. It remains to be seen whether this attempt to keep habitual drinkers off the roads will prove successful.

CHAPTER 16

BLOOD ALCOHOL LEVELS ABROAD

There is now substantial international agreement that blood-alcohol levels in excess of 80 mg/100 ml are unacceptable in drivers but a number of countries apply more stringent rules. The following table sets out the present legal blood-alcohol limits so far as they can be discovered

No Blood Alcohol Allowed

Czechoslovakia (in practice levels up to 30 mg/100 ml are not prosecuted)

Turkey, and Moslem countries generally

50 mg/100 ml Limit

Australia (Victoria and Western Australia)	Iceland
	Japan
Finland	Norway
Greece	Poland
Holland	Sweden
	Yugoslavia

80 mg/100 ml Limit

Australia (N.S. Wales)	Northern Ireland
Austria	Portugal
Belgium	Republic of South
Canada (some provinces	Africa
suspend licences for 24 hours	Spain
over 50 mg/100 ml)	Switzerland
Denmark	West Germany
France	U.S.A. (Idaho and
Luxembourg	Utah)
New Zealand	

100 mg/100 ml LIMIT

U.S.A. (Alaska
   Arizona
   California
   Connecticut
   Delaware
   District of Columbia
   Florida
   Illinois
   Kansas
   Maine
   Michigan
   Minnesota
   Missouri

Nebraska
New Mexico
New York
North Carolina
Oklahoma
Oregon
Pennsylvania
Rhode Island
South Dakota
Vermont
Washington
Wisconsin)

Eire

130 mg/100 ml LIMIT

U.S.A. (Iowa)

150 mg/100 ml LIMIT

Swaziland

NO SPECIFIC LEGAL LIMIT

Cyprus
Italy
Malta
Monaco
U.S.A. (Arkansas
   Colorado
   Georgia
   Hawaii
   Indiana
   Kentucky
   Louisiana
   Maryland
   Massachussets

Mississippi
Montana
Nevada
New Hampshire
New Jersey
North Dakota
Ohio
South Carolina
Tennessee
Texas
Virginia
West Virginia
Wyoming)

U.S.S.R.

A number of countries have a first degree offence for blood-alcohol levels exceeding 125 or 150 mg/100 ml and a second degree offence carrying a lesser penalty for blood-alcohol levels exceeding 80 mg/100 ml but falling short of the higher threshhold. This is the case for example in Belgium, France, Northern Ireland, Portugal, Spain, Sweden and West Germany.

Special mention should also be made of New Zealand where, alongside the blood-alcohol limit of 80 mg/100 ml, the Transport Amendment Act (No. 3) of 1978 introduced a statutory breath-alcohol limit of 50 micrograms/100 ml so creating an independent offence of driving with excessive breath-alcohol. Unlike the United Kingdom offence (as it was prior to May 6, 1983) there is no need to translate the breath-alcohol figure into a figure for blood-alcohol. The New Zealand experience is therefore of special interest to the United Kingdom.

REFERENCES

The Blennerhassett Report, *Drinking & Driving*: H.M.S.O. (1976).
Denney Ronald C. (1979) *Drinking & Driving*.
Gradwohl's Legal Medicine Ed. Camps, 1976 Ch. 35.
Stone, H.M. (1982) *Alcohol Drugs & the New Zealand Driver*.
Department of Transport; personal communication.
Ivanov S.V. and Uljanov, V.A.; personal communication.

EXAMPLES OF MACHINE PRINT-OUTS

A: SCOTTISH PRINT-OUT: CAMIC BREATH-ANALYSER
EXAMPLE
A

```
CAMIC BREATH
ANALYSER (S)


NAME OF SUBJECT


** RESULTS **

CAL CHECK NO.1
    033UG/100ML
* ZERO CHECK *
    000UG/100ML

BREATH TEST NO.1
    079UG/100ML
DATE   14/03/84
TIME   16:28

 * ZERO CHECK *
    000UG/100ML

BREATH TEST NO.2
    077UG/100ML
DATE   14/03/84
TIME   16:30

CAL CHECK NO.2
    033UG/100ML

ABOVE PARTICULARS
CERTIFIED AS CORRECT

CONSTABLES NAME


--------------------
      SIGNATURE


--------------------
```

Reproduced with permission of Mr. A. M. Mather, Car and Medical Instrument Company Limited.

B: English Print-Out: Camic Breath-Analyser Examiner

B

```
-----------------------
POLICE STATION


NAME OF SUBJECT


SUBJECT'S SIGNATURE


        ** RESULTS **

CAL CHECK NO. 1
        032UG/100ML
        *ZERO CHECK*
        000UG/100ML

    BREATH TEST NO. 1
        000UG/100ML
DATE   23/02/83
TIME   10:45 GMT.
        *ZERO CHECK*
        000UG/100ML

    BREATH TEST NO. 2
        000UG/100ML
DATE   23/02/83
TIME   10:46 GMT.
        *ZERO CHECK*
        000UG/100ML

CAL CHECK NO. 2
        033UG/100ML

OPERATOR


I CERTIFY THAT IN THIS
STATEMENT READING 1
RELATES TO THE FIRST
SPECIMEN OF BREATH
PROVIDED BY THE
SUBJECT NAMED ABOVE
AND READING 2 TO THE
SECOND, AT THE DATE
AND TIME SHOWN HEREIN

    *** CAMIC ***
-----------------------
```

Reproduced with permission of Mr. A. M. Mather, Car and Medical Instrument Company Limited.

C: Lion Intoximeter: Print-Out Example
C

Print-out	Description
TEST RECORD	
LION INTOX.3333 9990	Name and Number of Instrument
NORTHTOWN POLICE STN	
WESSEX CONSTABULARY	Location of Instrument
THU JUN 30,1993	Day and Date of Test
SUBJECT NAME=	
JONES,JOHN ALFRED	Subject's Name and Date of Birth
DOB.=160947	
J.A. Jones	Subject's Signature
SIGNATURE	
TEST UG% TIME	
	1st Simulator Reading
STD 36 16:47GMT	
BLK Ø 16:47GMT	Blank Reading
	1st Breath Reading
ONE 127 16:48GMT	
BLK Ø 16:48GMT	Blank Reading
TWO 125 16:49GMT	2nd Breath Reading
BLK Ø 16:49GMT	Blank Reading
STD 35 16:50GMT	2nd Simulator Reading
OPERATOR NAME=	
SGT1234WILLIAMS	Operator's Name
I CERTIFY THAT IN THIS STATEMENT, READING ONE RELATES TO THE FIRST SPECIMEN OF BREATH PROVIDED BY THE SUBJECT NAMED ABOVE; AND READING TWO TO THE SECOND, AT THE DATE AND TIME SHOWN HEREIN.	Legal Statement Certifying Readings for Court Purposes
D.Williams	Operator's Signature
SIGNATURE	

All alcohol readings are in micrograms of alcohol per 100ml (ug%) of breath. Both simulator readings must be between 32 and 37 ug% inclusive.

(Print-out example is not actual size.)
Reproduced with permission of Dr. P. M. Williams, Lion Laboratories Limited.

237

ROAD TRAFFIC ACT 1972

Driving, or being in charge, when under influence of drink or drugs

5.—(1) A person who, when driving or attempting to drive a motor vehicle on a road or other public place, is unfit to drive through drink or drugs shall be guilty of an offence.

(2) Without prejudice to subsection (1) above, a person who, when in charge of a motor vehicle which is on a road or other public place, is unfit to drive through drink or drugs shall be guilty of an offence.

(3) For the purposes of subsection (2) above a person shall be deemed not to have been in charge of a motor vehicle if he proves that at the material time the circumstances were such that there was no likelihood of his driving it so long as he remained unfit to drive through drink or drugs [but in determining whether there was such a likelihood the court may disregard any injury to him and any damage to the vehicle].

(4) For the purposes of this section a person shall be taken to be unfit to drive if his ability to drive properly is for the time being impaired.

[(5) A constable may arrest a person without warrant if he has reasonable cause to suspect that that person is or has been committing an offence under this section.

(6) For the purposes of arresting a person under the power conferred by subsection (5) above a constable may enter (if need be by force) any place where that person is or where the constable, with reasonable cause, suspects him to be.

(7) Subsection (6) above does not extend to Scotland and nothing in that subsection shall affect any rule of law in Scotland concerning the right of a constable to enter any premises for any purpose.]

DERIVATION

Subs. (1) replaces 1960, s. 6 (1). Subs. (2) replaces 1960, s. 6 (2); Road

Safety Act 1967, s. 32 (1), Sched. 1, para. 1. Subs. (3) replaces 1960, s. 6 (2). Subs. (4) replaces 1962, s. 1. Subs. (5) replaces 1960, s. 6 (4).

AMENDMENTS
Subs. (5) was substituted and the words in square brackets in subs. (3) and subss. (6) and (7) were inserted with effect from May 6, 1983, by the Transport Act 1981, s. 25 (1) and (2).

[Driving or being in charge of a motor vehicle with alcohol concentration above prescribed limit

6.—(1) If a person—
  (*a*) drives or attempts to drive a motor vehicle on a road or other public place; or
  (*b*) is in charge of a motor vehicle on a road or other public place; after consuming so much alcohol that the proportion of it in his breath, blood or urine exceeds the prescribed limit he shall be guilty of an offence.

(2) It is a defence for a person charged with an offence under subsection (1)(*b*) above to prove that at the time he is alleged to have committed the offence the circumstances were such that there was no likelihood of his driving the vehicle whilst the proportion of alcohol in his breath, blood or urine remained likely to exceed the prescribed limit; but in determining whether there was such a likelihood the court may disregard any injury to him and any damage to the vehicle.]

AMENDMENT
This section was substituted by the Transport Act 1981, s. 25(3) and Sched. 8, which came into force on May 6, 1983 (S.I. 1983 No. 576).

[Breath tests

7.—(1) Where a constable in uniform has reasonable cause to suspect—
  (*a*) that a person driving or attempting to drive or in charge of a motor vehicle on a road or other public place has alcohol in his body or has committed a traffic offence whilst the vehicle was in motion; or
  (*b*) that a person has been driving or attempting to drive or been in charge of a motor vehicle on a road or other public place with alcohol in his body and that that person still has alcohol in his body; or
  (*c*) that a person has been driving or attempting to drive or

been in charge of a motor vehicle on a road or other public place and has committed a traffic offence whilst the vehicle was in motion;

he may, subject to section 9 below, require him to provide a specimen of breath for a breath test.

(2) If an accident occurs owing to the presence of a motor vehicle on a road or other public place a constable may require any person who he has reasonable cause to believe was driving or attempting to drive or in charge of the vehicle at the time of the accident to provide a specimen of breath for a breath test, but subject to section 9 below.

(3) A person may be required under subsection (1) or subsection (2) of this section to provide a specimen either at or near the place where the requirement is made or, if the requirement is made under subsection (2) and the constable making the requirement thinks fit, at a police station specified by the constable.

(4) A person who, without reasonable excuse, fails to provide a specimen of breath when required to do so in pursuance of this section shall be guilty of an offence.

(5) A constable may arrest a person without warning if—

(*a*) as a result of a breath test he has reasonable cause to suspect that the proportion of alcohol in that person's breath or blood exceeds the prescribed limit; or

(*b*) that person has failed to provide a specimen of breath for a breath test when required to do so in pursuance of this section and the constable has reasonable cause to suspect that he has alcohol in his body;

but a person shall not be arrested by virtue of this subsection when he is at a hospital as a patient.

(6) For the purpose of requiring a person to provide a specimen of breath under subsection (2) above in a case where he has reasonable cause to suspect that the accident involved injury to another person or of arresting him in such a case under subsection (5) above a constable may enter (if need be by force) any place where that person is or where the constable, with reasonable cause, suspects him to be.

(7) Subsection (6) above does not extend to Scotland and nothing in that subsection shall affect any rule of law in Scotland concerning the right of a constable to enter any premises for any purpose.

(8) In this section "traffic offence" means an offence under any provision of this Act except Part V, or under any provision of Part

III of the Road Traffic Act 1960, the Road Traffic Regulation Act 1967 or Part I of the Transport Act 1980.]

AMENDMENT
This section was substituted by the Transport Act 1981, s. 25 (3) and Sched. 8, which came into force on May 6, 1983 (S.I. 1983 No. 576).

[Provision of specimens for analysis

8.—(1) In the course of an investigation whether a person has committed an offence under section 5 or section 6 of this Act a constable may, subject to the following provisions of this section and section 9 below, require him—

(a) to provide two specimens of breath for analysis by means of a device of a type approved by the Secretary of State; or

(b) to provide a specimen of blood or urine for a laboratory test.

(2) A requirement under this section to provide specimens of breath can only be made at a police station.

(3) A requirement under this section to provide a specimen of blood or urine can only be made at a police station or at a hospital; and it cannot be made at a police station unless—

(a) the constable making the requirement has reasonable cause to believe that for medical reasons a specimen of breath cannot be provided or should not be required; or

(b) at the time the requirement is made a device or a reliable device of the type mentioned in subsection (1)(a) is not available at the police station or it is then for any other reason not practicable to use such a device there; or

(c) the suspected offence is one under section 5 of this Act and the constable making the requirement has been advised by a medical practitioner that the condition of the person required to provide the specimen might be due to some drug;

but may then be made notwithstanding that the person required to provide the specimen has already provided or been required to provide two specimens of breath.

(4) If the provision of a specimen other than a specimen of breath may be required in pursuance of this section the question whether it is to be a specimen of blood or a specimen of urine shall be decided by the constable making the requirement, except that if a medical practitioner is of the opinion that for medical reasons a specimen of blood cannot or should not be taken the specimen shall be a specimen of urine.

(5) A specimen of urine shall be provided within one hour of the requirement for its provision being made and after the provision of a previous specimen of urine.

(6) Of any two specimens of breath provided by any person in pursuance of this section that with the lower proportion of alcohol in the breath shall be used and the other shall be disregarded; but if the specimen with the lower proportion of alcohol contains no more than 50 microgrammes of alcohol in 100 millilitres of breath the person who provided it may claim that it should be replaced by such a specimen as may be required under subsection (4), and if he then provides such a specimen neither specimen of breath shall be used.

(7) A person who, without reasonable excuse, fails to provide a specimen when required to do so in pursuance of this section shall be guilty of an offence.

(8) On requiring any person to provide a specimen in pursuance of this section a constable shall warn him that a failure to provide it may render him liable to prosecution.

(9) The Secretary of State may by regulations substitute another proportion of alcohol in the breath for that specified in subsection (6).]

AMENDMENT

This section was substituted by the Transport Act 1981, s. 25 (3) and Sched. 8, which came into force on May 6, 1983 (S.I. 1983 No. 576).

[Protection for hospital patients

9.—(1) While a person is at a hospital as a patient he shall not be required to provide a specimen of breath for a breath test or to provide a specimen for a laboratory test unless the medical practitioner in immediate charge of his case has been notified of the proposal to make the requirement; and—

    (*a*) if the requirement is then made it shall be for the provision of a specimen at the hospital; but

    (*b*) if the medical practitioner objects on the ground specified in subsection (2) below the requirement shall not be made.

(2) The ground on which the medical practitioner may object is that the requirement or the provision of a specimen or, in the case of a specimen of blood or urine, the warning required under section 8 (8) above, would be prejudicial to the proper care and treatment of the patient.]

AMENDMENT

This section was substituted by the Transport Act 1981, s. 25 (3) and Sched. 8, which came into force on May 6, 1983 (S.I. 1983 No. 576).

[Evidence in proceedings for an offence under s. 5 or s. 6

10.—(1) The following provisions apply with respect to proceedings for an offence under section 5 or section 6 of this Act.

(2) Evidence of the proportion of alcohol or any drug in a specimen of breath, blood or urine provided by the accused shall, in all cases, be taken into account, and it shall be assumed that the proportion of alcohol in the accused's breath, blood or urine at the time of the alleged offence was not less than in the specimen; but if the proceedings are for an offence under section 6 of this Act, or for an offence under section 5 of this Act in a case where the accused is alleged to have been unfit through drink, the assumption shall not be made if the accused proves—

    (*a*) that he consumed alcohol after he had ceased to drive, attempt to drive or be in charge of a motor vehicle on a road or other public place and before he provided the specimen; and

    (*b*) that had he not done so the proportion of alcohol in his breath, blood or urine would not have exceeded the prescribed limit and, if the proceedings are for an offence under section 5 of this Act, would not have been such as to impair his ability to drive properly.

(3) Evidence of the proportion of alcohol or a drug in a specimen of breath, blood or urine may, subject to subsections (5) and (6) below, be given by the production of a document or documents purporting to be whichever of the following is appropriate, that is to say—

    (*a*) a statement automatically produced by the device by which the proportion of alcohol in a specimen of breath was measured and a certificate signed by a constable (which may but need not be contained in the same document as the statement) that the statement relates to a specimen provided by the accused at the date and time shown in the statement; and

    (*b*) a certificate signed by an authorised analyst as to the proportion of alcohol or any drug found in a specimen of blood or urine identified in the certificate.

(4) A specimen of blood shall be disregarded unless it was taken from the accused with his consent by a medical practitioner; but

evidence that a specimen of blood was so taken may be given by the production of a document purporting to certify that fact and to be signed by a medical practitioner.

(5) A document purporting to be such a statement or such a certificate, or both such a statement and such a certificate, as is mentioned in subsection (3) (*a*) above is admissible in evidence on behalf of the prosecution in pursuance of this section only if a copy of it either has been handed to the accused when the document was produced or has been served on him not later than seven days before the hearing, and any other document is so admissible only if a copy of it has been served on the accused not later than seven days before the hearing; but a document purporting to be a certificate (or so much of a document as purports to be a certificate) is not so admissible if the accused, not later than three days before the hearing or within such further time as the court may in special circumstances allow, has served notice on the prosecutor requiring the attendance at the hearing of the person by whom the document purports to be signed.

(6) Where, at the time a specimen of blood or urine was provided by the accused; he asked to be supplied with such a specimen, evidence of the proportion of alcohol or any drug found in the specimen is not admissible on behalf of the prosecution unless—

(*a*) the specimen in which the alcohol or drug was found is one of two parts into which the specimen provided by the accused was divided at the time it was provided; and

(*b*) the other part was supplied to the accused.

(7) In Scotland—

(*a*) a document produced in evidence on behalf of the prosecution in pursuance of subsection (3) or (4) above and, where the person by whom the document was signed is called as a witness, the evidence of that person, shall be sufficient evidence of the facts stated in the document; and

(*b*) a written execution purporting to be signed by the person who handed to or served on the accused or the prosecutor a copy of the document or of the notice in terms of subsection (5) above, together with, where appropriate, a post office receipt for the relative registered or recorded delivery letter shall be sufficient evidence of the handing or service of such a copy or notice.

(8) A copy of a certificate required by this section to be served on the accused or a notice required by this section to be served on

the prosecutor may be served personally or sent by registered post or recorded delivery service.

(9) In this section "authorised analyst" means any person possessing the qualifications prescribed by regulations made under section 89 of the Food and Drugs Act 1955 or section 27 of the Food and Drugs (Scotland) Act 1956 as qualifying persons for appointment as public analysts under those Acts, and any other person authorised by the Secretary of State to make analyses for the purposes of this section.]

AMENDMENT
This section was substituted by the Transport Act 1981, s. 25 (3) and Sched. 8, which came into force on May 6, 1983 (S.I. 1983 No. 576).

NOTE
Section 10 (2) (*a*) and (*b*). See further pp. 121 *et seq.*

[Detention of persons affected by alcohol or a drug

11.—A person required to provide a specimen of breath, blood or urine may thereafter be detained at a police station until it appears to a constable that, were that person then driving or attempting to drive a motor vehicle on a road, he would not be committing an offence under section 5 or section 6 of this Act; but—

(*a*) a person shall not be detained in pursuance of this section if it appears to a constable that there is no likelihood of his driving or attempting to drive a motor vehicle whilst his ability to drive properly is impaired or whilst the proportion of alcohol in his breath, blood or urine exceeds the prescribed limit; and

(*b*) a constable shall consult a medical practitioner on any question arising under this section whether a person's ability to drive properly is or might be impaired through drugs and shall act on the medical practitioner's advice.]

AMENDMENT
This section was substituted by the Transport Act 1981, s. 25(3) and Sched. 8, which came into force on May 6, 1983 (S.I. 1983 No. 576).

[Interpretation of sections 5 to 11

12.—(1) The following provisions apply for the interpretation of sections 5 to 11 of this Act.

(2) In those sections—

"breath test" means a preliminary test for the purpose of obtaining, by means of a device of a type approved by the Secretary of State, an indication whether the proportion of alcohol in a person's breath or blood is likely to exceed the prescribed limit;

"drug" includes any intoxicant other than alcohol;

"fail" includes refuse;

"hospital" means an institution which provides medical or surgical treatment for in-patients or out-patients;

"the prescribed limit" means, as the case may require—

(a) 35 microgrammes of alcohol in 100 millilitres of breath;

(b) 80 milligrammes of alcohol in 100 millilitres of blood; or

(c) 107 milligrammes of alcohol in 100 millilitres of urine;

or such other proportion as may be prescribed by regulations made by the Secretary of State.

(3) A person does not provide a specimen of breath for a breath test or for analysis unless the specimen is sufficient to enable the test or the analysis to be carried out [and provided in such a way as to enable the objective of the test or analysis to be satisfactorily achieved].

(4) A person provides a specimen of blood if and only if he consents to its being taken by a medical practitioner and it is so taken.]

AMENDMENT

This section was substituted by the Transport Act 1981, s. 25 (3) and Sched. 8, which came into force on May 6, 1983 (S.I. 1983 No. 576).

The words in square brackets in subs. (3) were added by the Transport Act 1982, s. 59, with effect from the coming into force of the substituted section (S.I. 1983 No. 577).

NOTE

"drug." See further Chapter 8, above.

LEGAL REFERENCES

ADAMS, J.N., "Doubts and the Breathalyzer," (1969) 51 *Law Guardian* 21.

"Alcohol Abuse and the Law" 94 *Harvard Law Review* 1660.

AMEY, P., "Drink/Drive: A new Initiative," 146 J.P. N. 480.

BARNETT, C.W.H., "Blood and Alcohol Test Procedures (1980)," 120 New L.J. 949.

BARNETT, C.W.H., "Drinking Driving Cases. Evidential Problems," (1982) 122 New L.J. 245.

"The Basingstoke Breathalyser—theory v. the real world," 148 J.P. N. 3.

BEAVAN, A., "Querying the Intoximeter," 80 L.S.Gaz. 2835.

BEAVAN, A., "Querying the Intoximeter again," 81 L.S.Gaz. 563.

BONNER, G.A., "The Breathalyzer and the Drink-Driving laws," 74 L.S.Gaz. 754.

BORKENSTEIN & SMITH, "Breathalyser," (1961) 1 Med. Sci. & Law 13.

BRASLAVSKY, N., "Technology and the Trespassing Police Officer," 146 J.P. N. 21.

"Breath Alcohol Analysis: Can it withstand Modern Scientific Scrutiny?" 5 *North Kentucky Law Review* 207.

"Breathalyser—Evidence to Contrary," 24 *Criminal Law Quarterly* 41.

BROWN, W.A., "Attempt in Road Traffic Offences," 1968 S.L.T. (News) 113.

BROWN W.A., "The Balloon goes up," (1969) 14 J.L.S. 126.

BROWN, W.A., "The Road Safety Act 1967 Pt 1," (1967) 12 J.L.S. 471.

BROWNLIE, Alistair R., "Drink Drugs & Driving—A Survey," (1975) 43 *Medico-Legal Journal* 143.

BURGES, S.H., JOHNSON, C.H. and LAWRENCE, R.A.A.R., "Alcohol Intoxication and Driving," in *The New Police Surgeon*, Chapter 15 p. 380. (1978).

CALDWELL, J.L., "Blood-Alcohol Offences the Judicial Approach," [1983] *New Zealand Law Journal* 286.

COLEMAN, R.F. and WALLS, H.J., "The Evaluation of Scientific Evidence," [1976] Crim. L.R. 344.

"Consultation Paper on Drinking and Driving—British Academy of Forensic Sciences," (1980) 20 Med. Sci. & Law 151.

COOPER, H.E. and BAMFORD, B.R., *South African Motor Law* (1965) containing Chapter 18 "Medico-Legal Aspects of Acute Alcoholic Intoxication," by H.A. Shapiro.

CROMPTON, W. RUFUS, "Alcohol and Fatal Road Traffic Accidents," (1982) 22 Med. Sci. & Law 189.

DOSSETT, J.A. "The Significance of a Difference between Two Successive Readings on the Lion Intoximeter 3000." (1984) 81 L.S. Gaz. 2840.

"Drinking & Driving in Communist Europe digested," (1964) 4 Med. Sci. & Law 71.

"Drinking and Driving: Procedure or Penalties," (1976) 21 J.L.S. 388.

ELLIOTT, D.W. and STREET, H., *Road Accidents*, (Penguin Books, 1968).

ERWIN, R.E., *Defence of Drunk Driving Cases: Criminal/Civil*, (3rd Ed. Matthew Bender, New York, 1984).

FELDMAN, J. and COHEN, H., "The Questionable Accuracy of the Breathalyzer Tests," 19 *Trial* 54.

FELDSTEIN, A., "Blood-Alcohol concentrations in Drinking/Driving Prosecutions," (1983) 133 N.L.J. 36.

FITZGERALD, P.J. and POLE, K.F.M. "The Road Safety Act 1967," (1969) 119 New L.J. pp. 43 and 61.

FLANNAGAN, N.G. and OTHERS, "Blood Alcohol and Social Drinking," (1979) 19 Med. Sci. & Law 180.

FLANNAGAN, N.G. and OTHERS, "The Effects of Low Doses of Alcohol on Driving Performance," (1983) 23 Med. Sci. & Law 203.

FLANNAGAN, N.G. and OTHERS, "Further Observations in the Validity of Urine Alcohol Levels in Road Traffic Offences," (1977) 17 Med. Sci. & Law 269.

GATT, J.A., "The Effect of Temperature on Blood/Breath Ratio: An Interpretation of Breath Alcohol Results," (1984) 134 New L.J. 249.

GORDON, G.H., "The Breathalyser in Scotland," [1974] Crim. L.R. pp. 165 and 209.

HAGAN & OSBOROUGH, N. "The Drinking Motorist and the Road Traffic Act (N.I.) 1964," (1967) 18 *Northern Ireland Law Quarterly* 395.

HARPER, R., "Drinking & Driving in 1980: a Good Year?" (1981) 125 S.J. 507.

HARVEY, F.C., "Roadside Screening: A Police Officer's Views," (1968) *Criminal Law Quarterly* 415.

HAVARD, J.D.J., "Alcohol and Road Accidents," 1962 *Practitioner* pp. 188 and 498.

HAVARD, J.D.J., *Alcohol in Relation to Road Traffic*, in Gradwohl's Legal Medicine, Chapter 35, p. 532, (3rd Ed. 1976).

HAVARD, J.D.J., "Recent Developments in the Alcohol and Road Traffic Situation," (1963) *British Journal of Addiction* 55.

HERXHEIMER, A., "Driving under the Influence of Oxazepam: Guilt without responsibility?" (1982) 132 New L.J. 718.

ISAACS, M.D.J. and OTHERS, "Impressions of the First Six Months of the Transport Act 1981," delivered at 9th International Conference on Alcohol, Drugs and Traffic Safety, Puerto Rico, 1983.

ISAACS, M.D.J. and OTHERS, "The Transition to Evidential Breath Testing in Great Britain," delivered at 9th International Conference on Alcohol Drugs and Traffic Safety, Puerto Rico, 1983.

JONES, A.W., "How Breathing Techniques Can Influence the Results of Breath Alcohol Analysis," (1982) 22 Med. Sci. & Law 275.

JOYE, R.I., "Drunk Driving," 19 *Trial* 60.

KEITH & CLARK, "What is a Road?" [1959] Crim. L.R. 326.

KINNIS, WILLIAM, "Breath Test Technicalities," (1975) 20 J.L.S. 38.

LADD, M. & GIBSON, R.B., "Legal-Medical Aspects of Blood Tests to Determine Intoxication," (1943) 18 Ann. Int. Med. 564.

LASOK, D., "The Problem of Criminal Responsibility of Drunken Drivers," (1962) 1 *Solicitors' Quarterly* 47.

LEEMING, J.J., "Doubt and Hunch" in *Road Accidents: Prevent or Punish*, Chapter 13. (Cassell, London 1969).

McINTOSH, John H.B., "Self-Incrimination and the Breathalyser," 36 *Saskatchewan Law Review* 22.

MAHER, G. and OTHERS, "Diabetes Mellitus and Criminal Responsibility," (1984) 24 Med. Sci. & Law 95.

MASON, J.K., (1984) 128 S.J. 539.

MATHERS, J.M.F., "The Drinking Driver," (1983) 80 L.S.Gaz. 1041.

MURPHY, H.F., "Chemical Tests for Intoxication: A Criticism," [1964] *New Zealand Law Journal* pp. 491 and 511.

NEWARK, M., "Failure to Object to an Irregularity," [1968] Crim. L.R. 310.

NEWARK, M. and SAMUELS, A., "Disastrously Complicated Offence," (1970) 10 Med. Sci. & Law pp. 59 and 160.

NOKES, G.D., "Real Evidence," (1949) 65 *Law Quarterly Review* 57.

NOKES, G.D., "Self-Incrimination by the Accused in English Law," (1966) 2 *University of British Columbia Law Review* 316.

OLIVER, J.S., SLOAN, E., HAMILTON SMITH and RODGER, W.J., "Alcohol and Driving: a Survey of Prosecution and Defence Alcohol Estimations," (1975) 15 Med. Sci. & Law 211.

OLSON, J.S., "Effective use of expert testimony in defence of Drink Driving cases," 54 *Wisconsin Bar Bull.* 17.

"Pilots who Drink": 45 *Journal of Air Law* 1089.

POLE, Dr. K.F.M., "The Driver as the Doctor Sees Him," in *Road Accidents: Prevent or Punish* J.J. Leeming, Chapter 11 (Cassels, London, 1969).

"The Price for Driving while Intoxicated: Should it be Blood?" 4 *Price Law Rev.* 115.

ROBERTSON, W. and OTHERS, "Jail sentences for Driving while Intoxicated in Chicago: a Judicial Policy that failed," 8 *Law & Society Review* 55.

ROBINSON, Ann E., "Alcohol and the Drinking Driver's Blood Sample," (1974) 71 *Guardian Gazette* 8.

ROSS, H.L., "Deterring the Drinking Driver: A critique of Blennerhassett," 3 *British Journal of Law & Society* 255.

ROSS, H.L., "Law Science and Accidents: The British Road Safety Act 1967," 2 *Journal of Legal Studies* 1.

ROSS, H.L., "Sanctions for the Drinking Driver: An Experimental Study," 3 *Journal of Legal Studies* 53.

ROSS, H.L., "Scandinavian Myth: the Effectiveness of Drink and Driving Legislation in Sweden and Norway," 4 *Journal of Legal Studies* 285.

RYAN, S., "Use of Chemical Tests to Prove Impairment by Alcohol," (1959) 2 *Criminal Law Quarterly* 41.

SAEED, S., "The drunken drivers: a new approach," (1982) 55 *Police Journal* p. 373.

SAMUELS, A., "Defence to the new Drunken Driving Laws," (1983) 133 New L.J. 435.

SAMUELS, A., "Drunken Driving: all the Known Defences," (1975) 125 New L.J. 838.

SAMUELS, A., "Drunken Driving: Challenging the Blood or Urine Analysis," (1980) 20 Med. Sci. & Law 14.

SAMUELS, A., "Drunken Driving: has the juridical nature of the offence changed?" (1983) 133 New L.J. 426.

SEAGO, P., "Breathalyser Re-blown," [1973] Crim.L.R. 153.

SEAGO, P., "Driving to Drink," [1970] Crim.L.R. 683.

SEAGO, P., "Offences under the Road Safety Act 1967," [1969] Crim.L.R. 292.

"Self Incrimination and the Breathalyser," 36 *Saskatchewan Law Review* 22.

"Sentencing in Drink/Driving Cases," 142 J.P. N. 188.

SIMON, M., "Driving with Excess Blood Alcohol: Recent Developments in French Law," 29 C.L.Q. 166.

SIMPSON, Sir J., "Police Procedure in Relation to the Drinking Driver," in *Alcohol and Road Traffic*, p. 49 (B.M.A. 1963).

SLOUGH & WILSON, "Alcohol and the Motorist: Practical and Legal Problems of Chemical Testing," (1960) 44 Minnesota Law Review 673.

SMITH, H. WARD, "Drinking and Driving," (1960) 3 *Criminal Law Quarterly* 65.

SMITH, J.C., "Alcohol and Road Traffic—the English Law and its Reformation," *Alcohol and Road Traffic*, p. 299 (B.M.A. 1963).

SMITH, J.C. and HOGAN, *Criminal Law* Chap. 14 (Butterworth, 5th Ed., 1983).

SPENCER, J., "Drinking & Driving Laws Revisited," 127 S.J. 772.

STATISTICS OF BREATH TESTS—ENGLAND, WALES, 1983, Home Office Statistical Bulletin, 20/84.

STENNING, P.C., "Breathalyser Reference," 12 *Criminal Law Quarterly* 394.

STEWART, J.B., "Smoking and the Breathalyser," (1975) S.L.T. (News) 197.

"Submission to the Blennerhassett Committee on Drinking and Driving—British Academy of Forensic Sciences," (1975) 15 Med. Sci. & Law 218.

SWEENY, J., "Sound Motion Pictures as Evidence of Intoxication," (1965) 52 *Cornell Law Quarterly* 323.

TAYLOR, Eric, "The Non-Driving Drinker," [1975] Crim.L.R. 670.

TAYLOR, Lawrence E., *Drunk Driving Defense*, (Little Brown & Co. Boston, 1981): First supplement 1984.

"True Blood-Alcohol Level: Drink and Driving," 45 A.L.J. 360.

TURNER, A., "The Transport Act 1981: Excess alcohol provisions," 147 J.P. N. 341.

VOTEY, H.L., "Scandinavian Drinking-Driving Control: Myth?" 11 *Journal Legal Studies* 93.

WILLIAMS, Glanville, "Absolute Liability in Traffic Offences," [1967] Crim.L.R. 194.
WILLIAMS, Glanville, "Reckless Driving and Intoxication," (1978) 128 New L.J. 276.
WRIGHT, B.M., "Alcohol the Motorist and the Law," (1967) 117 New L.J. pp. 631 and 659.
WRIGHT, B.M., JONES, T.P. and JONES, A.W., (1975) 15 Med. Sci. & Law 295.
YOUNG, N., "Special Reasons," 1966 S.L.T. (News) 113.

APPENDIX IV

SCIENTIFIC REFERENCES

The list starting on p. 255 contains all of the scientific references cited in the text. It is NOT a complete bibliography of the subject, which would be several times as long.

The publications cited are of three kinds:

(A) Papers in scientific and medical journals.

(B) Books and other "one-off" publications.

(C) Reports of conferences containing contributions by many authors.

(A) **TEXT** references to papers in journals consist of
Name(s) of author(s), date of publication.

Full references in the list starting on p. 255 consist of
NAME(s) (date of publication): *Title of Journal,* **volume no.**, (part, in some cases), page.

Some long journal titles which occur frequently are abbreviated as follows:

Accid. Anal. Prev.: *Accident Analysis and Prevention*

B.M.J.: *British Medical Journal*

Clin. Pharm. Ther.: *Clinical Pharmacology and Therapeutics*

Dt. Z. ges. ger. Med.: *Deutsche Zeitschrift für die gesamte gerichtliche Medizin.* (This journal has now been re-named *Zeitschrift für Rechtsmedizin*—q.v., below)

J.A.M.A. : *Journal of the American Medical Association*

J. For. Sc.: *Journal of Forensic Sciences* (American)

J. For Sc. Soc. Journal of the Forensic Science Society (British)

Med. Sci. Law: *Medicine, Science and the Law* (organ of the British Academy of Forensic Sciences)

Pharmakopsych.: *Pharmakopsychiatrie* (*Neuro-Psycholpharmakologie* appears to be an additional or alternative title for the same journal.)

Quart. Jl. Stud. Alc.: *Quarterly Journal of Studies on Alcohol*

TRRL Reports: Transport and Road Research Laboratory reports

Zeitschr. f. Rechtsmed.: *Zeitschrift für Rechtsmedizin* (formerly *Deutsche Zeitschrift für die ges. ger. Medizin*—q.v., above. Now uses German and English as alternative languages, and *Journal of Legal Medicine* as an alternative title.)

Note: The journal *Blutalkohol*, published by Verlag Deutsche Polizei, Hamburg, should not be confused with the book of the same name by H. Elbel and F. Schleyer. In the text and the list below the journal is referred to by that name, and the book as *Elbel and Schleyer*.

(B) References to books and other "one-off" publications are given in the **TEXT** by

Name(s) of author(s), page

and in the list below by

Names(s) of Author(s) (date of publication), *Title*, (Publisher, **place of publication**).

(C) In recent decades international conferences on the general subject of alcohol and road traffic have been held every few years and their proceedings published as reports. So far, eight such reports have appeared, and a ninth is on the way. The first eight are:

1. Proceedings of the 1st International Conference, **Stockholm**, 1951.

2. Proceedings of the 2nd International Conference, 1953.

Any reference to either of these conferences will rarely be encountered nowadays.

3. *Alcohol and Road Traffic*. Proceedings of the 3rd International Conference on Alcohol and Road Traffic, **London** 1962. Published B.M.A. 1963.

4. *Alcohol and Traffic Safety*. Proceedings of the 4th International Conference on Alcohol and Traffic Safety, **Indiana**, 1965. Published Indiana University, Bloomington, Indiana.

5. *Alkohol und Verkehrssicherheit*. Konferenzbericht der 5. Internationalen Konferenz über Alkohol und Verkenhrssicherheit, **Freiburg im Breisgau**, 1969. Published Hans Ferdinand Schulz Verlag, Freiburg.

6. *Alcohol, Drugs and Traffic Safety*. (1974) Proceedings of the 6th International Conference on Alcohol, Drugs and Traffic Safety, **Toronto**, 1974. Published by Addiction Research Foundation of Ontario, 1975.

7. *Proceedings, Seventh International Conference on Alcohol,*

Drugs and Traffic Safety, **Melbourne**, 1977. Australian Government Publishing Service, Canberra, 1979.

8. *Alcohol, Drugs and Traffic Safety* (1980). International Conference on Alcohol, Drugs and Traffic Safety, **Stockholm**, 1980. Published in 2 vols., Almqvist & Wiksell, Stockholm, 1981.

References here to these reports give the date of the conference, not that of publication, which is usually a year later.

References appear in the **TEXT** as

       Author, place and date of conference, page

and in the list below as

AUTHOR(S) (date of conferernce): Brief identification of conference, **Place**, page in report.

ABELE, G. AND KROPP, R. (1958): *Dt. Z. ges. ger. Med*, **48**, 69.

ADERJAHN R. AND SCHMIDT, G. (1980): Proc. 8th Internat. Conf. **Stockholm**, p. 996.

ALHA, A.R., KARLSSON, M., LINNOILA, M. AND LUKKARI, I. (1977): *Zeitschr. f. Rechtsmed*. **79**, 225.

ALOBAIDI, T.A.A., HILL, D.W. AND PAYNE, J.P. (1976) *B.M.J.* **2**, 1479.

ANDERSSON, K. ET AL. (1977): *Blutalkohol*, **14**, 366.

ANTEBI, D. (1982): *Med., Sci. and the Law*, **22**(3), 181.

APEL, G. (1960): *Dt. Z. ges. ger. Med.*, **49**, 388.

ARNOLD, W. AND BRINKMANN, B. (1980) : Proc. 8th Internat. Conf., **Stockholm**, p. 506.

BAILEY, J.P.M., WILLIAMS, P.P., NORRIS, R.J. AND CAMERON, B.J. (1982) : See STONE (New Zealand), p. 37.

BASKETT, P.J.F. (1979): *Lancet*, **1**, 490.

BATT, R.D. AND COUCHMAN, K.G. (1977): Proc. 7th Internat. Conf., **Melbourne**, p. 200.

BEGG, T.B., HILL, L.D. AND NICKOLLS, L.C. (1972): Proc. 3rd Internat. Conf., **London**, p. 277.

BESSERER, K. AND SPRINGER, E. (1971): *Blutalkohol*, **8**, 122.

BETTS, T.A., CLAYTON, A.B. AND MACKAY, G.M. (1972): *B.M.J.*, **4**, 580.

BILZER, N. AND KÜHNHOLZ, B. (1979): *Blutalkohol*, **16**, 220.

BJERVER, K. AND GOLDBERG, L. (1950): *Quart. Jl. Stud. Alc.*, **11**, 1.

BLACKMORE, D.J. (1968): *J. For. Sc. Soc.*, **8**, 73.

BLENNERHASSETT, F. (1976): (Chairman, D.O.E. Departmental Committee), *Drinking & Driving*. (H.M.S.O., 1976).

BODE, J.C. (1974): In *Alcohol and Acetaldehyde Metabolising Systems* (Academic Press, New York,).

BOGEN, J. (1927): *J. A. M. A.*, **98**, 1508.

BONNISCHSEN, R., DIMBERG, R. AND SJOBERG, L. (1964): *Meddelande Nr. 12 från Institutet för Maltdryckforskning* (Stockholm, 1964).

BONNICHSEN, R., DIMBERG, R., MAEHLY, A. AND ÅQVIST, S. (1967): *Meddlelande Nr. 16 från Institutet för Maltdryckforskning* (Stockholm, 1967).

BONNICHSEN, R., DIMBERG, R., MAEHLY, A. AND ÅQVIST, S., (1968): *Blutalkohol*, **5**, 301.

BONNICHSEN, R., MAEHLY, A. AND ÅQVIST, S. (1970): *Blutalkohol*, **7**, 1.

BONNICHSEN, R., MAEHLY, A., MÖLLER, M. AND ÅQVIST, S. (1972): *Blutalkohol*, **9**, 8.

BONTE, W. ET AL. (1978 & 1979): *Blutalkohol*, (1978), **15**(5), 323 and (1979), **16**(2), 108.

BORKENSTEIN, R.F. (1960): *J. For. Sc.*, **5**, 395.

BORKENSTEIN, R.F., CROWTHER, R.F., SHUMATE, R.P., ZIEL, W.B. AND ZYLMAN, R. (1964): *Report on the Grand Rapids Survey* (Department of Police Administration, Indiana University,).

BRADFORD, L.W. (1966): *J. For. Sc. Soc.*, **6**, 204.

BRETTEL, H.-F. (1975): *Zeitschr. f. Rechtsmed.*, **76**, 31.

BRINKMANN, B., NAEVE, W., EICHEN, R. AND REHNER, M. (1970), *Blutalkohol*, **7**, 358.

BROWN, G.A., NEYLAND, D., REYNOLDS, W.J. AND SMALLDON, K.W. (1973): *Analytica Chimica Acta*, **66**, 271.

BURFORD, R., FRENCH, I.W. AND LEBLANC, A.E. (1974): Proc. 6th Internat. Conf., Toronto, p. 423.

CAMPS, F.E. AND ROBINSON, A.E. (1968): *Med., Sci. and Law*, **8**, 153,

Canadian Medical Association Journal (1972): Editorial, **107**, 269.

CASSWELL, S. (1977): Proc. 7th Internat. Conf., Melbourne, p. 238.

CHORLTON, P. (1983): *Guardian*, 28.1.'83, p. 16.

CLARKE, DR. J.A.C., DUDLEY (1982): Private Communication.

CLAYTON, A.B., HARVEY, P.G. AND BETTS, T.A. (1977): Proc. 7th Internat. Conf., Melbourne, p. 230.

CLAYTON, A.B. (1980): In *Psychopharmacology of Alcohol*, p. 73 (Ed. Merton Sandler, Raven Press, New York, 1980).

COHEN, J., DEARNALEY, E.J. AND HANSEL, C.E.M. (1958) *B.M.J.* **1**, 1438.

COLDWELL, B.B., PENNER, D.W., SMITH, H.W., LUCAS,

G.H.W., RODGERS, R.F. AND DARROCH, F. (1958): *Quart. Jl. Stud. Alc.*, **19**, 590.

COLDWELL, B.B., AND SMITH, H.W. (1959): *Canadian Journal of Biochemistry*, **37**, 43.

COLDWELL, B.B. AND GRANT, G.L. (1963): *J. Foren. Sci.* **8**, 220.

COLLISTER, RUBY M. (1962): Proc. 3rd Internat. Conf., **London**, p. 31.

COOPER, W.E., SCHWÄR, T.G. AND SMITH, L.S. (1979): *Alcohol, Drugs and Road Traffic.* (Juta and Co., South Africa).

CRANCER ET AL. (1969): *Science* (Washington), **164**, 851,

CROMPTON, M.R. (1982): *Med., Sci. Law* **22**(3), 189.

CURRY, A.S., WALKER, G.W. AND SIMPSON, G.S. (1966): *Analyst*, **91**, 742.

DAL MONTE—See MONTE.

DAVIS, J.H. (1972): *J.A.M.A.*, **221**, 714.

DENNEMARK, H.-G. (1962): *Blutalkohol* **2**, 166.

DENNEY, R.C. (1979): *Drinking and Driving* (Robert Hale, London).

DENNEY, R.C. (1980): *Chemistry in Britain*, **16**, 428.

Deutsche medizinsche Wochenschrift (1971): Editorial, **96**(23), 1027.

DITT, J. & SCHULZ, G. (1962): *Blutalkohol*, **1**, 183.

DITT, J. (1963): *Blutalkohol*, **2**, 68.

DREW, G.C., COLQUHOUN, W.P. AND LONG, H.A. (1959): *Effect of Small Doses of Alcohol on a Skill Resembling Driving* (Medical Research Council Memorandum no. 38, H.M.S.O., London, 1959).

DUBOWSKI, K.M. (1975): *Zeitschr. f. Rechtsmed.*, **76**, 93.

DUBOWSKI, K.M. (1979–1): *Journal of Analytical Toxicology*, **3**, 177.

DUBOWSKI, K.M. (1979–2): *Clinical Chemistry*, **25**(6), 1144.

DUNDEE, J.W., BOVILL, J. AND ISAAC, M. (1971): *Med., Sci., Law*, **11**(3), 146,

DUSSAULT, P. AND CHAPPEL, C.I. (1974): Proc. 6th Internat. Conf., **Toronto**, p. 365,

EBBEL, H. AND SCHLEYER, F. (1956): *Blutalkohol* (Georg Thieme Verlag, Stuttgart). This book should not be confused with the journal of the same name.

EMERSON, V.J., HOLLEYHEAD, R., ISAACS, M.D.J., FULLER, N.A. AND HUNT, D.J. (1980): *J. For. Sc. Soc.*, **20**(1), 3. Also published separately as a hardback (Forensic Science Society, Harrogate).

EMERSON, V.J. (Home Office—1982): Private communication.

ENTICKNAP, J.B. AND WRIGHT, B.M. (1965): Proc. 4th Internat. Conf., **Indiana**, p. 161.

ERWIN, R.E., MINZER, M.K., GREENBERG, L.A., GOLDSTEIN, H.M. AND BERGH, A.K. (1982): *Defence of Drunk Driving Cases* (Bender, New York; 3rd. edn., 1982).

ETZLER, K., JOSWIG, E.H. AND MALLACH, H.J. (1968): *Archiv für Kriminologie*, **141**, 142.

FAZEKAS, I.G. AND RENGEL, B. (1969): *Blutalkohol*, **6**, 1.

FINKLE, B.S. (1980): *Alcohol, Drugs and Driving* (Paper presented to the National Safety Congress, Traffic Division, Oct. 1980).

FLANAGAN, N.G., LOCHRIDGE, G.K., HENRY, J.G., HADLOW, A.J. AND HAMER, P.S. (1979): *Med., Sci., Law*, **19**(3), 180.

FLOM, M.C., BROWN, B., ADAMS, R.J. AND JONES, R.T. (1976): *American Journal of Optometry and Physical Optics*, **53**(12), 764.

FORNEY, R.B., HARGER, R.N., HUGHES AND RICHARDS (1964): *Quart. Jl. Stud. Alc.*, **25**, 205.

FORNEY, R.B. (1973): *Pharmakopsych.* **6**(2), 104.

FORNEY, R.B. (1979): *Report of Sub-Committee on Human Factors* (National Safety Council's Committee on Alcohol and Drugs, Chicago, 1979).

FORSTER, G., SCHULZ, G. AND STARCK, H.J. (1961): *Blutalkohol*, **1**, 2.

FOX, B.H., HALLETT, R.A., MAKOWSKI, W., SCHNALL, A.M. AND PELCH, A. (1965): Proc. 4th Internat. Conf., **Indiana**, p. 128.

FRANKS, H.M., STARMER, G.A., CHESHER, G.B., JACKSON, D.M., HENSLEY, V.R. AND HENSLEY, W.J. (1974): Proc. 6th Internat. Conf., **Toronto**, p. 461.

FROENTJES, W. (1962): Proc. 3rd Internat. Conf., **London**, p. 179.

GARRIOTT, J.C., DIMAIO, V.J.H., ZUMWALT, R.E. AND PETTY, C.S. (1977): *J. For. Sci.*, **22**(2), 383.

GEHM, E. AND SCHMIDT, W. (1962): *Dt. Z. ges. ger. Med.*, **52**, 424.

GELBKE, H.P., SCHLICHT, H.J. AND SCHMIDT, G. (1978): *Zeitschr. f. Rechtsmed.*, **80**(4), 319.

GERCHOW, J. AND SACHS, V. (1961): *Dt. Z. ges. ger. Med.*, **51**, 32.

GERLACH, D. (1973): *Blutalkohol*, **9**, 239.

GHIMICESCU, G., COTRAU, M., DUMBRAVA, E., PROCA, M.,

DIMA, E., BAZGAN, L. & PIROZINSCKI, T. (1969): Proc. 5th Internat. Conf., **Freiburg im Breisgau**, p. II–9.

GOLDBERG, L. (1951): Proc. 1st Internat. Conf., **Stockholm**, p. 85.

GOLDBERG, L. (1965): Proc. 4th Internat. Conf., **Indiana**, p. 235.

GOLDBERG, L. AND HAVARD, J.D.J. (1968): *Research on the Effects of Alcohol and Drugs on Driver Behaviour* (Organisation for Economic Co-operation and Development, Paris).

GOLDBERG, L., WAYNE-JONES, A. AND NERI, A. (1979): *Blutalkohol*, **16**, 431.

GOLDMAN, V. ET AL. (1969): *Nature*, **224**, 1175.

GORDON, N.B. (1976): *Accid. Anal. Prev.*, **8**, 3.

GOSTOMZYK, J.G., REINEKE, H., NEUMANN, G.K. AND LEITHOFF, H. (1974): *Zeitschr. f. Rechtsmed.*, **75**, 37.

GREENBERG, L.A. AND LESTER, D. (1954): *Quart. Jl. Stud. Alc.*, **15**, 16.

GRÜNER, O. (1959): *Dt. Z. ges. ger. Med.*, **49**, 235.

GRÜNER, O., LUDWIG, O. AND TRABANT, G. (1970): *Blutalkohol*, **7**, 338.

HAISMAN, M.F., KIMBER, K.J. AND WALLS, H.J. (1963): *British Journal of Addiction*, **59**, 24.

HANSTEEN, R.W. AND JONES, R. (1976): *Annals of New York Academy of Sciences*, **282**, 240.

HARGER, R.N., FORNEY, R.B. AND BARNES, H.B. (1950): *Journal of Laboratory and Clinical Medicine*, **36**(2), 306.

HARGER, R.N., FORNEY, R.B. AND BAKER, R.S. (1956): *Quart. Jl. Stud. Alc.*, **17**, 1.

HARGER, R.N. (1956): *Alcoholism*, p. 103 (ed. G. N. Thompson; pub. Chas. C. Thomas, Springfield, Ill.).

HARGER, R.N. (1961): in *Toxicology: Mechanisms and Analytical Methods*, ed. C. P. Stewart and A. Stolman, p. 85 (Academic Press, New York).

HARGER, R.N. (1962): Proc. 3rd. Internat. Conf., **London**, p. 212.

HARGER, R.N. (1965): Proc. 4th Internat. Conf., **Indiana**, p. 182.

HARGER, R.N. AND FORNEY, R.B. (1967): Chapter *Aliphatic Alcohols*, in *Progress in Chemical Toxicology*, vol 3 (ed. A. Stolman, Academic Press, New York).

HARGER, R.N. AND FORNEY, R.B. (1969): Proc. 5th Internat Conf, **Freiburg im Breisgau**, p. II–73.

HARTMANN, H.P. (1980): *Der Kranke als Fahrzeuglenker* (Springer Verlag, Berlin).

HARVEY, D.J., LEUSCHNER, J.A.A. AND PATON, W.D.M. (1980): *Journal of Chromatography*, **202**, 89.

HARVEY, D.J. (1982): *Report on the Effects of Cannabis* to the Advisory Council on the Misuse of Drugs (H.M.S.O., London).

HAUCK, G. AND SPANN, W. (1974): *Medizinische Klinik*, **69**(13), 525.

HAVARD, J.D.J. (1973): *Pharmakopsych.*, **6**(2), 67.

HAVARD, J.D.J. (1976): *Medical Aspects of Fitness to Drive*: A guide for Medical Practitioners (B.M.A., London).

HELMER, R., WUNDER, K., ZELLMANN, K. AND HAESSEN, D. (1972): *Blutalkohol*, **9**, 213.

HICKEY, M., HAYDEN, P.M., LAYDEN, M.T. AND HEARNE, R. (1975): *Journal of the Irish Medical Association*, **68**, 583.

HOLCOMB, R.L. (1938): *J.A.M.A.*, **111**, 1076.

HUFFMANN, W.J., FLORIO, A.E., PAYNE, J.L. AND BOYS, F.E. (1963): *American Journal of Psychiatry*, **119**, 888.

HUNTLEY, M.S. AND CENTYBEAR, T.M. (1974): *Human Factors*, **16**(1), 19.

ISAACS, M.D.J., EMERSON, V.J., FULLER, N.A. AND HOLLYHEAD, R. (1980): Proc. 8th Internat. Conf., **Stockholm**, p. 442.

ISAACS, M.D.J., JACOBS, J.M., EMERSON, V.J., BROSTER, G.C. AND HUNT, D. (1982): *Field Trial of Three Substantive Breath Alcohol Testing Instruments* (H.M.S.O., London).

IVANOV, S.V. (Scientific Attaché, U.S.S.R. Embassy) and Uljanov, V.A. (Ministry of Internal Affairs, Moscow) (1983): Private Communication.

JACOBSEN, E. (1952): *Nature*, **169**, 645.

J.A.M.A. (1972): editorial, **220**(1), 139.

JEFFCOATE, G.O. (1958): *British Journal of Addiction*, **55**, 37.

JOACHIM, H., FRIEDRICH, G. AND ULLMANN, H. (1974): *Blutalkohol*, **11**, 88.

JOACHIM, H. AND WEYER, H.H. (1975): *Zeitschr. f. Rechtsmed.*, **76**, 187.

JONES, A.W. AND JONES, T.P. (1971): *Counter-Measures to Driver Behaviour under the Influence of Alcohol and other Drugs*. Proceedings O.E.C.D. International Symposium, London).

JONES, A.W., WRIGHT, B.M. AND JONES, T.P. (1974): Proc. 6th Internat. Conf., **Toronto**, p. 509.

JONES, A.W. (1978): *Forensic Science International*, **12**, 11.

JONES, A.W. (1982): *Med. Sci. Law*, **22**(4), 275.

JONES, T.P., JONES, A.W. AND WILLIAMS, P.M. (1977): Proc. 7th Internat. Conf., **Melbourne**, p. 259.

JOYCE, C.R.B., EDGECOMBE, P.C.E., KENNARD, D.A., WEATHERALL, M. AND WOODS, D.P. (1959): *Journal of Mental Science.*, **105**, 51.

KAYE, S. (1974): Proc. 6th Internat. Conf., **Toronto**, p. 85.

KIBRICK, E. AND SMART, R.G. (1970): *Journal of Safety Research*, **2**, 73.

KIELHOLZ, P., HOBI, V., LADEWIG, D., MIEST, P. AND RICHTER, R. (1973): *Pharmakopsych.* **6**(2), 91.

KITIGAWA, T. AND WRIGHT, B.M. (1962): *B.M.J.*, **2**, 652.

KLEBELSBERG, D. (1973): *Pharmakopsych.*, **6**(2), 83.

KLEIN, A.W., DAVIS, J.H. AND BLACKBOURNE, B.D. (1971): *Journal of Drug Issues*, **1**, 18.

KLONOFF, H. (1974): *Science* (Washington), **186** (4161), 317.

KOLENDA, K.B. (1975): *Medizinische Klinik* **70**, 516.

KRAULAND, W., VIDIC, E., FREUDENBERG, K., SCHMIDT, K. AND LENK, V. (1960): *Dt.Z. ges. ger. Med.*, **50**, 34.

KRAULAND, W., MALLACH, H.J., GOSSOW, H. AND FREUDENBERG, K. (1964): *Blutalkohol*, **2**, 293.

KRAULAND, W., MALLACH, H.J., MELLEROWICZ, H. AND MÜLLER, J. (1965): *Blutalkohol*, **3**, 63.

KRAULAND, W. (1966): *Dt. Z. ges. gr. Med.*, **57**, 263.

KREUZER, A. (1974): *Blutalkohol*, **11**, 329.

KRICKA, L.J. AND CLARK, P.M.S. (1979): *Biochemistry of Alcohol and Alcoholism.* (pub. Ellis Horwood, Chichester).

KULPE, W. AND MALLACH, H.J. (1961): *Zeitschrift für klinische Medizin*, **156**, 432.

LANDAUER, A.A. AND MILNER, G. (1969): *Science* (Washington), **163**, 1467.

LANDAUER, A.A. AND MILNER, G. (1971): *Psychopharmacology*, **4**(5), 265; and *Journal of Forensic Medicine* (Johannesburg), **18**(4), 127.

LANDAUER, A.A., LAURIE, N. AND MILNER, G. (1973): *Forensic Science*, **2**(3), 275.

LANDAUER, A.A., POCOCK, D.A. AND PROTT, F.M. (1974): *Psychopharmacology*, **37**(4), 159.

LAURELL, H. (1977): Proc. 7th Internat. Conf., **Melbourne**, p. 157; and *Accid. Anal. Prev.*, **8**, 19.

LEGG, N.J., MALPAS, A. AND SCOTT, D.F. (1973): *B.M.J.*, **1**, 417.

LESTER, D. (1961 & 1962): *Quart. Jl. Stud. Alc.*, **22**, 554 and **23**, 17.

LESTER, D. (1965): Proc. 4th Internat. Conf., **Indiana**, p. 267.

LEWRENZ, H., BERGHAUS, G. AND DOTZAUER, G. (1974): *Blutalkohol*, **11**, 104.

LIEBER, CHAS. (1976): *Scientific American*, **234**, 26.

LILJESTRAND, G. AND LINDE, P. (1930); *Skandinavisches Archiv für Physiologie*, **60**, 273.

LIN, L-J, ET AL. (1976): *Research Communications in Chemical Pathology and Pharmacology*, **13**, 713.

LINNOILA, M. (1973–1): *Annals of Medical and Experimental Biology* (Fen.), **51**(3), 118, 125.

LINNOILA, M. AND MATTILA, M.J. (1973–2): *British Journal of Pharmacology*, **47**(3), 671P.

LINNOILA, M. AND MATTILA, M.J. (1973–3): *European Journal of Clinical Pharmacology*, **5**, 186.

LINNOILA, M. AND MATTILA, M.J. (1973–4): *Pharmakopsych.*, **6**(2), 127.

LINNOILA, M. (1974–1): *Annals of Clinical Research*, **6**(1), 7.

LINNOILA, M., SEPPÄLÄ, T. AND MATTILA, M.J., (1974–2): *British Journal of Clinical Pharmacology*, **1**, 477.

LINNOILA, M. ET AL. (1974–3): *Clin. Pharm. Ther.*, **5**, 368.

LINNOILA, M. (1976): *Accid. Anal. Prev.*, **8**(1), 15.

LINNOILA, M., ERWIN, C.W., RAMM, D., CLEVELAND, W.P. AND BREDLE, A. (1980): *Alcoholism: Clinical and Experimental Research*, **4**(3), 302.

LINS, G. AND RAUDONAT, H.W. (1962): *Dt. Z. ges. ger. Med.*, **52**, 242.

LION LABORATORIES, BARRY, S.Glam. (1982): *Intoximeter* 3000 *Instruction Manual*.

LITTLE, J.W. (1972): *Journal of Criminal Law, Criminology and Police Science*, **63**(2), 278.

LOOMIS, T. AND WEST, T.C. (1958): *Quart. Jl. St. Alc.*, **19**, 30.

LOVIBOND, S.M. (1977): Proc. 7th Internat. Conf., **Melbourne**, p. 168.

LOWENSTEIN, L.M., SIMONE, R., BOULTER, P. AND NATHAN, P. (1970): *J.A.M.A.*, **213**(11), 1899.

LUCAS, C.H.W., KALOW, W., McCOLL, J.D., GRIFFITH, B.A. AND SMITH, H.W. (1953): Proceedings Second International Conference on Alcohol and Road Traffic, p. 139.

LUND, A. (1976): *Blutalkohol*, **13**, 166.

LUNDBERG, G.D., WHITE, J.M. AND HOFFMAN, K.I. (1979): *J. For. Sc.*, **24**(1), 207.

LUNDQUIST, F. (1961): *Acta Pharmacologica et Toxicologica*, **18**, 231.

LUNDQUIST, F. AND WOLTHERS, H. (1958): *Acta Pharmacologica et Toxicologica*, **14**, 265.

LUTZ, P. AND LEU, R. (1975): *Blutalkohol*, **12**, 116.

LUTZE, J. AND SCHACHER, E. (1979): *Blutalkohol*, **16**, 49.

MCCALLUM, N.E.W. AND SCROGGIE, J.G. (1963): *Quart. Jl. Stud. Alc.*, **24**, 195.

MCCARROLL, J.R. AND HADDON, W. (1962): *Journal of Chronic Diseases*, **15**, 811.

MCCLEAN, A.J. AND HOLUBOWYCZ, O.T. (1980): Proc. 8th Internat. Conf., **Stockholm**, p. 113.

MACDONALD, I.R.C., STONE, H.M. AND DICK, G.L. (1982): See Stone, (1982), p. 1

MACHATA, G. (1967): *Blutalkohol*, **4**, 252.

MACHATA, G. AND PROKOP, L. (1971 and 1978): *Blutalkohol*, **8**, 281 and **17**, 49.

MALLACH, H.J. (1966): *Blutalkohol*, **3**, 308.

MALPAS, A. (1970): *B.M.J.*, **2**, 762.

MANNO, J.E. ET AL. (1971): *Clin. Pharm. Ther.*, **12**, 202.

MANTON, J.C. (1979): Proc. 7th Internat. Conf., **Melbourne**, p. 247.

MARTIN, G. (1971): *Journal of Safety Research*, **3**(1), 21.

MASON, J.K. AND BLACKMORE, D.J. (1972): *Med., Sci. & Law*, **12**(3), 205.

MASON, M.F. (1974): *J. For. Sc.*, **19**(2), 325.

MASON, M.F. AND HUTSON, D. (1974): Proc. 6th Internat. Conf., **Toronto**, p. 533.

MASON, M.F. AND DUBOWSKI, K.M. (1976): *J. For. Sc.*, **21**(1), 9.

MATTILA, M.J. (1980): Proc. 8th Internat. Conf., **Stockholm**, p. 909.

MILLER, A.I., D'AGOSTINO, A. AND MINSKY, R. (1963): *Quart. Jl. Stud. Alc.*, **24**, 9.

MILLER, J.G. (1962): *J.A.M.A.*, **179**(12), 940.

MILNER, G. AND LANDAUER, A.A. (1971): *British Journal of Psychiatry*, **118**, 351.

MILNER, G. (1972): *Drugs and Driving* (Vol. 1 of Monographs on Drugs, pub. S. Karger, Basel, etc.).

MILNER, G. AND LANDAUER, A.A. (1973): *Medical Journal of Australia*, **1**(17), 837, and *Blutalkohol*, **10**(4), 247.

MISSEN, A.W., CLEARY, W.T., ENG, L., MCDONALD, K.S. AND WATTS, D.T. (1982): see Stone (1982), p. 45.

MOFFAT, A.C. (1980): *J. For. Sc. Soc.*, **20**, 183.

DAL MONTE, P.R., FORMICA, G., MILANDRI, G. AND RUGGIERI, M. (1980): Proc. 8th Internat. Conf., **Stockholm**, p. 160.

MORGAN, W.H.D. (1965): *J. For. Sc. Soc.*, **5**, 15.

MOSKOWITZ, H. (1973): *Pharmakopsych.*, **6**(2), 114.

MOSKOWITZ, H. AND MURRAY, J. (1974): Proc. 6th Internat. Conf., **Toronto**, p. 399.

MOSKOWITZ, H. (1976): *Accid. Anal. Prev.*, **8**(1), 3 and 21.

MOSKOWITZ, H., DAILY, J. AND HENDERSON, R. (1977): Proc. 7th Internat. Conf., **Melbourne**, p. 184.

MOSKOWITZ, H. AND BURNS, M. (1980): Proc. 8th Internat. Conf., **Stockholm**, p. 969.

MOSKOWITZ, H. (1980): *ibid.* p. 881.

MULLEN, P.W. (1977): *J. For. Sc. Soc.*, **17**, 49.

MYERS, R.A.M., TALJAARD, J.J.F. AND PENMAN, K. (1977): *South African Medical Journal*, **52**, 328.

NAESS-SCHMIDT, T.E. (1971): *Blutalkohol*, **8**(5), 318.

NAEVE, W. ET AL. (1974): *Blutalkohol*, **11**, 145.

NEWMAN, H.W., SMITH, M.E. AND NEWMAN, E.J. (1959): *Quart. Jl. Stud. Alc.*, **20**, 213.

NEYLAN, D. (Home Office Forensic Science Labortory, Aldermaston—1982): Private Communication.

NICKOLLS, L.C. (1956): *The Scientific Investigation of Crime* (Butterworth & Co., London).

Nouvelle presse medicale (1972): editorial, **1**(25), 1685.

NPL (NATIONAL PHYSICAL LABORATORY) (1983): *NPL Report BCS 2* (BCS Scheme for Evidential Breath Testing).

ODESAMNI, W.O. (1978): *J. For. Sc. Soc.*, **19**, 131.

OLIVER, DR. J.S., (Glasgow–1982): Private Communication.

VAN OOIJEN, D. (1981): Proc. 8th Internat. Conf., **Stockholm**, p. 342.

OSSELTON, M.D., HAMMOND, M.D. AND MOFFAT, A.C. (1980): *J. For. Sc. Soc.*, **20**, 187.

OSTERHAUS, E. AND JOHANNSMEIER, K. (1966): *Dt. Z. ges. ger. Med.*, **57**, 281.

OSTERWALDER, C. AND SCHMIDT, P. (1973): *Blutalkohol*, **10**(2), 80.

OTTIS L. (1963): *Blutalkohol*, **2**, 25.

PATEL, A.R. (1969): *Scottish Medical Journal*, **14**, 268.

PATMAN, J., LANDAUER, A.A. AND MILNER, G. (1969): *Medical Journal of Australia*, **2**, 946.

PATSCHNEIDER, H. (1975): *Blutalkohol*, **12**, 291.

PAWAN, G.L.S. (1968): *Nature*, **218**, 966.

PAYNE, J.P., HILL, D.W. AND KING, N.W. (1966): *B.M.J.*, **1**, 196.

PAYNE, J.P., FOSTER, D.V., HILL, D.W. AND WOOD D.G.L. (1967): *B.M.J.*, **3**, 819.

PAYNE, J.P., HILL, D.W. AND WOOD, D.G.L. (1968): *Nature*, **217**, 963.

PAYNE, J.P. (1970): *Annals of the Royal College of Surgeons*, **47**, 3.

PAYNE, J.P. (1975): *Proceedings of the Royal Society of Medicine*, **68**, 375.

PERRINE, M.W. (1976): *Modern Problems of Pharmacopsychiatry*, Vol. **11**, (pub. S. Karger, Basel, etc.).

POLKIS, A. AND PEARSON, M.A. (1977): *Clinical Toxicology*, **10**, 429.

PONSOLD, A. (1965): Proc. 4th Internat. Conf., *Indiana*, p. 127.

PONSOLD, A. AND HEITE, H.J. (1960): *Dt. Z. ges. ger. Med.*, **50**, 228.

PRICE, D.L. AND HICKS, T.G. (1979): *Ergonomics*, **22**(1), 37.

PÜSCHEZ, K. (1979): *Blutalkohol*, **16**, 217.

RAFAELSEN, O.J. (1973–1): *Science* (Washington), **179** (4076), 920.

RAFAELSEN, O.J., BECH, P. AND RAFAELSEN, L. (1973–2): *Pharmakopsych*, **6**(2), 71.

RENTOUL, E., SMITH, H. AND BEAVERS, R. (1962): *J. For. Sc. Soc.*, **3**, 2.

RICHTER, R. AND HOBI, V. (1975): *Schweizerische medizinische Wochenschrift*, **165**(27), 884.

ROSE, C. AND GLASS, F. (1970): *Archiv für Kriminologie*, **145**, (3, 4), 109.

RUSSELL, M.A.H., COLE, P.V. AND BROWN, E. (1973): *Lancet*, **1**, 576.

SAARIO, I. AND LINNOILA, M. (1975): *Journal of Clinical Pharmacology*, **15**, 52.

SAARIO, I. AND LINNOILA, M. (1976): *Acta Pharmacologica et Toxicologica*, **38**, 382.

SABEY, B.E. AND CODLING, P.J. (1974); Proc. 6th. Internat. Conf., **Toronto**, p. 73.

SABEY, B.E. (1978): *Transport and Road Research Supplementary Report* No. 441.

SAURY, A., BOULETREAU, P., RACHELIER-NOTTER, J. AND ROCHE, L. (1966): *Annales de Médecine Légale*, **46**, 179.

SCHELLMANN, B., REINHARDT, G. AND LÖSER (1979 and 1980): *Blutalkohol*, **16**(3), 186 and **17**(2), 89.

SCHLEYER, F. AND WICHMANN, D. (1962): *Blutalkohol*, **1**, 234.

SCHLEYER, H. (1966): *Blutalkohol*, **3**, 571.

SCHWEITZER, H. (1968): *Blutalkohol*, **5**, 73.

SCHWERD, W., DIMMLING, T. AND KREBS, J. (1967): *Blutalkohol*, **4**, 260.

SEPPÄLÄ, T. ET AL. (1975): *Clin. Pharm. Ther.*, **17**, 515.

SEPPÄLÄ, T., SAARIO, I. AND MATTILA, M.J. (1976–1): *Modern Problems of Pharmacopsychiatry*, **11**, 85.

SEPPÄLÄ, T. ET AL. (1976–2): *Acta Pharmacologica et Toxicologica*, **38**(3), 209.

SEPPÄLÄ, T., LINNOILA, M. AND MATTILA, M.J.: (1979): *Drugs*, **17**, 389.

SHARMA, S.: (1976): *Accid. Anal. Prev.*, **8**, 27.

SHEEHAN, T.M.T. AND BOWEN, D.A. Ll. (1980): Proc. 8th Internat.Conf., **Stockholm**, p. 180.

SHUMATE, R.P., CROWTHER, M. AND ZARAFSHAN, M. (1967): *Journal of Forensic Medicine* (South Africa), **14**, 83.

SILVERSTONE, J.T. (1974): *British Journal of Clinical Pharmacology*, **1**, 451.

SILVERSTONE, J.T. (1977): *Pharmaceutical Journal*, **219**, 309.

SLEMEYER, A. (1980): Proc. 8th Internat. Conf., **Stockholm**, p. 456.

SMALLDON, K.W. (1973): *Nature*, **245** (5423), 266.

SMALLDON, K.W. AND BROWN, G.A. (1973): *Analytica Chimica Acta*, **66**, 285.

SMILEY, A., LeBLANC, A.E., FRENCH, I.W. AND BURFORD, R. (1974): Proc. 6th Internat. Conf., **Toronto**, p. 433.

SMITH, H.W. AND POPHAM, R.E. (1951): Proc. 1st Internat. Conf., **Stockholm**, p. 150.

SMITH, H.W. AND LUCAS, D.M. (1963): Proc. 3rd Internat. Conf., **London**, p. 189.

SMITH, R.N. (1980): Proc. 8th Internat. Conf., **Stockholm**, p. 469.

SMITH, R.N. (1981): *J. For. Sc. Soc.*, **21**, 142.

SOTERAKIS, J. AND IBER, F.L. (1975): *American Journal of Clinical Nutrition*, **28**(3), 254.

SPAN, W. ET AL. (1977): *Blutalkohol*, **14**, 205.

SPRIGGS, N.I. (1958): *The Medical Press*, **240**, 933.

SPRUNG, R. ET AL. (1981): *Blutalkohol*, **18**, 65.

STAAK, M., SPRINGER, E. AND SCHOOK, P. (1972): *Blutalkohol*, **9**, 441.

STAAK, M., MALLACH, H.J. AND MOOSMEYER, A. (1976): *Beiträge gerichtliche Medizin*, **34**, 91.

STONE, H.M. (1982): Compiler of *Alcohol, Drugs and the New Zealand Driver*, (pub. Dept of Scientific and Industrial Research, Wellington, N.Z.).

STONE, H.M., NORRIS, R.J., CAMERON, B.J., MUIRHEAD, J.M. AND MISSEN, A.W. (1982). See Stone 1982, p. 17.

STONE, H.M., NORRIS, R.J., MUIRHEAD, J.M. AND SINGERS, W.A. (1982): See Stone 1982, p. 23.

STUHLFAUTH, K. AND NEUMAIER, H. (1951): *Medizinische Klinik*, **46**, 541.

SUNSHINE, I., HODNETT, N., HALL, C.R. AND RIEDERS, F. (1968): *Postgraduate Medicine*, **43**, 152.

TAYLOR, J.D. AND STEVENS, S.L. (1965): Proc. 4th Internat. Conf., **Indiana**, p. 252.

TAYLOR, J.F. (1980): Proc. 8th Internat. Conf., **Stockholm**, p. 478.

TERHUNE, K.W. AND FELL, J.C. (1981): *Quarterly Journal of the American Association of Automotive Medicine*, Oct. 1981.

TURK, R.F., MCBAY, A.J. AND HUDSON, P. (1974): *J. For. Sc.*, **19**(1), 90.

TRRL (TRANSPORT AND ROAD RESEARCH LABORATORY) (1975): Supplementary Report No. 134.

ULJANOV, V.A.: See Ivanov.

VAMOSI, M. (1958): *Soudni Lékarvstvi*, **3**, 133; (1960) *Traffic Safety*, **4**(3), 8.

VAN OOIJEN: See Ooijen.

VEERHAEGEN, P., AND KERR, E. AND GAMBART, R. (1974): Proc. 6th Internat. Conf., **Toronto**, p. 405.

VESSELL, E.S. ET AL. (1971): *Clin. Pharm. Ther.*, **12**, 192.

WALLS, H.J. (1958 and 1962): *B.M.J.*, **1**, 1442; Proc. 3rd Internat. Conf., **London**, p. 239.

WATSON, J.M. (1978): *Med. Sci. Law*, **18**(1), 40.

WAYNE, E.J. (1962): Proc. 3rd Internat. Conf., **London**, p. 113.

WEINIG, E., ZINK, P. AND REINHARDT, G. (1970): *Blutalkohol*, **7**, 307.

WELLING, P.G. ET AL. (1977): *Journal of Clinical Pharmacology*, **17**, 199; and *Journal of Pharmacokinetics and Biopharmaceutics*, **5**(4), 291.

WETHERALL, A. (1979): *Psychopharmacology*, **63**, 259.

WILHELM, F. ET AL. (1972): *Blutalkohol*, **9** 473.

WILLIAMS, P.L., MOFFAT, A.C. AND KING, L.J. (1978): *Journal of Chromatography*, **155**, 273.

WILLIAMS, DR. R.L. (Metropolitan Police Forensic Science Laboratory 1982): Private Communication.

WRIGHT, B.M. (1963): *B.M.J.*, **1**, 814.

WRIGHT, B.M., JONES, T.P. AND JONES, A.W. (1975): *Med. Sci. Law.* **15**(3), 205.

YLIKHARI ET AL. (1976): *European Journal of Clinical Investigation*, **6**, 93.

ZINK, P. AND REINHARDT, G. (1975, 1976, 1980, 1981): *Blutalkohol*, **12** 100; **13**, 327; **17**, 400; **18**, 377.

ZINK, P. AND REINHARDT, G. (1977): *Beiträge gerichtliche Medizin*, **35**, 119.

ZINK, P. AND WENDLER, K. (1978): *Blutalkohol*, **15**, 409.

ZWAHLEN, H.T. (1976): *Journal of Occupational Accidents*, **1**, 21.

APPENDIX V

VOLUMES AND MEASURES

See also Table 1 and footnote (p. 6).

Metric units are increasingly being used in Great Britain for volumes of liquor sold and consumed, but until this process is complete (and it looks as though the pint will be with us for some time yet), we are stuck with an awkward combination of metric and British Imperial units.

The basic units are the *pint*, the *litre* and (in popular usage) the *bottle*.

1 pint = 20 fluid ounces = 4 gills = 570 millilitres (see below)
approximately = $\frac{3}{4}$ of traditional wine bottle.

The *gill* is not in everyday use, but the unit is of legal importance in connection with the sale of spirits for consumption on the premises (see Table 1, footnote); these are normally dispensed in *optics* delivering $\frac{1}{6}$ gill (i.e., $\frac{5}{6}$ fluid ounce). 32 such optics can be got from a spirits bottle. Another (unofficial) unit based on the pint is the *nip*, which is used for extra-strong bottled beers and ciders ("barley wines," etc.).

1 nip = $\frac{1}{3}$ pint = $6\frac{2}{3}$ fluid ounces = about 180 millilitres (see below).

1 litre = approximately $1\frac{3}{4}$ pints or $35\frac{1}{4}$ fluid ounces or $1\frac{1}{3}$ ordinary wine bottles.

1 millilitre (see below) of water weighs 1 gram = $\frac{1}{28}$ ounce approximately.

269

The most commonly used multiples and sub-multiples of metric units are designated thus:

kilo-	1,000 times
deci-	one tenth
centi-	one hundredth (1 centilitre (cl) = $\frac{1}{3}$ fluid ounce roughly)
milli-	one thousandth (1 millilitre is nearly the same as, and was formerly designated, 1 cubic centimetre (c.c.))
micro-	one millionth.

The capacities of *bottles* have in most cases no scientific or legal authority, but they form convenient units in everyday usage. The standard spirits bottle holds one-sixth of an Imperial gallon—that is, $1\frac{1}{3}$ pints or $26\frac{2}{3}$ fluid ounces or about 75 centilitres—and wine and aperitif bottles sometimes have the same capacity. However, table wines are more usually sold in bottles contaning 70 centilitres (cl), and litre bottles are also becoming increasingly common for all types of liquor. "Quart" flagons of beer and cider are now usually litres, and these are being replaced by 2-litre flagons. Table wines are now available in 3-litre plastic-lined cartons. *Cans* of beer are labelled with their capacities in millilitres, most frequently 275 or 440 (about $\frac{1}{2}$ or $\frac{3}{4}$ pint respectively).

INDEX

271

In charge—*cont.*
  disqualification optional, 162
  hip-flask defence and, 208, 243
  re-defined, 158
  separated, 147
  sleeping, 159
  while impaired, 159
Infra-red radiation, use of,
  for analysis, 88, 90–93, 94
Inhalation of alcohol vapour, 25
Instrumental breath analysis. *See*
    Analysis, 195
  camic, 114
  change to, 194
  Intoximeter, 194
Insulin, 21
Integrator,
  in gas chromatography, 83
Interpretation,
  of analysis, 216
Intoxilyzer. See C.M.I. Intoxilyzer.
Intoximeter. See Lion Intoximeter 3000.
Isaacs, M. D. J., 32, 95

Jones, A. W., 33, 34, 41, 96
Journey finished, 156, 157
Juries,
  option for, 146
  sympathetic to motorist, 145
Justice, perverting course of, 207

Karolinska Institut, 21, 34

Laboratory specimens,
  divided into two parts, 197
  option for lies with police, 197
  must be capable of analysis, 197
  part supplied at the time, 197
  too late later, 197
Laboratory tests,
  absconding before, 191
  at hospital, 190, 196
  at police station, 196
  failure to provide, 192, 210
  request for, 190, 192, 194, 241
  "please yourself" not compliance, 198
Laced drinks, 205
  special reasons, 212, 214
Laevulose. *See* Fructose.
Lapse of time, 222
Lawnmower, powered, 153

Legal references, 247
Liberty, inroads upon, 172
Librium. See Chlordiazepoxide.
Likelihood of driving, 197, 203, 238, 239
Liljestrand, G., 31
Linnoila, M., 25, 126, 128, 136, 138, 143
Lion Auto-Alcometer, 95
Lion Intoximeter 3000, 95, 96, 114, 194, 198
  adverse publicity, 197
  leap year, 194
  print out, 237
Lion Laboratories Ltd.,
  address of, 100
Liquors,
  alcoholic,
    laws about, 4–6
    types and strengths of, 4–7
    volumes of sold and dispensed, 6
  sparkling, 16
  various,
    rate of absorption of, 16
Liver,
  dysfunction,
    and alcohol metabolism, 25
  role of, 9
Loomis, T., and *West, T.C.*, 44
Loopholes, 150, 202
Lucas, C. H. W., 63

Macro analysis, 149
Marihuana. *See* Cannabis.
Mason, M. F., 30, 32, 34, 72, 87, 100
Measures,
  liquor, 269
Mechanical dumpers, 152
Medical advice,
  police to have and follow for drugs, 198
Medical examination of driver, 164, 201, 231
Medical Research Council, 58
Mellanby Effect, 48, 55
Menstruation, 25
Methanol, traces of, in blood, 87
Methyl alcohol. *See* Methanol.
Metric units, 269
Micrometre, definition of, 90
Milner, G., 43, 130
Mini cars, 152
Mistake, distinction of, from error, 101
Morgan, W. H. D., 40